DOUGLAS JOB
19 APRIL 1990
KIERNAN'S IN CHICAGO
$2.25

THE MODERN LIBRARY
OF THE WORLD'S BEST BOOKS

The Journals of
RALPH WALDO EMERSON

The publishers will be pleased to send, upon request, an illustrated folder setting forth the purpose and scope of The Modern Library, and listing each volume in the series. Every reader of books will find titles he has been looking for, handsomely printed, in definitive editions, and at an unusually low price.

The Journals of

Ralph Waldo

EMERSON

Abridged and Edited, with an Introduction, by

Robert N. Linscott

THE MODERN LIBRARY · NEW YORK

Random House IS THE PUBLISHER OF *The Modern Library*
BENNETT CERF · DONALD S. KLOPFER
Manufactured in the United States of America by H. Wolff

INTRODUCTION

I

I confine my ambition to true reporting. I write anecdotes of the intellect, a sort of Farmers' Almanac of mental moods.

For more than half a century, Emerson kept a journal in which he recorded his thoughts, moods, meditations and observations; sometimes daily, sometimes at long intervals. The first volume that has survived is dated January, 1820 (Emerson was then sixteen and a junior at Harvard), and marked No. XVII. The writing in these early volumes is stiff and imitative; schoolboy practice work. Year by year the thoughts acquired depth; the style, individuality; the words, felicity. But he ripened late, and it was not till his thirties that the entries have the full Emersonian flavor.

After Emerson resigned as pastor of the Second Church in Boston, and began to lecture and write for a living, the journals took on a practical value. "This book," he said, "is my savings bank. I grow richer because I have somewhere deposited my earnings." As thoughts came to him during the mornings in his study, he would shape them into sentences and record them in its pages. On days when thoughts lagged, he would occupy himself by grouping and indexing the entries. When lectures were needed, appropriate entries would be copied out, and pruned or enlarged to the proper length. These lectures, after repeated testings and revisions ("The barber," he would say, "learns his trade on the orphan's chin."), were given a final polish, and printed as essays.

Twenty years after Emerson's death, his son and grandson undertook the long task of preparing the journals for publication. In 1909 they were issued in ten volumes, now out of print. Not all the journals were included. Extracts only were given from the earlier notebooks, and, throughout, those passages were omitted which had already appeared in the published works.

Emerson had a phenomenal gift for condensing his thoughts into aphorisms, epigrams, maxims, clipped and gnomic sayings. Bundled together in the essays, these sometimes lack coherence and a sense of organic growth, but in the journals, each thought stands alone and gains in impact thereby. Moreover, a large part of the journal entries—and many of the choicest—had no place in the essays; Emerson's self-appraisals, his hopes, fears, aspirations and mortifications; the shrewd analyses—surprisingly caustic for a man so outwardly urbane—of his friends, and of the great figures and events of the period.

As is inevitable in a journal of a million and a quarter words, many of Emerson's entries were perfunctory or repetitious; variant readings of passages now available in the published *Works*, casual observations on subjects of limited interest, and comments on, or quotations from, the books he was reading. Entries such as these, of value only to the specialist, have been omitted from this one-volume edition.

The outward facts of Emerson's life are given in the chronology that follows this Introduction, and in the biographical summaries that precede each of the seven sections into which the book is divided. But beyond these facts, some exposition of the intellectual and spiritual climate of the period is needed to clarify the sense of ferment everywhere apparent in these pages.

II

We are all a little wild here with numberless projects of social reform. Not a reading man but has a draft of a new community in his waistcoat pocket. I am gently mad myself, and am resolved to live cleanly.

"When I was born," wrote Emerson in 1849, "private and family prayer was in the use of all well-bred people, and now it is not known." During these years the cramping bonds of Puritanism had been loosened, and the harsh doctrines that for two centuries confined the New England mind had lost their authority. Tradition was out the window and freedom in the door. No longer was the world "a scaffold of Divine Vengeance" and a waiting room in which to prepare for eternity. The purpose of life, said Emerson, is "to acquaint man with himself. Let redemption be sought in the soul. All real good and evil that can befall him must be from himself." To the older generation the words were blasphemy; to the younger, a battle cry of freedom.

The seeds of this revolt had come from abroad. From Germany, by way of Carlyle and Coleridge in England, had come Transcendentalism, the belief that the nature of reality must be discovered by the individual through intuition and introspection. Plato, the neo-Platonists and the scriptures of the East had further emphasized the role of the individual as the creator of his own destiny. And, to add social to spiritual ferment, there had come from France the theories of Fourier, who had promised a new and better world through the reorganization of society into small, communistic and self-contained communities: a belief that his American disciples attempted to put into practice at Brook Farm, Fruitlands and other Utopias. All these influences, joined to a sense of buoyant liberation as the hold of Puritanism relaxed, produced an effervescence which was commonly referred to simply as The Newness.

More than any other factor it was Emerson's two great Harvard orations, the Phi Beta Kappa address of 1837 and the Divinity School address of 1838, that stirred the ferment, and *The Dial* magazine (edited first by Margaret Fuller and then by Emerson) that put into words the ideas, emotions, and aspirations of the young intellectuals.

But although Emerson inspired, he refused to lead. To his door came the lunatic fringe of reformers: those who renounced money, and those who denounced the State; those who believed that man should not work for man, and those who believed that animals should be equally free. To these moon-struck Peter the Hermits, each preaching his Little Crusade, Emerson listened, but went his own way, noting in his journal: "A man shares the new light that irradiates the world and promises the establishment of the Kingdom of Heaven—and ends by champing unleavened bread, or devoting himself to the nourishment of a beard." Brook Farm, he called, "A French Revolution in small; an Age of Reason in a patty-pan," and he wrote in his journal: "I do not wish to remove from my present prison to a prison a little larger. I wish to break all prisons. I have not yet conquered my own house. It irks and repents me. Shall I raise the siege of this hen-coop, and march baffled away to a pretended siege of Babylon?"

Gradually all reforms were subsumed in one. By 1850 the surge and storm of the Abolition Movement had swept aside all other crusades. Lukewarm at first, Emerson was soon caught up in the movement and his most eloquent speeches were directed against slavery. The denunciation of Daniel Webster for his support of the Fugitive Slave Act, with its magnificent peroration—"The word *liberty* in the mouth of Mr. Webster sounds like the word *love* in the mouth of a courtesan. . . . All the drops of his blood have eyes that look downward."—is perhaps the most striking passage in the journals. And in the last section, a long entry of historic interest describes a Sunday morning in the White House during the Civil War, and testifies to Emerson's admiration for Lincoln. But even before the War, The Newness had vanished, and, by its close, the Age of Iron had come.

III

In silence we must wrap much of our life, because it is too fine for speech, because also we cannot explain it to others, and because somewhat we cannot yet understand.

The mirror-glimpses of Emerson through his own eyes that one finds in these pages are fragmentary and tantalizing. In his early years he was a self-flagellator. "I am awkward, sour, saturnine, lumpish, pedantic, and thoroughly disagreeable and oppressive to the people around me," he writes in a characteristic passage. And as late as 1840 he notes: "Guy wished all his friends dead on very slight occasion." (Emerson was accustomed to refer to himself under various disguises.) "Whoever was privy to one of his gaucheries had the honor of this Stygian optation. Had Jove heard all his prayers, the planet would have been unpeopled." Yet the evidence of his contemporaries all, or almost all, contradicts his self-indictment. Oliver Wendell Holmes said: "His expression was calm, sedate, kindly; his manner noble and gracious." And James Russell Lowell noted "a majesty about him beyond all other men I have ever known." The truth would seem to lie between. Morbidly self-conscious in his youth, unsure and ill at ease with strangers, Emerson learned for self-protection to wear a mask: serene, benign, reserved —and a mask long worn shapes the man.

In appearance Emerson was tall, slender, and slightly stooped, with narrow shoulders, a thin, scholar's face, bright blue eyes, thick brown hair, a prominent nose, and a wide, firm mouth. His voice was musical and penetrating: a perfect instrument for a lecturer. He hated to be made to laugh, had little ear for music, and no mechanical aptitude. In his youth he was threatened with tuberculosis; in his middle age he was wiry, fond of long walks and able to endure without ill effects the rigors of midwinter lecture tours on the Western frontier—days in stagecoaches and canal boats, crossing the frozen Mississippi on foot, and forty-mile sleigh rides in sub-zero weather.

"In my strait and decorous way of living, native to my family and to my country, and more strictly proper to me," Emerson noted in his journal, "is nothing extravagant or flowing. I content myself with moderate, languid motions, and never transgress the staidness of village manners." He rose at six, breakfasted on pie and coffee, worked in the morning, walked in the afternoon, and went to bed at ten. He was an exemplary citizen, attending Town Meetings and serving on the Concord School Committee. Many visitors came to his house, and Lydia, his second wife (his first wife had died eighteen months after they were married) kept two hired girls to help with the housework as she was often ailing. His mother lived with them, and sometimes, while Emerson was away, Thoreau stayed at the house as handyman.

Emerson depended much on his friends for stimulation and four names recur again and again in the journals:— Bronson Alcott, educator, philosopher and indefatigable conversationalist; Henry D. Thoreau, his "wood-god" and young disciple; Ellery Channing, wayward poet and freakish, favorite walking companion; and, until she left for New York and Europe, Margaret Fuller, intellectual *femme fatale*.

To Emerson, Alcott was a constant tonic and occasional irritant; a "magnificent dreamer" and a "tedious archangel," "the highest genius of the time" and "a pail of which the bottom is taken out." Thoreau was sometimes patronized ("My good Henry Thoreau . . . his thoughts are my own, quite originally dressed"), sometimes berated ("Always some weary, captious paradox to fight you with, and time and temper wasted"), but always respected for his integrity as a man, his ability as a writer, and his knowledge of woods and river. Margaret Fuller, "whom I always admire and sometimes love—yet whom I freeze, and who freezes me to silence," he was wary of, skillfully warding off her urge for intimacy. And, overseas, was Carlyle, with whom he corresponded and for whom he arranged American publication.

On the whole, Emerson gives the impression of a sagacious Yankee who speculated, not on the market, but on the universe, "a cautious mystic," as Holmes said, "who never let go the string of his balloon." But how reconcile his serenity, his sense and sensibility, with the chilling entry in the journal of March 29, 1832, thirteen months after his first wife's death: "I visited Ellen's tomb and opened the coffin." No more; no further reference. Or this, of 1857: "This morning I had the remains of my son Waldo removed to my lot in Sleepy Hollow. Waldo's coffin was well preserved—now fifteen years. I ventured to look into the coffin." Of himself, Emerson wrote: "In the graveyard my muscles were twitched by some ludicrous recollection, and I am apt to be solemn at a ball." One of his brothers went insane, one was a half-wit. His aunt, Mary Moody Emerson, greeted friends with "I wish you joy of the worm," and rode horseback through Concord wrapped in her shroud. "There is no great genius," said Aristotle, "without a mixture of madness."

IV

I read my commission in every cipher of nature, and know that I was made for another office, a professor of the Joyous Science . . . an affirmer of the one Law, yet as one who should affirm it in music and dancing.

Emerson was a virtuoso of the English language, creator of the wildly imaginative phrase, selector of the precise, the perfect word. "The maker of a sentence launches out into the infinite, and builds a road into Chaos and old Night," and of no sentence-maker is this more true than of the man who wrote it. This verbal exuberance is the first principle of selection for the entries that follow. Here is Emerson the stylist, the poet, the master of words. Here, also, is Emerson the commentator: on himself, on his friends and acquaintances, and on the world in which he lived. The sometimes facile optimism of the essays, the flattery of mankind implicit in Emersonian ethics, is almost wholly absent. This is the Emerson who wrote: "I like dry light, and hard clouds, hard expressions, and hard manners," who called life "a one-cent farce . . . a country-muster full of noise, squibbs and egg-pop." The Emerson of these entries is shrewd, astringent, and greatly daring; a poet, and an adventurer in the world of the mind.

Emerson's strength lay in his flashing intuitions; in the quick, oblique thrust that penetrates to the heart of the matter. Truth was his aim, and there is hardly a page on which he fails to hit the target. To read the journals is to realize that, even more than the essays, these are Emerson's passport to immortality.

Robert N. Linscott

CHRONOLOGICAL TABLE

1803 Emerson born, in Boston, May 25.

1813-17 At the Boston Latin School.

1817-21 At Harvard College.

1821-28 Teaching school and studying Divinity at Harvard.

1829 Pastor of Second Church of Boston. Married, September, to Ellen Louisa Tucker.

1831 Death of his wife (February).

1832 Resigned his pastorate (September). Sailed for Europe (December).

1833 Returned from Europe (October).

1834 Death of Edward Emerson in Porto Rico.

1835 Married to Lydia Jackson (September).

1836 Charles Emerson died (May). *Nature* published (September). Emerson's son Waldo born (October).

1837 *Phi Beta Kappa Address* (*The American Scholar;* August 31).

1838 *Divinity School Address* (July 15).

1841 *Essays. First Series.*

1842 His son Waldo died (January). Editor of *Dial* (1842-44).

1844 *Essays. Second Series.*

1847 *Poems.* Second visit to Europe.

1850 *Representative Men.*

1856 *English Traits.*

1860 *Conduct of Life.*

1867 *May Day* (poems). Received degree of LL.D. from Harvard, and was elected an Overseer of the University.

1870 *Society and Solitude.*

1872 House burned; third visit to Europe.

1875 *Letters and Social Aims.*

1882 Died at Concord, April 27.

PART I

1820-1835

Emerson's earliest surviving journal is numbered XVII and dated 1820 when he was a Junior at Harvard. After graduation, his journal was abandoned for half a year while he taught at his brother William's school for young ladies. In 1823 his mother, with whom he had been living in Boston, moved to Canterbury, then a part of Roxbury. In August Emerson made a solitary walking trip to the Connecticut valley, and, the following spring, decided to become a minister. He entered the Harvard Divinity School early in 1825, but his health failed, and during most of that year and the next he taught school. In the autumn of 1826 he was "approbated to preach," but his health again failing, he went south for the winter. On his return he reëntered the Divinity School, and in 1829 became assistant pastor of the Second Church of Boston. That same year he married Ellen Louisa Tucker of Concord, New Hampshire, a frail girl of eighteen who died a year and a half later.

Increasing restiveness at church discipline and ritual led Emerson to resign his pastorate in 1832. In December he sailed for Europe, returning in October of the following year. In November, 1834, he moved to Concord, Mass., with his mother and his brother, Charles, boarding in the Old Manse, built by Emerson's grandfather and occupied by his step-grandfather, Dr. Ripley. The following August, Emerson bought the house in Concord where he was to live for the rest of his life, and in September married Lydia Jackson of Plymouth, Mass. During that winter he delivered, in Boston, ten lectures on English literature.

1820

Different mortals improve resources of happiness which are entirely different. This I find more apparent in the familiar instances obvious at college recitations. My more fortunate neighbours exult in the display of mathematical study, while I, after feeling the humiliating sense of dependence and inferiority, which, like the goading, soul-sickening sense of extreme poverty, palsies effort, esteem myself abundantly compensated, if with my pen, I can marshal whole catalogues of nouns and verbs, to express to the life the imbecility I felt.

I find myself often idle, vagrant, stupid and hollow. This is somewhat appalling and, if I do not discipline myself with diligent care, I shall suffer severely from remorse and the sense of inferiority hereafter. All around me are industrious and will be great, I am indolent and shall be insignificant. Avert it, heaven! avert it, virtue! I need excitement.

1821

I am sick—if I should die what would become of me? We forget ourselves and our destinies in health, and the chief use of temporary sickness is to remind us of these concerns. I must improve my time better. I must prepare myself for the great profession I have purposed to undertake. I am to give my soul to God.

1822

In twelve days I shall be nineteen years old; which I count a miserable thing. Has any other educated person lived so

many years and lost so many days? I am he who nourished
brilliant visions of future grandeur which may well appear
presumptuous and foolish now. My infant imagination was
idolatrous of glory, and thought itself no mean pretender
to the honours of those who stood highest in the community, and dared even to contend for fame with those who
are hallowed by time and the approbation of the ages. This
hope was fed and fanned by the occasional lofty communications which were vouchsafed to me with the Muses'
Heaven, and which have at intervals made me the organ
of remarkable sentiments and feelings which were far
above my ordinary train. Shall I resign every aspiration to
belong to that family of giant minds? No, I will yet a little
while entertain the angel.

Look next from the history of my intellect to the history
of my heart. A blank, my lord. I have not the kind affections of a pigeon. Ungenerous and selfish, cautious and
cold, I yet wish to be romantic; have not sufficient feeling to
speak a natural, hearty welcome to a friend or stranger.
There is not in the whole wide Universe of God (my relations to Himself I do not understand) one being to whom I
am attached with warm and entire devotion; and this I say
at the most susceptible age of man.

I love my Wide Worlds.*

1823

Once when *Vanity* was full fed, it sufficed to keep me at
work and to produce some creditable scraps; but alas! it has
long been dying of a galloping starvation, and the Muse, I
fear me, will die too. The dreams of my childhood are all
fading away and giving place to some very sober and very

* Early volumes of the *Journals* were so called by Emerson.

disgusting views of a quiet mediocrity of talents and condition.

Melons and plums and peaches, eating and drinking, and the bugle, all the day long. These are the glorious occupations which engross a proud and thinking being, running his race of preparation for the eternal world.

A nation, like a tree, does not thrive well till it is engraffed with a foreign stock.

1824

No man would consent to live in society if he was obliged to admit everybody to his house that chose to come.

Envy is the tax which all distinction must pay.

The common conversation that has place in a city for a year does not embrace more intelligence than one vigorous thinker might originate.

The kingdom of thought is a proud aristocracy.

I am beginning my professional studies. In a month I shall be legally a man. And I deliberately dedicate my time, my talents, and my hopes to the Church. In Divinity I hope to thrive. I inherit from my sire a formality of manner and speech, but I derive from him, or his patriotic parent, a passionate love for the strains of eloquence. In my better hours, I am the believer (if not the dupe) of brilliant promises, and can respect myself as the possessor of those powers which command the reason and passions of the multitude.

Every wise man aims at an entire conquest of himself. I am not assuredly that excellent creature. A score of words and deeds issue from me daily, of which I am not the master. They are begotten of weakness and born of shame. In my frequent humiliation, even before women and children, I am compelled to remember the poor boy who cried, "I told you, Father, they would find me out."

I cannot accurately estimate my chances of success, in my profession, and in life. Were it just to judge the future from the past, they would be very low. In my case, I think it is not. My trust is that my profession shall be my regeneration.

There is a dreaminess about my mode of life (which may be a depravity) which loosens the tenacity of what should be most tenacious—this my grasp on heaven and earth. I am the servant more than the master of my fates. They seem to lead me into many a slough where I do no better than despond. And as to the life I lead, and the works and the days, I should blush to recite the unprofitable account. But prophets and philosophers assure me that I am immortal, and sometimes my own imagination goes into a fever with its hopes and conceptions.

Why has my motley diary no jokes? Because it is a soliloquy and every man is grave alone.

I confess I am a little cynical on some topics, and when a whole nation is roaring Patriotism at the top of its voice, I am fain to explore the cleanness of its hands and purity of its heart. I have generally found the gravest and most useful citizens are not the easiest provoked to swell the noise, though they may be punctual at the polls.

1825

I will not believe because I cannot unite dignity, as many can, to folly, that I am not born to fill the eye of great expectation.

It is the evening of February eighth, which was never renowned that I know. But, be that as it may, 't is the last evening I spend in Canterbury. I go to my College Chamber to-morrow a little changed for better or worse since I left it in 1821. I have learned a few more names and dates, additional facility of expression, the gauge of my own ignorance, its sounding-places and bottomless depths. I have inverted my inquiries two or three times on myself, and have learned what a sinner and a saint I am. My cardinal vice of intellectual dissipation—sinful strolling from book to book, from care to idleness—is my cardinal vice still; is a malady that belongs to the chapter of Incurables. I have written two or three hundred pages that will be of use to me. I have earned two or three thousand dollars which have paid my debts and obligated my neighbors, so that I thank Heaven I can say none of my house is the worse for me. In short, I have grown older and have seen something of the vanity and something of the value of existence, have seen what shallow things men are, and how independent of external circumstances may be the states of mind called good and ill.

1826

I am cold, and when shall I kindle? I was born cold. My bodily habit is cold. I shiver in and out; don't heat to the good purposes called enthusiasm a quarter so quick and kindly as my neighbours. Yet, so depraved is self-conceit, that I sometimes imagined this very seed of wrath to be one of my gifts, though not graces.

1827

When the man is at home, his standing in society is well known and quietly taken; but when he is abroad, it is problematical, and is dependent on the success of his manners.

I have found my ideas very refractory to the usual bye-laws of Association. In the graveyard my muscles were twitched by some ludicrous recollections, and I am apt to be solemn at a ball. But, whilst places are alike to me, I make great distinction between states of mind. My days are made up of the irregular succession of a very few different tones of feeling. These are my feasts and fasts.

1828

If I were richer, I should lead a better life than I do; that is, better divided and more able. I should ride on horseback a good deal; I should bowl, and create an appetite for my studies by intermixing some heat and labour in affairs. The chief advantage I should propose myself in wealth would be the independence of manner and conversation it would bestow and which I eagerly covet and seldom quite attain, and in some companies never.

It is a peculiarity (I find by observation upon others) of humour in me, my strong propensity for strolling. I deliberately shut up my books in a cloudy July noon, put on my old clothes and old hat and slink away to the whortleberry bushes and slip with the greatest satisfaction into a little cowpath where I am sure I can defy observation. This point gained, I solace myself for hours with picking blueberries and other trash of the woods, far from fame, behind the birch-trees. I seldom enjoy hours as I do these. I remember them in winter; I expect them in spring.

When I consider the constitutional calamity of my family which, in its falling upon Edward,* has buried at once so many towering hopes—with whatever reason, I have little apprehension of my own liability to the same evil. I have so much mixture of *silliness* in my intellectual frame that I think Providence has tempered me against this. My brother lived and acted and spoke with preternatural energy. My own manner is sluggish; my speech sometimes flippant, sometimes embarrassed and ragged; my actions (if I may say so) are of a passive kind. Edward had always great power of face. I have none. I laugh; I blush; I look ill-tempered against my will and against my interest. But all this imperfection, as it appears to me, is a *caput mortuum,* is a ballast—as things go, is a defence.

I like a man who likes to see a fine barn as well as a good tragedy.

'T is a striking proof of the power of *situation* to drop a penknife or a glove upon the ground and see how they look there.

In a tavern everybody puts on airs except the landlord: he is the poor devil, and the commonest sot of a teamster thinks he has the advantage of him.

December 21

I have now been four days engaged to Ellen Louisa Tucker. Will my Father in Heaven regard us with kindness, and as

---

* Emerson's brother had had a mental breakdown.

he hath, as we trust, made us for each other, will he be pleased to strengthen and purify and prosper and eternize our affection!

The great majority of men are bundles of beginnings.

1829

Every man contemplates an angel in his future self.

1830

I hate steady labour from morn till night, and therefore am not a learned man, but I have an omnivorous curiosity and facility of new undertaking.

If a man be asked if he is happy, on his conscience, he will not affirm it; he will feel a scruple, I apprehend, precisely like that he would feel if he were about to say that he was sinless.

If a man loves the city, so will his writings love the city, and if a man loves sweet fern and roams much in the pastures, his writings will smell of it.

The mind performs a penitential act of perceiving its deficiency, but there it stops. It declares war against the enemy, but it does not levy a troop nor make an excursion into his country. It languishes in inaction, and, at the end of a year, or of seven years, it is found no better, and therefore far worse than at the beginning—far worse, because the demand runs on increasing and the performance does not.

One man talks of the abolition of slavery with perfect coolness, whilst all around him sneer or roar at his ludicrous benevolence. They with their sinful eyes cannot see society without slaves. He sees distinctly the difference, and knows that the crime is unnecessary.

There is a time when a man distinguishes the idea of felicity from the idea of wealth; it is the beginning of wisdom.

Most young men had rather run in debt or tell a lie than be known by the most elegant young man of their acquaintance to have made their dinner on onions from economy.

It has often occurred to me that a man was a reflection of my own self. I understand his smile and his scowl. So far we go along together and have one nature. The moment I do not understand him, the moment he departs from me, I am pained, for I feel that either he is wrong or I am. As long as that difference subsists, so long will our uneasiness on that point. It is an unshaken conviction of both, that both cannot be right.

1831

Ellen Tucker Emerson died, 8th February, Tuesday morning, 9 o'clock.

Five days are wasted since Ellen went to heaven to see, to know, to worship, to love, to intercede. Reunite us, O thou Father of our spirits.

There is that which passes away and never returns. This miserable apathy, I know, may wear off. I almost fear when it will. Old duties will present themselves with no more repulsive face. I shall go again among my friends with a tranquil countenance. Again I shall be amused, I shall stoop again to little hopes and little fears and forget the graveyard. But will the dead be restored to me? Will the eye that was closed on Tuesday ever beam again in the fulness of love on me? Shall I ever again be able to connect the face of outward nature, the mists of the morn, the star of eve, the flowers, and all poetry, with the heart and life of an enchanting friend? No. There is one birth, and one baptism, and one first love, and the affections cannot keep their youth any more than men.

Her end was blessed and a fit termination to such a career. She prayed that God would speedily release her from her body, and that she might not make her prayer to be rid of her pains, "but because thy favour is better than life." "Take me, O God, to thyself," was frequently on her lips. Never anyone spake with greater simplicity or cheerfulness of dying. She said, "I pray for sincerity, and that I may not talk, but may realize what I say." She did not think she had a wish to get well.

The Religion that is afraid of science dishonours God and commits suicide.

The spring is wearing into summer, and life is wearing into death; our friends are forsaking us, our hopes are declining; our riches are wasting; our mortifications are increasing, and is the question settled in our minds, what objects we pursue with undivided aim? Have we fixed ourselves by principles? Have we planted our stakes?

The days go by, griefs, and simpers, and sloth and disappointments. The dead do not return, and sometimes we

are negligent of their image. Not of yours, Ellen. I know
too well who is gone from me.

The love of novels is the preference of sentiment to the
senses. Who are they that love an ideal world and dwell
in it? The young, the pure, who believe that love is stronger
than lust. What you seek in these novels is the friendships
you would form with tempers so true and majestic on
which an infinite trust might be reposed. They would act
for you across the earth and could not be bribed or scared,
or cooled. Now in every mind is the material of all this romance and that is the way in which every mind is heir of
heaven. Have you not ever felt the pleasure, the tossing, the
turmoil of a lofty sentiment? When your pillow would not
give rest to your head because of the delight of what you
had done or determined. How was life ennobled, and
death in that hour lost much of his dread. Is there not living
in the world the person for whose advantage you would
eagerly have made costliest sacrifices? That sentiment, that
occasion, was the beginning of all good to you, if only per-
severed in; and if you have left that way, you have wandered; and how have you fared? *Therefore* is life stale and
cheap. It is wonderful that men do not learn this lesson
from love, so familiar in its lower stages, but seldom carried
to any heights.

There is a capacity of virtue in us, and there is capacity of
vice to make your blood creep.

Every popinjay blows with the wind. The thunder cloud
sails against it.

Went to-night to the Sunday School meeting, but was myself a dumb dog that could not bark.

A sect or party is an elegant incognito devised to save a man from the vexation of thinking.

Since to govern my passions with absolute sway is the work I have to do, I cannot but think that the sect for the suppression of Intemperance, or a sect for the suppression of loose behaviour to women, would be a more reasonable and useful society than the Orthodox sect, which is a society for the suppression of Unitarianism, or the Unitarian, which is a society for the diffusion of useful knowledge.

Religion is the relation of the soul to God, and therefore the progress of Sectarianism marks the decline of religion. For, looking at God instantly reduces our disposition to dissent from our brother. A man may die by a fever as well as by consumption, and religion is as effectually destroyed by bigotry as by indifference.

President Monroe died on the fourth of July,—a respectable man, I believe.

No man can write well who thinks there is any choice of words for him.

In good writing, words become one with things.

I sit alone from month to month filled with a deep desire to exchange thoughts with a friend who does not appear.

The things taught in colleges and schools are not an education, but the means of education.

Let me embark in political economy, in repartee, in fiction, in verse, in practical counsels and I am soon run aground; but let my bark head its own way toward the law of laws, toward the compensation or action and reaction of the moral universe, and I sweep serenely over God's depths in an infinite sea.

1832

It is the best part of the man, I sometimes think, that revolts most against his being a minister. His good revolts from official goodness. The difficulty is that we do not make a world of our own, but fall into institutions already made, and have to accommodate ourselves to them to be useful at all, and this accommodation is, I say, a loss of so much integrity and, of course, of so much power.

But how shall the droning world get on if all its *beaux esprits* recalcitrate upon its approved forms and accepted institutions, and quit them all in order to be single minded? The double refiners would produce at the other end the double damned.

There are men whose language is strong and defying enough, yet their eyes and their actions ask leave of other men to live.

Be as beneficent as the sun or the sea, but if your rights as a rational being are trenched on, die on the first inch of your territory.

No man gains credit for his cowardly courtesies. Every one makes allowance for so much bowing and smiling and compliment as he supposes was insincere, and rates the character so much the worse for that heavy subtraction.

Finney can preach, and so his prayers are short; Parkman can pray, and so his prayers are long; Lowell can visit, and so his church service is less. But what shall poor I do, who can neither visit nor pray nor preach to my mind?

I believe a hundred dollars a year would support me in the enjoyment of what I love best. Why toil I then for twenty times as much? Might I cut and run? Might I dignifiedly walk away, and keep the man nor turn cat?

The sermon which I write inquisitive of truth is good a year after, but that which is written because a sermon must be writ is musty the next day.

What can we see, read, acquire, but ourselves. Take the book, my friend, and read your eyes out, you will never find there what I find.

It is idle in us to wonder at the bigotry and violence of the persecution of Galileo. Every man may read the history of it in himself when he is contradicted and silenced in argument by a person whom he had always reckoned his inferior.

Many a profound genius, I suppose, who fills the world with fame of his exploding renowned errors, is yet every day posed by trivial questions at his own supper-table.

This year I have spent say $20. in wines and liquors which are drunk up, and the drinkers are the worse. It would have bought a beautiful print that would have pleased for a century; or have paid a debt.

March 29

I visited Ellen's tomb and opened the coffin.

You had better begin small, sail in an eggshell, make a straw your mast, a cobweb all your cloth. Begin and proceed on a settled and not-to-be-shaken conviction that but little is permitted to any man to do or to know, and if he complies with the first grand laws, he shall do well.

Count from yourself in order the persons that have near relation to you up to ten or fifteen, and see if you can consider your whole relation to each without squirming. That will be something. Then, have you paid all your debts? Then, have you paid to the world as much kindness as you received from early benefactors? It were a sort of baseness to die in the world's debt. Then, can you not, merely for the very elegancy, the *eruditus luxus* of the thing, do an unmixed kindness or two?

He that rides his hobby gently must always give way to him that rides his hobby hard.

Is not affluence,—or at least easy circumstances,—essential to the finish of the female character? Not to its depth and resources, perhaps, but to the *beauty* of mind and manners. Is it not because woman is not yet treated properly, but some taint of Indian barbarity marks yet our civilization? She was made, not to serve, but to be served, and only wealth admits among us of that condition. Or is it that an eye to interest is a fatal blot to the female character, and the poor scarce can help it?

Shakespeare's creations indicate no sort of anxiety to be understood. There is the Cleopatra, an irregular, unfinished, glorious, sinful character, sink or swim, there she is, and not one in the thousand of his readers apprehends the noble dimensions of the heroine. Then Ariel, Hamlet, and all; all done in sport with the free, daring pencil of a master of the World. He leaves his children with God.

Admiration warms and exalts. The lover is made happier by his love than the object of his affection.

The vanishing, volatile froth of the Present which any shadow will alter, any thought blow away, any event annihilate, is every moment converted into the Adamantine Record of the Past. We walk on molten lava on which the claw of a fly or the fall of a hair makes its impression, which being received, the mass hardens to flint and retains every impression forevermore.

"You send out to the Sandwich Islands one missionary and twenty-five refutations in the crew of the vessel," said Mr. Sturgis.

A lobster is monstrous, but when we have been shown the reason of the case and the colour and the tentacula and the proportion of the claws, and seen that he has not a scale nor a bristle nor any quality but fits to some habit and condition of the creature, he then seems as perfect and suitable to his sea-house as a glove to a hand. A man in the rocks under the sea would be a monster, but a lobster is a most handy and happy fellow there.

June 2

Cold, cold. Thermometer says temperate. Yet a week of moral excitement.*

* Emerson, then serving as pastor of the Second Church, had proposed that Communion be modified by the omission of the use of the elements, and had offered to resign if the church authorities were unwilling to do so. His proposal was rejected and his resignation accepted. (See entry of October 28.)

I have sometimes thought that, in order to be a good minister, it was necessary to leave the ministry. The profession is antiquated.

The hour of decision. It seems not worth while for them who charge others with exalting forms above the moon to fear forms themselves with extravagant dislike. I am so placed that my *aliquid ingenii* may be brought into useful action. Let me not bury my talent in the earth in my indignation at this windmill. I know very well that it is a bad sign in a man to be too conscientious, and stick at gnats. The most desperate scoundrels have been the over-refiners. Without accommodation society is impracticable. But this ordinance is esteemed the most sacred of religious institutions, and I cannot go habitually to an institution which they esteem holiest with indifference and dislike.

The truth of truth consists in this, that it is self-evident, self-subsistent. It is light. You don't get a candle to see the sun rise.

Instead of making Christianity a vehicle of truth, you make truth only a horse for Christianity. It is a very operose way of making people good. You must be humble because Christ says, "Be humble." "But why must I obey Christ?" "Because God sent him." But how do I know God sent him? Because your own heart teaches the same thing he taught. Why then shall I not go to my own heart at first?

It does not shock us when ordinary persons discover no craving for truth, and are content to exist for years exclusively occupied with the secondary objects of house and lands and food and company, and never cast up their eyes to inquire whence it comes and what it is for, wholly occupied with the play, and never ask after the design. But we cannot forgive it in the ——s and ——s that they who have souls to comprehend the magnificent secret should utterly neglect it and seek only huzzas and champagne. My quarrel with the vulgar great men is that they do not generously give themselves to the measures which they meddle with; they do not espouse the things they would do, live in the life of the cause they would forward and faint in its failure, but they are casting sheep's eyes ever upon their own by-ends; their pert individuality is ever and anon peeping out to see what way the wind blows, and where this boat will land them, whether it is likely they will dine nicely and sleep warm.

"Ah me," said the mourner to me, "how natural he looked when they had put on his dickey!"

"It was this that caught him," said the wife to me, touching her pearl earring.

It is awful to look into the mind of man and see how free we are, to what frightful excesses our vices may run under the whited wall of a respectable reputation. Outside, among your fellows, among strangers, you must preserve appearances, a hundred things you cannot do; but inside, the terrible freedom!

My aunt [MARY MOODY EMERSON] had an eye that went through and through you like a needle. "She was endowed," she said, "with the fatal gift of penetration." She disgusted everybody because she knew them too well.

To live in a field of pumpkins, yet eat no pie!

October 28

The vote on the question proposed to the proprietors of the Second Church this evening stood thus, Ayes 25; nays

34; blanks 2. On the acceptance of the pastor's letter, ayes 30; nays 20; blanks 4.

The chief mourner does not always attend the funeral.

1833

At Sea. January 2

Sailed from Boston for Malta, December 25, 1832, in Brig Jasper, Captain Ellis, 236 tons, laden with logwood, mahogany, tobacco, sugar, coffee, beeswax, cheese, etc. A long storm from the second morn of our departure consigned all the five passengers to the irremedial chagrins of the stateroom, to wit, nausea, darkness, unrest, uncleanness, harpy appetite and harpy feeding, the ugly "sound of water in mine ears," anticipations of going to the bottom, and the treasures of the memory. I remembered up nearly the whole of *Lycidas,* clause by clause, here a verse and there a word, as Isis in the fable the broken body of Osiris.

Out occasionally crawled we from our several holes, but hope and fair weather would not; so there was nothing for it but to wriggle again into the crooks of our transom. Then it seemed strange that the first man who came to sea did not turn round and go straight back again. Strange that because one of my neighbours had some trumpery logs and notions which would sell for a few cents more here than there, he should thrust forth this company of his poor countrymen to the tender mercies of the northwest wind.

We study the sailor, the man of his hands, man of all work; all eye, all finger, muscle, skill and endurance: a tailor, a carpenter, cooper, stevedore and clerk, and astronomer besides. He is a great saver, and a great quiddle, by the necessity of his situation.

The Captain believes in the superiority of the American to every other countryman. "You will see," he says, "when you get out here how they manage in Europe; they do everything by main strength and ignorance. Four truckmen and four stevedores at Long Wharf will load my brig quicker than a hundred men at any port in the Mediterranean."

Dr. Johnson rightly defends conversation upon the weather. With more reason we at sea beat that topic thin. We are pensioners of the wind. The weathercock is the wisest man. All our prosperity, enterprise, temper, come and go with the fickle air. If the wind should forget to blow, we must eat our masts. Sea-farmers must make hay when the sun shines. The gale collects plenty of work for the calm. Now are we all awaiting a smoother sea to stand at our toilette. A head wind makes grinning Esaus of us. Happy that there is a time for all things under the moon, so that no man need give a dinner-party in a brig's cabin, nor shave himself by the gulf lightning.

I like the latitude of 37° better than my bitter native 42°. We have sauntered all this calm day at one or two knots the hour, and nobody on board well pleased but I, and why should I be pleased? I have nothing to record. I have read little. I have done nothing. What then? Need we be such barren scoundrels that the whole beauty of heaven, the main, and man, cannot entertain us unless we too must needs hold a candle and daub God's world with a smutch of our own insignificance. Not I, for one. I will be pleased, though I do not deserve it. I will act in all up to my conceit

of last week, when I exulted in the power and art with
which we rode tilting over this January ocean, albeit, to
speak truth, our individual valors rode very sick the while,
lodged each in the waistcoat pocket of the brave brig's
transom. So that each passenger's particular share in the
glory was much the same as the sutler's or grocer's who
turns his penny in the army of Leonidas or Washington.
The southing latitude does not yet make early mornings.
The steward's lanthorn and trumpery matutinal preparations are to me for the rosy ray, the silver cloud, or chaunt
of earliest bird. But days will come.

What is a passenger? He is a much-enduring man who
bends under the load of his leisure. He fawns upon the
captain, reveres the mate, but his eye follows the steward;
scans accurately, as symptomatic, all the motions of that respectable officer. The species is contemplative, given to imitation, viciously inquisitive, immensely capable of sleep,
large eaters, swift digesters, their thoughts ever running on
men and things ashore, and their eye usually squinting over
the bulwark to estimate the speed of the bubbles.

Sailors are the best dressed of mankind. Convenience is
studied from head to heel, and they have a change for every emergency. It seems to me they get more work out of
the sailor than out of any other craftsman. His obedience is
prompt as a soldier's, and willing as a child's, and reconciles
me to some dim remembrances of authority I wondered at.
Thin skins do not believe in thick. Jack never looks an inch
beyond his orders. "Brace the yards," quoth the master;
"Ay, ay, sir," answers Jack, and never looks over the side
at the squall or the sea that cometh, as if it were no more
to him than to the capstan.

But though I do not find much attraction in the seaman,

yet I can discern that the naval hero is a hero. It takes all the thousand thousand European voyages that have been made to establish our faith in the practicability of this our hodiurnal voyage. But to be Columbus, to steer WEST steadily day after day, week after week, for the first time, and wholly alone in his opinion, shows a mind as solitary and self-subsistent as any that ever lived. A sea voyage at the best is yet such a bundle of perils and inconveniences that no person as much a lover of the present moment as I am would be swift to pay that price for any commodity which anything else would buy. Yet if our horses are somewhat wild, and the road uneven and lonely and without inns, yet experience shows us that the coward eye magnifies the dangers.

Calm, clear, warm, idle day; holiday to the senses, rest to the sailor, vexation to the captain, dubiously borne by the passenger.

I learn in the sunshine to get an altitude and the latitude, but am a dull scholar as ever in real figures. Seldom, I suppose, was a more inapt learner of arithmetic, astronomy, geography, political economy, than I am, as I daily find to my cost. It were to brag much if I should there end the catalogue of my defects. My memory of history—put me to the pinch of a precise question—is as bad; my comprehension of a question in technical metaphysics very slow, and in all arts practick, in driving a bargain, or hiding emotion, or carrying myself in company as a man for an hour, I have no skill. What under the sun canst thou do then, pale face? Truly not much, but I can hope.

The good Captain rejoices much in my ignorance. He confounded me the other day about the book in the Bible where God was not mentioned, and last night upon St. Paul's shipwreck. Yet I comforted myself at midnight with *Lycidas*. What marble beauty in that classic pastoral. I should like well to see an analysis of the pleasure it gives. That were criticism for the gods.

The inconvenience of living in a cabin is that people become all eye. 'T is a great part of well-being to ignorize a good deal of your fellow man's history and not count his warts nor expect the hour when he shall wash his teeth.

Straits of Gibraltar, January 20

Last evening they saw land from the masthead, and this morn broke over the bold and picturesque mountains of Africa behind Cape Spartel and Tangiers. On the left was Cape Trafalgar and Spain. The passengers greeted each other and mused, each in his own way, on this animating vision.

Honour evermore aboard ship to the man of action,—to the brain in the hand. Here is our stout master, worth a thousand philosophers,—a man who can strike a porpoise, and make oil out of his blubber, and steak out of his meat, who can thump a mutineer into obedience in two minutes; who can bleed his sick sailor, and mend the box of his pump; who can ride out the roughest storm on the American coast, and, more than all, with the sun and a three-cornered bit of wood, and a chart, can find his way from Boston across three thousand miles of stormy water into a little gut of inland sea, nine miles wide, with as much precision as if led by a clue.

Malta, February 3

Here in the precincts of St. John, the isle of old fame under the high battlements, once of the Knights and now of England, I spend my Sunday, which shines with but little Sabbath light. *"Tout commence,"* as Père Bossuet says. It is hardly truer of me at this point of time, when I am setting foot on the Old World and learning two languages, than it is of every day of mine, so rude and unready am I sent into this world. I seem, on all trivial emergencies, to be oppressed with an universal ignorance. If I rightly consider that for this point of time which we call a Life, *tout commence*, I shall rejoice in the omen of a boundless future and not be chagrined. Oh heavens! no. It is, however, a substantial satisfaction to benefit your companions with your knowledge,—a pleasure denied me. "Time," said friend Carlyle, "brings roses"; a capital *mot*, putting a little rouge on the old skeleton's cheek.

Perhaps it is a pernicious mistake, yet, rightly seen, I believe it is sound philosophy, that wherever we go, whatever we do, self is the sole subject we study and learn. Montaigne said, himself was all he knew. Myself is much more than I know, and yet I know nothing else. I bring myself to sea, to Malta, to Italy, to find new affinities between me and my fellow men, to observe narrowly the affections, weaknesses, surprises, hopes, doubts, which new sides of the panorama shall call forth in me. Mean, sneakingly mean, would be this philosophy, a reptile unworthy of the name, if *self* be used in the low sense, but as self means Devil, so it means God.

Everything intercepts us from ourselves.

La Valetta, February 16

Yesterday we took *pratique*, and found lodgings once more on dry ground with great joy. All day with my fellow travellers I perambulated this little town of stone. It is from end to end a box of curiosities, and though it is very green and juvenile to express wonder, I could not hinder my eyes from rolling continually in their sockets, nor my tongue from uttering my pleasure and surprise. It is an advantage to enter Europe at the little end, so we shall admire by just degrees from the Maltese architecture up to St. Peter's.

How beautiful to have the church always open, so that every tired wayfaring man may come in and be soothed by all that art can suggest of a better world when he is weary with this. How could anybody who had been in a Catholic church devise such a deformity as a pew?

Through the politeness of Mr. Eynaud, the American consul, I received a card of invitation from Sir Frederick Ponsonby, the governor, to attend a fancy dress ball at the Palace. A very gay and novel scene, but hardly equal to the place and expectation. As the consul did not appear very early, my friends and I presented each other to Sir Frederick, who conversed a few moments very pleasantly. We thought he resembled George IV. A few beautiful faces in the dancing crowd; and a beautiful face is worth going far to see. That which is finest in beauty is *moral*. The most piquant attraction of a long-descended maiden is the imputation of an immaculate innocence, a sort of wild virtue (if I may so term it), wild and fragrant as the violets. And the imagination is surprised and gratified with the strong contrast, meeting the Divinity amidst flowers and trifles.

I am my own comedy and tragedy.

Naples, March 12

And what if it is Naples, it is only the same world of cake and ale, of men and truth and folly. I won't be imposed upon by a name. It is so easy, almost so inevitable, to be overawed by names, that on entering this bay it is hard to keep one's judgment upright, and be pleased only after your own way. Baiæ and Misenum and Vesuvius, Procida and Posilipo and Villa Reale sound so big that we are ready to surrender at discretion and not stickle for our private opinion against what seems the human race. Who cares? Here's for the plain old Adam, the simple, genuine self against the whole world. Need is, that you assert yourself, or you will find yourself overborne by the most paltry things. A young man is dazzled by the stately arrangements of the hotel, and jostled out of his course of thought and study of men by such trumpery considerations. The immense regard paid to clean shoes and a smooth hat impedes him, and the staring of a few dozens of idlers in the street hinders him from looking about him with his own eyes; and the attention which he came so far to give to foreign wonders is concentrated instead on these contemptible particulars. Therefore it behoves the traveller to insist first of all upon his simple human rights of seeing and of judging here in Italy, as he would in his own farm or sitting-room at home.

When I was at home and felt vaunty, I pestered the good folks with insisting on discarding every motive but the highest. I said you need never act for example's sake; never give pledges, etc. But I think now that we need all the advantages we can get, that our virtue wants all the crutches; that we must avail ourselves of our strength, and weakness, and want of appetite, and press of affairs, and of calculation, and of fear, as well as of the just and sublime considerations of the love of God and of self-respect. Not that any others will bear comparison with these, but because the temptations are so manifold and so subtle and assail archangels as well as coarser clay, that it will not do to spare any strength.

One must be thoroughly reinforced with the spirit of antiquity to preserve his enthusiasm through all the annoyances that await the visitor of these ruins. Long ago when I dreamed at home of these things, I thought I should come suddenly in the midst of an open country upon broken columns and fallen friezes, and their solitude would be solemn and eloquent. Instead of this, they are carefully fenced round like orchards, and the moment the unhappy traveller approaches one of them this vermin of ciceroni and padroni fasten upon him; a class of people whose looks and manners are more like those of MacGuffog and the Duke of Alsatia than the vain and flippant character I had imagined as the exhibitor *con amore*. What with these truculent fellows, and the boys, and the beggars and the coachmen, all sentiment is killed in the bud, and most men clap both hands on their pockets and run.

Judge of your natural character by what you do in your dreams. If you yield to temptation there, I am afraid you will, awake. If you are a coward then, I jalouse of your courage by day.

Rome, March 27

It is even so; my poor feet are sore with walking all this day amongst the ruins of Rome. I was led in the evening, so easy is it to be led, to a violin concert. I was glad, however, to learn the power of a fiddle. It wailed like a bugle, and reminded me of much better things and much happier hours.

What is more pathetic than the studio of a young artist? Not rags and disease in the street move you to sadness like the lonely chamber littered round with sketches and canvas and colour-bags. There is something so gay in the art itself that these rough and poor commencements contrast more painfully with it. Here another enthusiast feeds himself with hope, and rejoices in dreams, and smarts with mortifications. The melancholy artist told me that, if the end of painting was to please the eye, he would throw away his pallet. And yet how many of them not only fail to reach the soul with their conceptions, but fail to please the eye.

Plain good manners and sensible people—how refreshing they are! A bashful man is cramped among the fine people who have polished manners but dull brains; but he is relieved and recreated by a better influence and regains his natural shape and air and powers.

To-night I heard the *Miserere* sung in St. Peter's and with less effect than yesterday. But what a temple! When night was settling down upon it and a long religious procession moved through a part of the church, I got an idea of its immensity such as I had not before. You walk about on its ample, marble pavement as you would on a common, so free are you of your neighbors; and throngs of people are lost upon it. And what beautiful lights and shades on its mighty gilded arches and vaults and far windows and brave columns, and its rich-clad priests that look as if they were the pictures come down from the walls and walking.

Thence we came out (I was walking with two painters, Cranch and Alexander) under the moon and saw the planet shine upon the finest fountain in the world, and upon all the stone saints on the piazza and the great church itself. This was a spectacle which only Rome can boast,— how faery beautiful! An Arabian Night's tale.

I do not yet fall in with that class of English I had hoped to see, those best educated gentlemen, namely, who are not bred with a view to any profession, nor even to politics, but only to maintain the old honours of their houses. In such a class one would hope to find chivalry and learning and sense; but I am not so fortunate as to meet them, but of dandies an abundance. A gentleman, I suppose, is as rare as a genius. Those who usurp the name are often masses of selfishness and littleness.

No man should travel until he has learned the language of the country he visits. Otherwise he voluntarily makes himself a great baby,—so helpless and so ridiculous.

I never get used to men. They always awaken expectations in me which they always disappoint, and I am a poor asteroid in the great system, subject to disturbances in my orbit, not only from all the planets, but from all their moons. The wise man, the true friend, the finished character, we seek everywhere, and only find in fragments. Yet I cannot persuade myself that all the beautiful souls are fled out of the planet, or that always I shall be excluded from good company and yoked with green, dull, pitiful persons.

God's greatest gift is a Teacher, and when will he send me one full of truth and of boundless benevolence and of heroic sentiments? I can describe the man. I know the idea well, but where is its real blood-warm counterpart? I know whilst I write thus that the creature is never to dawn upon me like a sunburst. I know too well how slowly we edge along sideways to everything good and brilliant in life, and how casually and unobservedly we make all our most valued acquaintances. And yet I saw Ellen at once in all her beauty, and she never disappointed me, but in her death.

All giving and receiving is reciprocal; you entertain angels unawares, but they cannot impart more or higher things than you are in a state to receive.

Florence, May 11

Last night I went to the Pergola, and to my eyes, unused to theatres, it was a glorious show. The whole scenery and the dresses of the performers were in admirable taste, everything good but the strutting of the actors. Is it penal for an actor to *walk?* Before the play was done, my eyes were so dazzled with the splendor of light and colors that I was obliged to rest them and look at my shoes for half an hour, that I might keep them for the last act.

I ought not to forget the ballet between the acts. Goethe laughs at those who force every work of art into the narrow circle of their own prejudices and cannot admire a picture as a picture, and a tune as a tune. So I was willing to look at this as a ballet, and to see that it was admirable, but I could not help feeling the while that it were better for mankind if there were no such dancers.

To-day I dined with Mr. Landor at his villa at San Domenica di Fiesole. He lives in a beautiful spot in a fine house full of pictures and with a family most engaging: he has a wife and four children. He said good and pleasant things, and preferred Washington to all modern great men. He is very decided, as I might have expected, in all his opinions, and very much a connoisseur, in paintings.

I met the fair Erminia to-day. These meetings always cost me a *grazie,* and it is fit that she should not be slighted in the journal. Erminia is a flower-girl who comes to the *caffè* every morning, and if you will not buy her flowers she gives them to you and with such a superb air. She has a fine expression of face and never lets her customers pass her in the street without a greeting. Every coach too in Florence that ventures to stop near the Piazza di Trinità is a tributary of Erminia's. I defy them to escape from her nosegays.

Went again to the opera to see a piece called *Ivanhoe*. What a miserable abuse, to put a woman of dignity and talent into man's clothes. They had spoiled a fine woman to make a bad knight. I came home disgusted.

I like the sayers of No better than the sayers of Yes.

Perhaps the most satisfactory and most valuable impressions are those which come to each individual casually and in moments when he is not on the hunt for wonders.

No man can have society upon his own terms. If he seek it, he must serve it too. He immediately and inevitably contracts debts to it which he must pay, at a great expense, often, of inclination, and of time, and of duty.

Venice, June 2

The ancient metropolis of the merchants. In coming into it, it seemed a great oddity but not at all attractive. Under the full moon, later in the evening, St. Mark's Piazza showed like a world's wonder, but still I pity the people, who are not beavers, and yet are compelled to live here.

But what matter where and how, as long as all of us are estranged from truth and love, from Him who is truth and love. Sometimes I would hide myself in the dens of the hills, in the thickets of an obscure country town. I am so vexed and chagrined with myself,—with my weakness, with my guilt. Then I have no skill to live with men, that is, with such men as the world is made of; and such as I delight in I seldom find. It seems to me, no boy makes so many blunders or says such awkward, contrary, disagreeable speeches as I do. In the attempt to oblige a person I wound and disgust him. I pity the hapless folks that have to do with me. But would it not be cowardly to flee out of society and live in the woods?

A great man will find a great subject, or which is the same thing, make any subject great.

Milan, June 10

Architecture—shall I speak what I think?—seems to me ever an imitation. Accustomed to look at our American churches as imitative, I cannot get it out of my head that these which I now see are only more splendid and successful imitations also. I am perplexed with my inveterate littleness; I must and will see the things in detail and analyse all, every noble sentiment to the contrary notwithstanding. It seems to me nothing is truly great, nothing impresses us, nothing overawes, nothing crowds upon us, and kills calculation. We always call in the effect of imagination, coax the imagination to hide this and enlarge that, and not even St. Peter's, nor this frost-work cathedral at Milan, with its 5000 marble people all over its towers, can charm down the little Imp.

I arrived in Paris at noon on Thursday, 20 June. My companions, who had been in the *belle ville* before, and wished it to strike me as it ought, are scarce content with my qualified admiration.

I have wandered round the city, but I am not well pleased. I have seen so much in five months that the magnificence of Paris will not take my eye to-day. The gardens of the Louvre looked pinched and the wind blew dust in my eyes, and before I got into the Champs Élysées I turned about and flatly refused to go farther. I was sorry to find that in leaving Italy I had left forever that air of antiquity and history which her towns possess, and in coming hither had come to a loud, modern New York of a place.

How does everybody live on the outside of the world! All young persons thirst for a *real* existence for an object—for something great and good which they shall do with all their heart. Meantime they all pack gloves, or keep books, or travel, or draw indentures, or cajole old women.

Does any man render written account to himself of himself? I think not. Those who have anything worth repeating— ah! the sad confession! Those who are innocent have been employed in tape and pins. When will good work be found for great spirits? When shall we be able without a blush and without harm to utter to the world our inmost thought?

Thus shall I write memoirs? A man who was no courtier, but loved men, went to Rome,—and there lived with boys. He came to France, and in Paris lives alone, and in Paris seldom speaks. If he do not see Carlyle in Edinburgh, he may go to America without saying anything in earnest, except to Cranch and to Landor.

The errors of traditional Christianity as it now exists, the popular faith of many millions, need to be removed to let men see the divine beauty of moral truth. I feel myself pledged, if health and opportunity be granted me, to demonstrate that all necessary truth is its own evidence; that no doctrine of God need appeal to a book; that Christianity is wrongly received by all such as take it for a system of doctrines,—its stress being upon moral truth; it is a rule of life, not a rule of faith.

And how men can toil and scratch so hard for things so dry, lifeless, unsightly, as these famous dogmas, when the divine beauty of the truths to which they are related lies behind them; how they can make such a fuss about the case, and never open it to see the jewel, is strange, pitiful.

Be cheerful. What an insane habit is this of groping always into the past months, and scraping together every little pitiful instance of awkwardness and misfortune, and keeping my nervous system ever on the rack. It is the disease of a man who is at the same time too idle, and respectful to the opinion of others.

I carried my ticket from Mr. Warden to the Cabinet of Natural History in the Garden of Plants. How much finer things are in composition than alone. 'T is wise in man to make cabinets. When I was come into the Ornithological Chambers I wished I had come only there. The fancy-coloured vests of these elegant beings make me as pensive as the hues and forms of a cabinet of shells, formerly. It is a beautiful collection and makes the visitor as calm and genial as a bridegroom. The limits of the possible are enlarged, and the real is stranger than the imaginary.

Here we are impressed with the inexhaustible riches of nature. The universe is a more amazing puzzle than ever, as you glance along this bewildering series of animated forms,—the hazy butterflies, the carved shells, the birds, beasts, fishes, insects, snakes, and the upheaving principle of life everywhere incipient, in the very rock aping organized forms. Not a form so grotesque, so savage, nor so beautiful but is an expression of some property inherent in man the observer,—an occult relation between the very scorpions and man. I feel the centipede in me,—cayman, carp, eagle, and fox. I am moved by strange sympathies; I say continually "I will be a naturalist."

Young men are very fond of Paris, partly, no doubt, because of the perfect freedom,—freedom from observation as well as interference,—in which each one walks after the sight of his own eyes; and partly because the extent and variety of objects offers an unceasing entertainment. So long as a man has francs in his pocket he needs consult neither time, nor place, nor other men's convenience; wherever in the vast city he is, he is within a stone's throw of a *patissier*, a *café*, a restaurant, a public garden, a theatre, and may enter when he will.

I went this evening into Frascati's, long the most noted of the gambling houses or hells of Paris, and which a gentleman had promised to show me. This establishment is in a very handsome house on the *Rue Richelieu*. Several servants in livery were waiting in the hall, who took our hats on entering, and we passed at once into the suite of rooms in all of which play was going on. The most perfect decorum and civility prevailed, the table was covered with little piles of napoleons which seemed to change masters very rapidly, but scarce a word was spoken. Servants carry about lemonade, etc., but no heating liquor. The house, I was told, is always one party in the game. Several women were present, but many of the company seemed to be mere spectators like ourselves. After walking round the tables, we returned to the hall, gave the servant a franc for our hats, and departed. Frascati has grown very rich.

London, July 20

We know London so well in books and pictures and maps and traditions that I saw nothing surprising in this passage up the Thames. A noble navigable stream, lined on each side by a highly cultivated country, full of all manner of good buildings. Then Greenwich and Deptford, hospital, docks, arsenals, fleets of shipping, and then the mighty metropolis itself, old, vast and still. Scarce anybody was in the streets. It was about 7 o'clock Sunday morning, and we met few persons until we reached St. Paul's. A porter carried our baggage, and we walked through Cheapside, Newgate Street, High Holborn, and found lodgings (according to the direction of my friend in Paris) at Mrs. Fowler's, No. 63 Russell Square. It was an extreme pleasure to hear English spoken in the streets; to understand all the words of children at play, and to find that we must not any longer express aloud our opinion of every person we met, as in France and Italy we had been wont to do.

Happy the man who never puts on a face, but receives every visitor with that countenance he has on.

Carlisle in Cumberland, August 26

I am just arrived in merry Carlisle from Dumfries. A white day in my years. I found the youth I sought in Scotland, and good and wise and pleasant he seems to me. Thomas Carlyle lives in the parish of Dunscore, 16 miles from Dumfries, amid wild and desolate heathery hills, and without a single companion in this region out of his own house. There he has his wife, a most accomplished and agreeable woman. Truth and peace and faith dwell with them and beautify them. I never saw more amiableness than is in his countenance.

Ambleside, August 28

This morning I went to Rydal Mount and called upon Mr. Wordsworth.

The poet is always young, and this old man took the same attitudes that he probably had at seventeen, whilst he recollected the sonnet he would recite.

His egotism was not at all displeasing, obtrusive, as I had heard. To be sure it met no rock. I spoke as I felt, with great respect of his genius.

Liverpool, September 1

I thank the Great God who has led me through this European scene, this last schoolroom in which he has pleased to instruct me, from Malta's isle, through Sicily, through Italy, through Switzerland, through France, through England, through Scotland, in safety and pleasure, and has now brought me to the shore and the ship that steers westward. He has shown me the men I wished to see,—Landor, Coleridge, Carlyle, Wordsworth; he has thereby comforted and confirmed me in my convictions. Many things I owe to the sight of these men. I shall judge more justly, less timidly, of wise men forevermore. To be sure not one of these is a mind of the very first class, but what the intercourse with each of these suggests is true of intercourse with better men, that they never *fill the ear*—fill the mind—no, it is an *idealized* portrait which always we draw of them. Upon an intelligent man, wholly a stranger to their names, they would make in conversation no deep impression, none of a world-filling fame,—they would be remembered as sensible, well-read, earnest men, not more. Especially are they all deficient, all these four,—in different degrees, but all deficient,—in insight into religious truth. They have no idea of that species of moral truth which I call the first philosophy.

The comfort of meeting men of genius such as these is that they talk sincerely, they feel themselves to be so rich that they are above the meanness of pretending to knowledge which they have not, and they frankly tell you what puzzles them. But Carlyle—Carlyle is so amiable that I love him.

But I am very glad my travelling is done. A man not old feels himself too old to be a vagabond. The people at their work, the people whose avocations I interrupt by my letters of introduction, accuse me by their looks for leaving my business to hinder theirs.

These men make you feel that fame is a conventional thing, and that man is a sadly "limitary" spirit. You speak to them as to children, or persons of inferior capacity whom it is necessary to humour; adapting our tone and remarks to their known prejudices and not to our knowledge of the truth.

I believe in my heart it is better to admire too rashly, as I do, than to be admired too rashly, as the great men of this day are. They miss by their premature canonization a great deal of necessary knowledge, and one of these days must begin the world again (as to their surprise they will find needful) poor. I speak now in general, and not of these individuals. God save a great man from a little circle of flatterers. I know it is sweet, very sweet, ratsbane.

Could not Wordsworth have kept to himself his intimations that his new edition was at the bookseller's and contained some improvements. John Milton was a poet, not a bookmaker.

I am thankful that I am an American as I am thankful that I am a man.

No sailing today. I am at a dead stand. I can neither write

nor read more. If the vessel do sail, they say we shall be
drowned on the lee shore; if she do not sail I perish waiting. What's the odds? I have plainly said my last word; it is
the prodigality of ink, the wanton destruction of paper
to add another syllable, and withal a singular exhibition of
what fatuity a man is capable who reckons himself sometimes an educated and thinking man. Yet must I write
still. Why? these lines are the expectants of the dinner; and
it is cold and I cannot go out. Why should I? I have bid
goodbye to all the people. Shall I make them repeal their
tears and benedictions? There are no books in the house, I
have digested the newspaper. I have no companion.

Ah me! Mr. Thomas Carlyle, I would give a gold pound
for your wise company this gloomy eve. Ah, we would
speed the hour. Ah, I would rise above myself—what self-
complacent glances casts the soul about in the moment of
fine conversation, esteeming itself the author of all the fine
things it utters, and the master of the riches the memory
produces, and how scornfully looks it back upon the plain
person it was yesterday without a thought.

It occurs forcibly, yea, somewhat pathetically, that he
who visits a man of genius out of admiration for his parts
should treat him tenderly. 'T is odds but he will be disappointed. That is not the man of genius's fault. He was honest and human, but the fault of his own ignorance of the
units of human excellence. Let him feel that his visit was
unwelcome, and that he is indebted to the tolerance and
good nature of his idol, and so spare him the abuse of his
own reacting feelings, the back-stroke.

No sailing still, but sitting still. I went to the railroad and
saw Rocket and Goliath and Pluto and Firefly and the rest
of that vulcanian generation. Mr. Perkins says they should
not go faster than fifteen miles the hour. It racks the en-

gines to go faster. He says that he confidently expects the time when the ocean will be navigated by merchantmen by *steam* as the most economical means, but there is a great deal to be done first; that now very little advantage is taken for the *expansion* of steam, its most important property.

We were towed out of Liverpool Harbor by steamboat. Admirable contrivance for ports in deep bays like this, or Philadelphia, or Baltimore, for they might lie weeks waiting to get out with the wind fair for the voyage all the time.

It is such a narrow line that divides an awkward act from the finish of gracefulness. Every man eats well alone. Let a stranger come in, and he misses his mouth, and spills his butterboat, and fails of finding the joint in carving, and that by so little.

I like my book about Nature, and wish I knew where and how I ought to live. God will show me. I am glad to be on my way home, yet not so glad as others, and my way to the bottom I could find perchance with less regret, for I think it would not hurt me,—that is, the ducking or drowning.

The road from Liverpool to New York, as they who have travelled it well know, is very long, crooked, rough, and eminently disagreeable. Good company even, Heaven's best gift, will scarce make it tolerable. Four meals a day is the usual expedient (and the wretchedness of the expedient will show the extremity of the case) and much wine and porter,—these are the amusements of wise men in this sad place. The purest wit may have a scurvy stomach.

The wise man in the storm prays God, not for safety from danger, but for deliverance from fear. It is the storm within which endangers him, not the storm without.

In this world, if a man sits down to think, he is immediately asked if he has the headache?

Milton describes himself in his letter to Diodati as enamoured of moral perfection. He did not love it more than I. That which I cannot yet declare has been my angel from childhood until now. It has separated me from men. It has watered my pillow, it has driven sleep from my bed. It has tortured me for my guilt. It has inspired me with hope. It cannot be defeated by my defeats. It cannot be questioned, though all the martyrs apostatize.

God defend me from ever looking at a man as an animal. God defend me from the vice of my constitution, an excessive desire of sympathy. Let me be content with the consciousness of innocency and the desire of worth, without stretching myself upon the rack whenever any man, woman, or child passes by until he, she or it is possessed of my intention.

An impulse as irresistible as is the acorn to germinate is in the soul of the prophet to speak.

I am sure of this, that by going much alone a man will get more of a noble courage in thought and word than from all the wisdom that is in books.

When a man goes into the woods he feels like a boy without loss of wisdom. To be sure a dandy may go there, and Nature will never speak to a dandy.

[QUAKER CONVERSATIONS]
"Thomas, I know what thee is thinking of." "If you do, Micah, you don't feel flattered."

"Mary it has been revealed to me that I should marry thee." "Abner, when it is revealed to me I will tell thee."

The old jail in Cambridge was immediately back of Mrs. Kneeland's house. The inmates of the prison were very bad neighbors and used to take delight in pestering Mrs. Kneeland with foul names and profane language. Professor Hedge took great pains to get the nuisance removed, and at last the old jail was pulled down. Someone congratulated Mrs. K. upon the happy deliverance, but found her quite sad at the loss of her stimulus. "She kind o' missed 'em," she said.

I will not refer, defer, confer, prefer, differ. I renounce the whole family of *fero*. I embrace absolute life.

My children, said my Grandfather, you will never see anything worse than yourselves.

We walk about in a sleep. A few moments in the year, or in our lifetime, we truly live; we are at the top of our being; we are pervaded, yea, dissolved by the Mind; but we fall back again presently. Those who are styled Practical Men are not awake, for they do not exercise the Reason; yet their sleep is restless. The most active lives have so much routine as to preclude progress almost equally with the most inactive. We bow low to the noted merchants whose influence is felt, not only in their native cities, but in most parts of the globe; but our respect does them and ourselves great injustice, for their trade is without system, their affairs unfold themselves after no law of the mind, but are bubble built on bubble without end; a work of arithmetic, not of commerce, much less of humanity. They add voyage to voyage, and buy stocks,—that they may buy stocks, —and no ulterior purpose is thought of. When you see their dexterity in particulars, you cannot overestimate the resources of good sense; and when you find how empty they are of all remote aims, you cannot underestimate their philosophy.

The man of letters puts the same cheat upon us, bestirring himself immensely to keep the secret of his littleness. He spins his most seeming surface directly before the eye, to conceal the universe of his ignorance.

All our writings are variations of one air. Books for the most part are such expedients as his who makes an errand for the sake of exercise.

Such is the inaction of men. We have an obscure consciousness of our attributes. We stand on the edge of all that is great, yet are restrained in inactivity and unconscious of our powers.

Much preparation, little fruit. But suddenly in any place, in the street, in the chamber, will the heavens open and the regions of wisdom be uncovered, as if to show how thin the veil, how null the circumstances. As quickly, a Lethean stream washes through us and bereaves us of ourselves.

What a benefit if a rule could be given whereby the mind, dreaming amid the gross fogs of matter, could at any moment CAST ITSELF *and* FIND THE SUN! But the common life is an endless succession of phantasms; and long after we have deemed ourselves recovered and sound, light breaks in upon us and we find that we have yet had no sane hour. Another morn rises on mid-noon.

1834

This Book is my Savings Bank. I grow richer because I have somewhere to deposit my earnings; and fractions are worth more to me because corresponding fractions are waiting here that shall be made integers by their addition.

Whole process of human generation how bifronted! To one it is bawdry, to another pure. In the mother's heart every sensation, from the nuptial embrace, through the uncertain symptoms of the quickening, to the birth of her child, is watched with an interest more chaste and wistful than the contemplations of the nun in her cloister; yet the low-minded visitor of a woman in such circumstances has the ignorant impertinence to look down and feel a sort of shame.

How often our nature is conscious of and labours with its own limits! In the very act of pretension it is oppressed with secret humiliation.

Times of eloquence are times of terror.

How imbecile is often a young person of superior intellectual powers for want of acquaintance with his powers; bashful, timid, he shrinks, retreats before every confident person, and is disconcerted by arguments and pretensions he would be ashamed to put forward himself. Let him work, as many merchants do, with the forces of millions of property for months and years upon the wills of hundreds of persons, and you shall see him transformed into an adroit, fluent, masterful gentleman, fit to take and keep his place in any society of men. This is the account to be given of the fine manners of the young Southerners brought up amidst slaves, and of the concession that young Northerners make to them,—yes, and old Northerners to old Southerners. This part of education is conducted in the nursery and the playground in fights, in frolics, in business, in politics. My manners and history would have been very different, if my parents had been rich, when I was a boy at school.

The days and months and years flit by, each with his own black riband, his own sad reminiscence. Yet I look at the almanack affectionately as a book of Promise. These three last years of my life are not a chasm—I could almost wish they were—so brilliantly sometimes the vision of Ellen's beauty and love and life come out of the darkness.

When a village Lyceum Committee asks me to give a lecture, and I tell them I will read one I am just writing, they are pleased. Poor men, they little know how different that lecture will be when it is given in New York, or is printed. I "try it on" on them; *"The barber learns his trade on the orphan's chin."*

A seaman in the coach told the story of an old sperm-whale, which he called a white whale, which was known for many years by the whalemen as Old Tom, and who rushed upon the boats which attacked him, and crushed the boats to small chips in his jaws, the men generally escaping by jumping overboard and being picked up. A vessel was fitted out at New Bedford, he said, to take him. And he was finally taken somewhere off Payta Head by the *Winslow* or the *Essex*.

I count no man much because he cows or silences me. Any fool can do that. But if his conversation enriches or rejoices me, I must reckon him wise.

Is it possible that, in the solitude I seek, I shall have the resolution, the force, to work as I ought to work, as I project in highest, most far-sighted hours? Well, and what do you project? Nothing less than to look at every object in its relation to myself.

Went yesterday to Cambridge and spent most of the day at Mount Auburn; got my luncheon at Fresh Pond, and went back again to the woods. After much wandering and seeing many things, four snakes gliding up and down a hollow for no purpose that I could see—not to eat, not for love, but only gliding; then a whole bed of *Hepatica triloba*, cousins of the Anemone, all blue and beautiful, but constrained by niggard nature to wear their last year's faded jacket of leaves; then a black-capped titmouse, who came upon a tree, and when I would know his name, sang *chick-a-dee-dee;* then a far-off tree full of clamorous birds, I know not what, but you might hear them half a mile. I forsook the tombs, and found a sunny hollow where the east wind would not blow, and lay down against the side of a tree to most happy beholdings. At least I opened my eyes and let what would pass through them into the soul. I saw no more my relation, how near and petty, to Cambridge or Boston; I heeded no more what minute or hour our Massachusetts clocks might indicate—I saw only the noble earth on which I was born, with the great Star which warms and enlightens it. I saw the clouds that hang their significant drapery over us. It was Day—that was all Heaven said. The pines glittered with their innumerable green needles

in the light, and seemed to challenge me to read their riddle. The drab oak-leaves of the last year turned their little
somersets and lay still again. And the wind bustled high
overhead in the forest top. This gay and grand architecture,
from the vault to the moss and lichen on which I lay,—who
shall explain to me the laws of its proportions and adorn-
ments?

See the perpetual generation of good sense: nothing
wholly false, fantastic, can take possession of men who, to
live and move, must plough the ground, sail the sea, have
orchards, hear the robin sing, and see the swallow fly.

We are always on the brink of an ocean of thought into
which we do not yet swim. We are poor lords,—have immense powers which we are hindered from using. I am
kept out of my heritage.

Are we not ever postponing great actions and ineffable wisdom? We are ever coming up with a group of angels still
in sight before us, which we refer to when we say "the
Truth" and the Wise Man, and the corrections these shall
make in human society. All the mistakes I make arise from
forsaking my own station and trying to see the object from
another person's point of view. I read so resolute a self-
thinker as Carlyle, and am convinced of the riches of
wisdom that ever belong to the man who utters his own
thought with a divine confidence that it must be true if he
heard it there.

We live, animals in the basement story, and when Shakspeare or Milton, or even my fantastical Scotchman who
fools his humor to the top of his bent, call us up into the
high region, we feel and say, "this is my region, they only
show me my own property. I am in my element. I thank
them for it." Presently we go about our business into the

basement again, cumbered with serving; and assured of our right to the halls above, we never go thither.

I had observed long since that, to give the thought a just and full expression, I must not prematurely utter it. Better not talk of the matter you are writing out. It was as if you had let the spring snap too soon.

Sabbath, April 13

There are some duties above courtesy: and were it not lawful for the discontented spirit sometimes to cry out, Husks, Husks! Ye feed the people with words, even in their solemn assembly? They distress me by their prayers, and all the discourse was an impertinence. There sat, too, the gifted man, and if he unlawfully withheld his word, this wearisome prose was his just punishment.

Elsewhere,—certainly not there, but from M.M.E.,* from Carlyle, or from this delicious day, or whatever celestial fingers touched the divine harp,—I woke to a strain of highest melody. I saw that it was not for me to complain of obscurity, of being misunderstood; it was not for me, even in the fifthy rags of my unrighteousness, to despond of what I might do and learn.

It occurs how much friction is in the machinery of society. The material is so much that the spiritual is overlaid and lost. A man meditates in solitude upon a truth which seems to him so weighty that he proposes to impart it to his fellow men. Immediately a society must be collected, and books consulted, and much paper blotted in preparation of his discourse. Alien considerations come in, personal considerations—and finally when he delivers his discourse, 'tis quite possible it does not contain the original message,

* Emerson's aunt.

so that it was no superfluous rule he gave who said, "When you write, do not omit the thing you meant to say." The material integuments have quite overlaid and killed the spiritual child. Not otherwise it falls out in education. A young man is to be educated, and schools are built, and masters brought together, and gymnasium erected, and scientific toys and monitorial systems and a college endowed with many professorships, and the apparatus is so enormous and unmanageable that the *e-ducation* or *calling out of his faculties* is never accomplished; he graduates a dunce.

Is it otherwise in our philosophic enterprises? They wish to heal the sick, or emancipate the African, or convert the Hindoo, and immediately agents are appointed, and an office established, and Annual Reports printed,—and the least streamlet of the vast contributions of the public trickles down to the healing of the original evil. The Charity becomes a job. Well now, is it otherwise with life itself? We are always getting ready to live, but never living. We have many years of technical education; then many years of earning a livelihood, and we get sick, and take journeys for our health, and compass land and sea for improvement by travelling, but the work of self-improvement,—always under our nose,—nearer than the nearest, is seldom seldom engaged in. A few, few hours in the longest life.

Set out to study a particular truth. Read upon it; walk to think upon it; talk of it; write about it;—the thing itself will not much manifest itself, at least not much in accommodation to your studying arrangements. The gleams you do get out, they will flash as likely at dinner, or in the roar of Faneuil Hall, as in your painfullest abstraction.

Very little life in a lifetime.

The whole secret of the teacher's force lies in the conviction that men are convertible.

In proportion as you penetrate facts for the law, and events for the cause, in that measure is your knowledge real, your condition gradually conformed to a stable idea, and the future forseen. I have laid my egg, but 'tis either old or empty.

In desert lands the bird alights on the barrel of the hunter's gun, and many other facts are there; but that which I would say is that every teacher acquires a cumulative inertia; the more forcible, the more eloquent, have been his innovating doctrines, the more eagerly his school have crowded around him, so much the more difficult is it for him to forfeit their love, to compromise his influence by advancing farther in the same track. Therefore the wise man must be wary of attaching followers. He must feel and teach that the best wisdom cannot be communicated; must be acquired by every soul for itself.

The Muses love the woods, and I have come hither to court the awful Powers in this sober solitude. Whatsoever is highest, wisest, best, favor me! I will listen and then speak.

Rain, rain. The good rain, like a bad preacher, does not know when to leave off.

I saw a hawk to-day wheeling up to heaven in a spiral flight, and every circle becoming less to the eye till he vanished into the atmosphere. What could be more in unison with all pure and brilliant images. Yet is the creature an unclean greedy eater, and all his geography from that grand observatory was a watching of barn-yards, or an inspection of moles and field-mice.

The air vibrates with equal facility to the thunder and to the squeak of a mouse; invites man with provoking indifference to total indolence and to immortal actions.

Many eyes go through the meadow, but few see the flowers in it.

"There are three things," said my worthy friend W. W. to me, "that make the gentleman,—the hat, the collar, and the boots."

A dim, venerable public decides upon every work. When it offers itself, a sort of perplexity, an uneasy waiting for judgment appears in the living literary judges; but the work presently takes its true place, by no effort, friendly or hostile, but by the real importance of its principles to the constant mind of man. And this in a way that no individual can much affect by blame or praise. It is the specific gravity of the atom.

There are persons both of superior character and intellect whose superiority quite disappears when they are put together. They neutralize, anticipate, puzzle, and belittle each other.

One has dim foresight of hitherto uncomputed mechanical advantages who rides on the railroad, and moreover a practical confirmation of the ideal philosopher that matter is phenomenal, whilst men and trees and barns whiz by you as fast as the leaves of a dictionary. As our teakettle hissed along through a field of mayflowers, we could judge of the sensations of a swallow who skims by trees and bushes with about the same speed. The very permanence of matter seems compromised, and oaks, fields, hills, hitherto esteemed symbols of stability, do absolutely dance by you. The countryman called it "Hell in harness."

I went to the menagerie Tuesday and saw 14 pelicans, a sacred ibis, a gazelle, zebras, a capibara, ichneumon, hyena, etc. It seems to me like "visiting the spirits in prison." Yet not to "*preach*." There was the mystery. No word could pass from me to them. Animals have been called by some German "the dreams of Nature." I think we go to our own dreams for a conception of their consciousness. In a dream I have the same instinctive obedience, the same torpidity of the highest power, the same unsurprised assent to the monstrous, as these metamorphosed men exhibit. The pelicans remind one of Nick Bottom. One has a kind of compassionate fear lest they should have a glimpse of their forlorn condition. What a horrible calamity would be to them one moment's endowment of reason! Yet sometimes the negro excites the same feeling, and sometimes the sharp-witted, prosperous white man. You think, if he could overlook his own condition, he could not be kept from suicide.

The finest poems of the world have been expedients to get bread, or else expedients to keep the writer from the madhouse and amuse him and his fellow men with the illusion that he knew; but the greatest passages they have writ, the infinite conclusions to which they owe their fame, are only confessions.

The rare women that charm us are those happily constituted persons who take possession of society wherever they go, and give it its form, its tone. If they sit, as we sit, to wait for what shall be said, we shall have no Olympus.

To their genius elegance is essential. It is enough that we men stammer and mince words and play the clown and pedant alternately. They must speak as clearly and simply as a song.

The thoughtful man laments perhaps the unpliancy of his organization, which draws down the corners of his mouth to ludicrous longitude, whilst all the company chat and titter around him. What matters it? He actually sympathizes with each of the company more truly than the liveliest chatterbox; for they are all going back from this smiling time to discipline, to silence, labor and anxiety, and then they recall the melancholy man with a fraternal remembrance.

I wish to be a true and free man, and therefore would not be a woman, or a king, or a clergyman, each of which classes, in the present order of things, is a slave.

The abomination of desolation is not a burned town, nor a country wasted by war, but the discovery that the man who has moved you is an enthusiast upon calculation.

What is there of the divine in a load of bricks? What is there of the divine in a barber's shop? . . . Much. All.

All society and government seems to be *making believe,* when we see such hollow boys with a grave countenance taking their places as legislators, presidents, and so forth.

Never assume. Be genuine. So wrote I for my own guidance months and years ago; but how vainly! Show me in the world the sincere man. Even the wit, the sentiment that seasons the dinner, is a sort of hypocrisy to hide the coarseness of appetite. The child is sincere, and the man when he is alone, if he be not a writer; but on the entrance of the second person, hypocrisy begins.

We sit down to write truly, and end with making a book that contains no thought of ours, but merely the tune of the time. Here am I writing a ϕ B K poem, free to say what I choose, and it looks to me now as if it would scarce express thought of mine, but be a sort of *fata morgana* reflecting the images of Byron, Shakspear, and the newspapers. We do what we can, and then make a theory to prove our performance the best.

So keep me heaven, I will love the race in general if I cannot in any particular.

My entire success, such as it is, is composed wholly of particular failures,—every public work of mine of the least importance, having been (probably without exception) noted at the time as a failure. The only success (agreeably to common ideas) has been in the country, and there founded on the false notion that here was a Boston preacher.

I never was on a coach which went fast enough for me.

It is extremely disagreeable, nay, a little fiendish to laugh amid dreams. In bed I would keep my countenance, if you please.

A poem is made up of thoughts, each of which filled the whole sky of the poet in its turn.

September 15

No art can exceed the mellow beauty of one square rood of ground in the woods this afternoon. The noise of the locust, the bee, and the pine; the light, the insect forms, butterflies, cankerworms hanging, balloon-spiders swinging, devils-needles cruising, chirping grasshoppers; the tints and forms of the leaves and trees,—not a flower but its form seems a type, not a capsule but is an elegant seed-box,—then the myriad asters, polygalas, and golden-rods, and through the bush the far pines, and overhead the eternal sky.

How despicable are the starts, sidelong glances, and lookings back of suspicious men. Go forward and look straight ahead, though you die for it. You have looked behind you at the passenger and caught his eye looking behind also. What dastards you both are for that moment! The unconscious forever, which turns the whole head or nothing!

New York, October 18

Received the tidings of the death of my dear brother Edward on the first day of this month at St. John, Porto Rico. So falls one pile more of hope for this life. I see I am bereaved of a part of myself.

Broadway is Trade and Vanity made flesh. Therein should the philosophers walk as the impersonations of States, as if Massachusetts, Carolina, Ohio, should go out to take an airing.

What is a man but a congress of nations. Just suppose for one moment to appear before him the whole host of his ancestors. All have vanished; he—the insulated result of all that character, activity, sympathy, antagonism, working for ages in all corners of the earth—alone remains.

If any eye rest on this page, let him know that he who blotted it could not go into conversation with any person of good understanding without being presently gravelled. The slightest question of his most familiar proposition disconcerted him, eyes, face and understanding, beyond recovery. Yet did he, not the less, respect and rejoice in this daily gift of vivacious common sense, which was so formidable to him. May it last as long as the world.

I rejoice in Time. I do not cross the common without a wild poetic delight, notwithstanding the prose of my demeanour. Thank God I live in the country.

The maker of a sentence launches out into the infinite and builds a road into Chaos and old Night, and is followed by those who hear him with something of wild, creative delight.

The domestic man loves no music so well as his kitchen clock and the airs which the logs sing to him as they burn in the fireplace.

The best means of mending a bad voice is to utter judicious remarks with it; the second best is to favor it by silence.

1835

There is no greater lie than a voluptuous book like Boccaccio. For it represents the pleasures of appetite, which only at rare intervals, a few times in a life-time, are intense, and to whose acme continence is essential, as frequent, habitual, and belonging to the incontinent.

Dr. H., Mr. B., Mr. S., Mr. I., the most powerful men in our community, have no theory of business that can stand scrutiny, but only bubble built on bubble without end. They skate so fast over a film of ice that it does not break under them. It seems, when you see their dexterity in particulars, as if you could not overestimate the resources of good sense, and when you find how utterly void they are of all remote aims, as if you could not underestimate their philosophy.

A wonderful sight is the inverted landscape. Look at the prospect from a high hill through your legs, and it gives the world a most pictorial appearance.

I fretted the other night at the hotel at the stranger who broke into my chamber after midnight, claiming to share it. But after his lamp had smoked the chamber full and I had turned round to the wall in despair, the man blew out his lamp, knelt down at his bedside, and made in low whisper a long earnest prayer. Then was the relation entirely changed between us. I fretted no more, but respected and liked him.

A writer appears ever to so much more advantage in the pages of another man's book than in his own. Coleridge, Wordsworth, Schelling are conclusive, when Channing or Carlyle or Everett quotes them, but if you take up their own books, then instantly they become, not lawgivers, but modest, peccable candidates for your approbation.

It is a happy talent to know how to play. Some men must always work if they would be respectable; for the moment they trifle, they are silly. Others show most talent when they trifle. Be it said of W.* that his excess of reverence made it impossible for him to realize ever that he was a man; he never assumed equality with strangers, but still esteemed them older than himself, though they were of his own age or younger. He went through life postponing his maturity and died in his error.

The order of things consents to virtue. Such scenes as luxurious poets and novelists often paint, where temptation has a quite overcoming force, never or very rarely occur in real life.

We are all wise for other people, none for himself.

Genius seems to consist merely in trueness of sight, in using such words as show that the man was an eye-witness, and not a repeater of what was told.

The young preacher is discouraged by learning the motives that brought his great congregation to church. Scarcely ten came to hear his sermon. But singing, or a new pelisse, or Cousin William, or the Sunday School, or a proprietors' meeting after church, or the merest anility in Hanover Street, were the beadles that brought and the bolts that hold his silent assembly in the church. Never mind how they came, my friend, never mind who or what brought them, any more than you do who or what set you down in Boston in 1835. Here they are, real men and

* Waldo; i.e., himself.

women,—fools, I grant, but potentially divine, every one of them convertible.

When I write a book on spiritual things I think I will advertise the reader that I am a very wicked man, and that consistency is nowise to be expected of me.

The advantage in Education is always with those children who slip up into life without being objects of notice. Happy then those who are members of large families.

The good of publishing one's thoughts is that of hooking to you like-minded men, and of giving to men whom you value, such as Wordsworth or Landor, one hour of stimulated thought. Yet, how few! Who in Concord cares for the first philosophy in a book? The woman whose child is to be suckled? The man at Nine-acre-Corner who is to cart sixty loads of gravel on his meadow? the stageman? the gunsmith? Oh, no! Who then?

We cross the ocean sweltering, sea-sick, reeling, week after week, with tar, harness-tub, and bilge, and, as an ingenious friend says, it is carrying the joke too far.

If you would know what nobody knows, read what everybody reads, just one year afterwards.

I study the art of solitude: I yield me as gracefully as I can to my destiny. Why cannot one get the good of his doom, and since it is from eternity a settled thing that he and society shall be nothing to each other, why need he blush so, and make wry faces and labor to keep up a poor beginner's place, a freshman's seat in the fine world?

Why do I still go to pasture where I never find grass; to these actors without a purpose, unless a poor mechanical one, these talkers without method, and reasoners without an idea? At the Divinity School this morning I heard what was called the best performance, but it was founded on nothing and led to nothing, and I wondered at the patience of the people. This afternoon the king of the House of Seem spoke, and made as if he was in earnest with pathetic tones and gestures, and the most approved expressions,—and all about nothing; and he was answered by others with equal apparent earnestness, and still it was all nothing. The building seemed to grudge its rent, if the assembly did not their time. They are all so solemn and vehement, that I listen with all my ears, and for my life can't find any idea at the foundation of their zeal.

I forgive desultoriness, trifling, vice even, in a young man, so long as I believe that he has a closet of secret thoughts to which he retires as to his home, and which have a sort of parents' interest in him wherever he is. At sight of them he bows. But if he is not in earnest about anything, if all his interest is good breeding and imitation, I had as lief not be as be him.

Humility is a great time-saver. The whole business must wait whenever each individual of the company has some personal recollection, some apology or explanation to make. All sit impatiently deferring till his impertinent vanity is adjusted and then go on.

When shall I be tired of reading? When the moon is tired of waxing and waning, when the sea is tired of ebbing and flowing, when the grass is weary of growing, when the planets are tired of going.

A system-grinder hates the truth. To make a step into the world of thought is given to but few men; to make a second step beyond his first, only one in a country can do; but to carry the thought out to three steps marks a great Teacher.

After thirty, a man wakes up sad ever morning, excepting perhaps five or six, until the day of his death.

Charles* wonders that I don't become sick at the stomach over my poor journal. Yet is obdurate habit callous even to contempt. I must scribble on, even if it were only to say in confirmation of Oegger's doctrine that I believe I never take a step in thought when engaged in conversation without some material symbol of my proposition figuring itself incipiently at the same time. My sentence often ends in babble from a vain effort to represent that picture in words.

While I thus talked, I *saw* some crude *symbols* of the thought with the mind's eye,—as it were, a mass of grass or weeds in a stream, of which the spears or blades shot out from the mass in every direction, but were immediately curved round to float all in one direction. When presently the conversation changed to the subject of Thomas à Kempis's popularity, and how Aristotle and Plato come safely down, as if God brought them in his hand (though at no time are there more than five or six men who read them), and of the Natural Academy by which the exact value of every book is determined, maugre all hindrance or furtherance; then saw I, as I spoke, the old pail in the Summer Street kitchen with potatoes swimming in it, some at the top, some in the midst, and some lying at the bot-

* Emerson's brother, Charles.

tom; and I spoiled my fine thought by saying that books take their place according to their specific gravity "as surely as potatoes in a tub."

A great tendency I like better than a small revelation, and I hate to be imprisoned in premature theories.

Yesterday I delighted myself with Michel de Montaigne. With all my heart I embrace the grand old sloven. He pricks and stings the sense of virtue in me.

August 15

I bought my house and two acres six rods of land of John T. Coolidge for 3,500 dollars.

September 14

I was married to Lydia Jackson.*

Thompson the abolitionist is inconvertible: what you say, or what might be said, would make no impress on him. He belongs, I fear, to that great class of the Vanity-stricken. An inordinate thirst for notice cannot be gratified until it has found in its gropings what is called a cause that men will bow to; tying himself fast to that, the small man is then at liberty to consider all objections made to him as proofs of folly and the devil in the objector, and, under that screen, if he gets a rotten egg or two, yet his name sounds through the world and he is praised and praised.

Go into one of our cool churches, and begin to count the words that might be spared, and in most places the entire sermon will go. One sentence kept another in countenance, but not one by its own weight could have justified the saying of it.

* Thereafter called, by Emerson, Lidian.

A man to thrive in literature must trust himself. The voice of society sometimes, and the writings of great geniuses always, are so noble and prolific, that it seems justifiable to follow and imitate. But it is better to be an independent shoemaker than to be an actor and play a king.

A meek self-reliance I believe to be the law and constitution of good *writing*. A man is to treat the world like children who must hear and obey the spirit in which he speaks, but which is not his. If he thinks he is to sing to the tune of the times, is to be the decorous sayer of smooth things to lull the ear of society, and to speak of religion as the great traditional *thing* to be either mutely avoided or kept at a distance by civil bows, he may make a very good workman for the booksellers, but he must lay aside all hope to wield or so much as to touch the bright thunderbolts of truth.

What's a book? Everything or nothing. The eye that sees it is all.

We form no guess, at the time of receiving a thought, of its comparative value.

Last Saturday night came hither Mr. Alcott, and spent the Sabbath with me. A wise man, simple, superior to display, and drops the best things as quietly as the least.

What can be truer than the doctrine of inspiration? of fortunate hours? Things sail dim and great through my head. Veins of rich ore are in me, could I only get outlet and pipe to draw them out. How unattainable seem to me these wild pleasantries of Shakespeare, yet not less so seem to me passages in old letters of my own.

What platitudes I find in Wordsworth!

> "I, poet, bestow my verse
> *On this and this and this.*"

Scarce has he dropped the smallest piece of an egg, when he fills the barnyard with his cackle.

C.* thinks that it is only by an effort like a Berserkir a man can work himself up to any interest in any exertion. All active life seems an *amabilis insania*. And when he has done anything of importance he repents of it, repents of virtue as soon as he is alone. Nor can he see any reason why the world should not burn up to-night. The play has been over some time.

* Charles.

PART II

1836-1838

During these years Emerson's first book, *Nature*, was published; Charles, his beloved brother, died of consumption; his son, Waldo, was born; and the names of new and valued friends, notably Bronson Alcott and Henry Thoreau, begin to appear in the journals. Lectures in Boston added to his slowly growing reputation as an original thinker, and he often preached at a nearby church at East Lexington. In 1837 he delivered in Cambridge his famous Phi Beta Kappa oration on *The American Scholar*, and the following year his plea to the graduating class of the Harvard Divinity School for freedom of thought raised a storm among the more conservative elements of the community that ruffles the pages of the journal. This was a period, not only of spiritual, but of financial crisis, and occasional echoes of the hard times will be heard in these entries.

1836

I take the law of hospitality to be this:—I confer on the friend whom I visit the highest compliment, in giving him my time. He gives me shelter and bread. Does he therewith buy my suffrage to his opinions henceforward? No more than by giving him my time, I have bought his.

The scholar works with invisible tools to invisible ends, so passes for an idler, or worse, brain-sick, defenceless to idle carpenters, masons, and merchants, that, having done nothing most laboriously all day, pounce on him fresh for spoil at night.

It is easy to solve the problem of individual existence. Why Milton, Shakspear, or Canova should be, there is reason enough. But why the million should exist, drunk with the opium of Time and Custom, does not appear. If their existence is phenomenal, they serve so valuable a purpose to the education of Milton, that, grant us the Ideal theory, and the universe is solved. Otherwise, the moment a man discovers that he has aims which his faculties cannot answer, the world becomes a riddle.

Society seems noxious. I believe that against these baleful influences Nature is the antidote. The man comes out of the wrangle of the shop and office, and sees the sky and the woods, and is a man again. He not only quits the cabal, but he finds himself. But how few men see the sky and the woods!

There is such an immense background to my nature that I must treat my fellow as Empire treats Empire, and God, God.

Let not a man guard his dignity, but let his dignity guard him.

A man should stand among his fellow men as one coal lies in the fire it has kindled, radiating heat, but lost in the general flame.

Last week I went to Salem. At the Lafayette Hotel where I lodged, every five or ten minutes the barkeepers came into the sitting-room to arrange their hair and collars at the looking-glass. So many joys has the kind God provided for us dear creatures.

Godliness. How strange that such a word exists applied to men! It was a masterpiece of wisdom to inoculate every biped crawling round after his bread with this sublime maggot.

Man is an analogist. He cannot help seeing everything under its relations to all other things and to himself. The most conspicuous example of this habit of his mind is his naming the Deity Father.

You must exercise your genius in some form that has essential life now; do something which is proper to the hour, and cannot but be done.

Concord, May 16

And here I am again at home, but I have come alone. My brother, my friend, my ornament, my joy and pride, has fallen by the wayside,—or rather has risen out of this dust. Charles died at New York, Monday afternoon, 9 May. Beautiful without any parallel in my experience of young men, was his life, happiest his death. Miserable is my own prospect from whom my friend is taken.

Now commences a new and gloomy epoch of my life. I have used his society so fondly and solidly. It was pleasant to unfold my thought to so wise a hearer. It opened itself genially to his warm and bright light, and borrowed color and sometimes form from him.

Who can ever supply his place to me? None. I may live long. I may (though 'tis improbable) see many cultivated persons, but his elegance, his wit, his sense, his worship of principles, I shall not find united—I shall not find them separate. The eye is closed that was to see nature for me, and give me leave to see.

The value of many persons is like that of a unit in decimal notation which is determined altogether by the *place* of the number.

I gladly pay the rent of my house because I therewith get the horizon and the woods which I pay no rent for. For daybreak and evening and night, I pay no tax. I think it is a glorious bargain which I drive with the town.

The pilgrim goes into the woods, but he carries with him the beauty which he visits. For the eye is the painter and the ear the singer. Where is not man is neither color nor sound. The man is the creator of his world. I choose to pursue certain thoughts, to enter certain states of mind, and forthwith I seem to walk into woods by known ways and to hear woodbirds and see pines and birches. I choose to pursue certain other thoughts, and lo! I seem to visit the wharves and market.

In rare society I dilate and am wise, good, and hopeful by sympathy, but in ordinary company I shrink and palter and apologize. I know not why, but I hate to be asked to preach here in Concord. I never go to the Sunday School Teachers without fear and shame.

If I study an ant-hill and neglect all business, all history, all conversation, yet shall that ant-hill, humbly and lovingly and unceasingly explored, furnish me with a parallel experience and the same conclusions to which business, history and conversation would have brought me.

Mr. Alcott has been here with his Olympian dreams. He is a world-builder. Evermore he toils to solve the problem, whence is the world? The point at which he prefers to begin is the mystery of the Birth of a child. I tell him it is idle for him to affect to feel an interest in the compositions of any one else. Particulars—particular thoughts, sentences, facts even—cannot interest him, except as for a moment

they take their place as a ray from his orb. The Whole,—
Nature proceeding from himself, is what he studies. But he
loses, like other sovereigns, great pleasures by reason of his
grandeur. I go to Shakspear, Goethe, Swift, even to Tennyson, submit myself to them, become merely an organ of
hearing, and yield to the law of their being. I am paid for
thus being nothing by an entire new mind, and thus, a
Proteus, I enjoy the universe through the powers and organs of a hundred different men. But Alcott cannot delight
in Shakspear, cannot get near him. And so with all things.
What is characteristic also, he cannot recall one word or
part of his own conversation or of any one's, let the expression be never so happy. He made here some majestic ut-
terances, but so inspired me that even I forgot the words
often.

Man is the point wherein matter and spirit meet and
marry.

There is something fearful in coming up against the walls
of a mind on every side, and learning to describe their
invisible circumference.

To-day came to me the first proof-sheet of *Nature* to be
corrected, like a new coat, full of vexations; with the first
sentences of the chapters perched like mottoes aloft in
small type! The peace of the author cannot be wounded
by such trifles, if he sees that the sentences are still good.
A good sentence can never be put out of countenance by
any blunder of compositors. It is good in text or note, in
poetry or prose, as title or corollary. But a bad sentence
shows all his flaws instantly by such dislocation.

If you go expressly to look at the moon, it becomes tinsel.

The man of talents who brings his poetry and eloquence to market is like the hawk which I have seen wheeling up to heaven in the face of noon, and all to have a better view of mice and moles and chickens.

We see much truth under the glitter and ribbons of a festival like Commencement. Each year the same faces come there, but each elongated or whitened or fallen a little. The courage too that is felt at presenting your own face before the well-known assembly, is not an extempore feeling, but is based on a long memory of studies and actions. An assembly is a sort of Judgment Day, before whose face every soul is tried. The scholar looks in at the door, but unwilling to face this ordeal to little purpose, he retreats and walks along solitary streets and lanes far from the show.

I found my old friends the same; the same jokes pleased, the same straws tickled; the manhood and offices they brought hither to-day seemed masks; underneath we were still boys.

"Dulness of the age." What age was not dull? When were not the majority wicked? or what progress was ever made by society? Society is always flat and foolish. The only progress ever known was of the individual. A great wit is, at any time, great solitude. A barnyard is full of chirping and cackle, but no fowl claps wings on Chimborazo.

Look into the stage-coach and see the faces! Stand in State Street and see the heads and the gait and gesture of the men; they are doomed ghosts going under Judgment all day long.

Want is a growing giant, and Have could never cut a coat large enough to cover him.

A very good discourse on Marriage might be written by him who would preach the nature of things. Let him teach how fast the frivolous external fancying fades out of the mind. Let him teach both husband and wife to mourn for the rapid ebb of inclination not one moment, to yield it no tear. As this fancy picture, these Fata-Morgana, this cloud scenery fades forever; the solid mountain chains whereupon the sky rests in the far perspective of the soul begin to appear. The parties discover every day the deep and permanent character each of the other as a rock foundation on which they may safely build their nuptial bower. They learn slowly that there is no luck, nor witchcraft, nor destiny, nor divinity in marriage that can produce affection, but only those qualities that by their nature extort it; that all love is mathematical.

He who seeks self-union is accused of injustice and inhospitality. People stretch out to him their mendicant arms, to whom he feels that he does not belong and who do not belong to him. He freezes them with his face of apathy, and they very naturally tax him with selfishness. He knows it is unjust. Send me, he says, cold, despised and naked, the man who loves what I love, the man whose soul is regulated and great, and he shall share my loaf and my cloak. But people of this class do not approach him, but the most unfit associates hasten to him with joy and confidence that they are the very ones whom his faith and philosophy invites; they mar all his days with their follies, and then with their tacit reproaches, so that his fair ideal of domestic life and serene household gods he cannot realize, but is afflicted instead with censures from the inmate, censures from the observer, and necessarily, if he be of a sympathetic character, censures from himself also.

For hospitality, however, the duties will clear themselves: give cake and lemons to those who come for such, and give them nothing else, and account yourself cheaply let off. And if those seek you whom you do not seek, hold them stiffly to their rightful claims. Give them your conversation; be to them a teacher, utter oracles, but admit them never into any infringement on your hours; keep state: be their priest, not their companion, for you cannot further their plans, you cannot counsel them on their affairs, and you have never pledged yourself to do so by confounding your relation to them.

The fine prints and pictures which the dentist hangs in his ante-room have a satirical air to the waiting patient.

The house praises the carpenter.

Poverty, Frost, Famine, Rain, Disease, are the beadles and guardsmen that hold us to Common Sense.

I sit alone and cannot arouse myself to thoughts. I go and sit with my friend and in the endeavor to explain my thought to him or her, I lay bare the awful mystery to myself as never before, and start at the total loneliness and infinity of one man.

How little masters we are of our wits! Mine run away with me. I don't know how to drive. I see them from far: then they whisk by me. I supplicate, I grieve, I point to the assembly that shall be, but the inexorable Thoughts will neither run in pairs, nor in strings, nor in any manageable system. But Necessity is lord of all, and when the day comes, comes always the old lord, and will harness the very air, if need be, to the cart.

So much lecturing, and now a little printing, has bronzed me, and I am growing very dogmatic and I mean to insist that whatsoever elements of humanity have been the subjects of my studies constitute the indisputable core of Modern History,—to such lengths of madness trot we, when we have not the fear of criticism before our eyes, and the literary man in this country has no critic.

Concord, October 31

Last night, at 11 o'clock, a son was born to me. Blessed child! a lovely wonder to me, and which makes the universe look friendly to me. How remote from my knowledge, how alien, yet how kind, does it make the Cause of causes appear! The stimulated curiosity of the father sees the graces and instincts which exist indeed in every babe, but unnoticed in others; the right to see all, know all, to examine nearly, distinguishes the relation, and endears this sweet child. Otherwise I see nothing in it of mine; I am no conscious party to any feature, any function, any perfection I behold in it. I seem to be merely a brute occasion of its being, and nowise attaining to the dignity even of a second cause, no more than I taught it to suck the breast.

Every day a child presents a new aspect, Lidian says, as the face of the sky is different every hour, so that we never get tired. The truth seems to be that every child is infinitely beautiful, but the father alone by position and by duty is led to look near enough to see. He looks with microscope. But what is most beautiful is to see the babe and the mother together, the contrast of size makes the little nestler appear so *cunning*, and its tiny beseeching weakness is compensated so perfectly by the happy patronizing look of the mother, who is a sort of high reposing Providence toward it, that they make a perfect group.

For form's sake, or for wantonness, I sometimes chaffer with the farmer on the price of a cord of wood, but if he said twenty dollars instead of five, I should think it cheap when I remember the beautiful botanical wonder—the bough of an oak—which he brings me so freely out of the enchanted forest where the sun and water, air and earth and God formed it.

Yesterday, the election of state and town officers. One must be of a robust temper and much familiar with general views to avoid disgust from seeing the way in which a young fellow with talents for intrigue can come into a peaceful town like this, besot all the ignorant and simple farmers and laborers, and ride on their necks until, as yesterday, they reject their long honoured townsman who had become a sort of second conscience to them, a Washington in his county, and choose in his place an obscure stranger whom they know not, and have no right to trust. Yet the philosopher ought to learn hence how greedy man is of fellowship and of guidance. The low can best win the low, and all men like to be made much of.

When fear enters the heart of a man at hearing the names of candidates and the reading of laws that are proposed, then is the State safe, but when these things are heard without regard, as above or below us, then is the Commonwealth sick or dead.

The very sentiment I expressed yesterday without heed, shall sound memorable to me to-morrow if I hear it from

another. My own book I read with new eyes when a
stranger has praised it.

The most fugitive deed or word, the mere air of doing a
thing, the intimated purpose, expresses character, and the
remote results of character are civil history and events that
shake or settle the world. If you act, you show character;
if you sit still, you show it; if you sleep.

But in analysing history do not be too profound, for
often the causes are quite superficial. In the present state
of Spain, in the old state of France, and in general in the
reigns of Terror, everywhere, there is no Idea, no Principle.
It is all scrambling for bread and money. It is the absence
of all profound views; of all principle. It is the triumph of
the senses, a total skepticism. They are all down on the
floor striving each to pick the pocket, or cut the throat that
he may pick the pocket, of the other, and the farthest
view the miscreants have is the next tavern or brothel
where their plunder may glut them. If presently one
among the mob possesses ulterior aims, and these inspire
him with skill, he masters all these brutes, as oxen and
dogs are mastered by a man, and turns them to work for
him and his thought.

The positive degree is the sinew of a speech, the superlative is the fat.

Pleasant walk yesterday, the most pleasant of days. At Walden Pond I found a new musical instrument which I call
the ice-harp. A thin coat of ice covered a part of the pond,
but melted around the edge of the shore. I threw a stone
upon the ice which rebounded with a shrill sound, and
falling again and again, repeated the note with pleasing

modulation. I thought at first it was the "peep, peep" of a bird I had scared. I was so taken with the music that I threw down my stick and spent twenty minutes in throwing stones single or in handfuls on this crystal drum.

A man's wife has more power over him than the state has.

1837

It occurred last night in groping after the elements of that pleasure we derive from literary compositions, that it is like the pleasure which the Prince Le Boo received from seeing himself for the first time in a mirror,—a mysterious and delightful surprise. A poem, a sentence, causes us to see ourselves. I be, and I see my being, at the same time.

Let a man behave in his own house as a guest.

I rode well; my horse took hold of the road as if he loved it.

I saw in Boston my fair young L., but so rashly grown that her sweet face was like a violet on the top of a pole.

My baby's lovely drama still goes forward, though he catches sad colds, and wheezes and grieves. Yet again he sputters and spurs, and puts on his little important faces, and looks dignified, and frets and sleeps again. We call him little Pharisee, who when he fasts, sounds a trumpet before him.

Any work looks wonderful to me except the one which I can do.

If we knew we were in a Purgatory, if we knew of crimes and are now in Hell, the lowness and filths of life were then explained.

The most tedious of all discourses are on the subject of the Supreme Being.

How wild and mysterious our position as individuals to the Universe. We understand nothing; our ignorance is abysmal, the overhanging immensity staggers us, whither we go, what we do, who we are, we cannot even so much as guess. We stagger and grope.

I see with joy the visits of heat and moisture to my trees, and please myself with this new property. I strangely mix myself with nature, and the Universal God works, buds, and blooms in my grove and parterre. I seem to myself an enchanter who by some rune or dumb-gesture compels the service of superior beings. But the instant I separate *my own* from the tree and the potato field, it loses this piquancy. I presently see that I also am but an instrument like the tree, a reagent. The tree was to grow; I was to transplant and water it, not for me, not for it, but for all.

Slowly I learn with amazement that in my wildest dream, in my softest emotion, in my tear of contrition, I but repeat moment for moment the impulses and experience of the fashionist, the buccaneer, the slave, or whatever other variety may be of the generic man.

Sad is this continual postponement of life. I refuse sympathy and intimacy with people, as if in view of some better sympathy and intimacy to come. But whence and when? I am already thirty-four years old. Already my friends and fellow workers are dying from me. Scarcely can I say that I see any new men or women approaching me; I am too old to regard fashion; too old to expect patronage of any greater or more powerful. Let me suck the sweetness of those affections and consuetudes that grow near me—that the Divine Providence offers me. These old shoes are easy to the feet.

The true medicine for hard times seems to be sleep. Use so much bodily labor as shall insure sleep, then you arise refreshed and in good spirits and in Hope. That have I this morn. Yesterday afternoon, I stirred the earth about my shrubs and trees and quarrelled with the piper-grass, and now I have slept, and no longer am morose nor feel twitchings in the muscles of my face when a visitor is by. The humble-bee and the pine-warbler seem to me the proper objects of attention in these disastrous times.

Yesterday Alcott left me after three days spent here. I had "lain down a man and waked up a bruise," by reason of a bad cold, and was lumpish, tardy and cold. Yet could I see plainly that I conversed with the most extraordinary man and the highest genius of the time. He is a Man. He is erect; he sees; let whoever be overthrown or parasitic or blind. Life he would have, and enact, and not nestle into any cast-off shell and form of the old time; and now proposes to preach to the people, or to take his staff and walk through the country conversing with the school-teachers, and holding conversations in the villages. And so he ought to go publishing through the land his gospel, like them of old times. Wonderful is his vision; the steadiness and scope of his eye at once rebukes all before it, and we little men creep about ashamed. It is amusing even to see how this great visual orb rolls round upon object after object, and threatens them all with annihilation,—seemeth to wither and scorch.

Coldly he asks "whether Milton is to continue to meet the wants of the mind"? and so Bacon, and so of all. He is, to be sure, monotonous; you may say, one gets tired of the uniformity,—he will not be amused, he never cares for the pleasant side of things, but always truths and their origin he seeketh after.

Society an imperfect union. Is it not pathetic that the action of men on men is so partial? We never touch but at points. The most I can have or be to my fellow man, is it the reading of his book, or the hearing of his project in conversation? I approach some Carlyle with desire and joy. I am led on from month to month with an expectation of some total embrace and oneness with a noble mind, and learn at last that it is only so feeble and remote and hiant action as reading a Mirabeau or Diderot paper, and a few the like. This is all that can be looked for. More we shall not be to each other. Baulked soul! It is not that the sea and poverty and pursuit separate us. Here is Alcott by my door, yet is the union more profound? No, the sea, vocation, poverty, are seeming fences, but man is insular and cannot be touched. Every man is an infinitely repelling orb, and holds his individual being on that condition.

I see a good in such emphatic and universal calamity as the times bring. That they dissatisfy me with society. Under common burdens we say there is much virtue in the world, and what evil coexists is inevitable. I am not aroused to say, "I have sinned; I am in the gall of bitterness, and bond of iniquity"; but when these full measures come, it then stands confessed,—society has played out its last stake; it is check-mated. Young men have no hope. Adults stand like day-laborers idle in the streets. None calleth us to labor. The old wear no crown of warm life on their gray hairs. The present generation is bankrupt of principles and hope, as of property. I see man is not what man should be. He is the treadle of a wheel. He is a tassel at the apron-string of society. He is a money-chest. He is the servant of his belly. This is the causal bankruptcy, this the cruel oppression, that the ideal should serve the actual, that the head should serve the feet.

Pride, and Thrift, and Expediency, who jeered and chirped and were so well pleased with themselves, and made merry with the dream, as they termed it, of Philosophy and Love,—behold they are all flat, and here is the Soul erect and unconquered still.

Among provocatives, the next best thing to good preaching is bad preaching. I have even more thoughts during or enduring it than at other times.

It is easy for the philosophic class to be poor. Poverty is their ornament, they wear with it a sort of silent protest, and challenge admiration. They need not immerse themselves in sense; they scorn to knit their brows on the merits of a sauce and a soup, because they are haunted with a thought that matter has higher uses, namely, its poetical use or language. But not so easy is it to the unphilosophical class to be poor. My friend has no books, no conversation, no fine insight, in short, no certificate that he is any better man than his thousand neighbors, except his great house and marble mantel-pieces, his superb centre-table, and the portfolio of engravings lying on it. These realize to him his inward merit. These are tough medals of his honesty and labor and the regard of fellow men. It is very cruel of you to insist, because you can very well forego them, that he shall.

You may regret calamities if you can thereby help the sufferer, but if you cannot, mind your own business.

If you go into the garden and hoe corn or kill bugs on the vines, or pick pease, when you come into the house you shall still for some time see *simulacra* of weeds and vines or pea-pods, as you see the image of the sun some time after looking at the sun. Both are disagreeable phenomena, as bad as laughing.*

Nature still solicits me. Overhead the sanctities of the stars shine forevermore, and to me also, pouring satire on the pompous business of the day which they close, and making the generations of men show slight and evanescent. A man is but a bug, the earth but a boat, a cockle, drifting under their old light.

I knew a man scared by the rustle of his own hat-band.

Hannah Haskins tells well the story of Aunt Mary's watcher, whilst she had a felon on her thumb. She had never a watcher in her life and was resolved to have one once, so seized the chance; all day was making preparations for her coming and requiring the family to have things in readiness. Twice or thrice she sent messages over to the woman's house to tell her to sleep, and to fix the hour of her coming. When at last she came, she first put the watcher to bed that she might be ready, and watched her herself, but presently woke her because she thought

* "Emerson hated to be made to laugh; he could not command his face well."

her head did not lie comfortably; then again because she snored, to forbid her making such a shocking noise. At last she became anxious lest her watcher should spend the night, and day break before she had got any service from her; so she determined to get up and have her own bed made for the sake of giving her something to do. But at last, growing very impatient of her attendance, she dismissed her before light, declaring she never would have a watcher again; she had passed the worst night she remembered. On the other part, Miss——, the watcher, declared that no consideration would tempt her to watch with Miss Emerson again.

The least effect of the oration is on the orator; yet it is something; a faint recoil; a kicking of the gun.

This morning Mr. Alcott and Mr. Hedge left me. Four or five days full of discourse, and much was seen. I incline to withdraw continually as from a surfeit, but the stomach of my wise guests being stronger, I strain my courtesy to sit by, though drowsy. In able conversation we have glimpses of the Universe, perceptions of the soul's omnipotence, but not much to record.

Meek young men grow up in colleges and believe it is their duty to accept the views which books have given, and grow up slaves. Some good angel in the shape of a turnkey bids them demand a *habeas corpus,* and the moment they come out of durance the heaven opens and the earth smiles.

I please myself with getting my nail-box set in the snuggest corner of the barn-chamber and well filled with nails, and gimlet, pincers, screwdriver and chisel. Herein I find an old joy of youth, of childhood, which perhaps all domestic children share,—the catlike love of garrets, barns and corn-chambers, and of the conveniences of long housekeeping.

The babe cheers me with his hearty and protracted laugh, which sounds to me like thunder in the woods.

There never was child so lovely but his mother was glad to get him asleep.

The young preacher preached from his ears and his memory, and never a word from his soul. His sermon was loud and hollow. It was not the report so much as the *rimbombo,* the reverberation of Calvinism. A solemn conclusion of a Calvinistic discourse imitated at the end of a Unitarian sermon is surely ludicrous, like grandfather's hat and spectacles on a rogue of six years.

I suppose there was seldom a person of my age and advantages whom so little people could pull down and overcrow. The least people do most entirely demolish me. I always find some quarter, and some orts of respect from the mediocre. But a snipper-snapper eats me whole.

A man is sometimes offended at the superfluous, supererogatory order and nicety of a woman who is the good housewife. But he must bear with little extremities and flourishes of a quality that makes comfort for all his senses throughout his house.

The young Southerner comes here a spoiled child, with graceful manners, excellent self-command, very good to be spoiled more, but good for nothing else,—a mere parader.

He has conversed so much with rifles, horses and dogs that he has become himself a rifle, a horse and a dog, and in civil, educated company, where anything human is going forward, he is dumb and unhappy, like an Indian in a church. Treat them with great deference, as we often do, and they accept it all as their due without misgiving. The proper way of treating them is not deference, but to say as Mr. Ripley does, "Fiddle faddle," in answer to each solemn remark about "The South." "It must be confessed," said the young man, "that in Alabama, we are dead to everything, as respects politics." "Very true," replied Mr. Ripley, "leaving out the last clause."

Be a football to Time and Chance, the more kicks, the better, so that you inspect the whole game and know its uttermost law.

We are carried by destiny along our life's course, looking as grave and knowing as little as the infant who is carried in his wicker coach through the street.

Men in society do not interest us because they are tame. We know all they will do, and man is like man as one steamboat is like another. Tame men are inexpressibly tedious, like the talking with a young Southerner who says, "Yes, sir," indifferently to every sort of thing you say, thinking Yes, sir, to mean nothing. From every man, even from great men as the world goes, a large deduction is to be made on account of this taming, or Conventions. His going to church does not interest me because all men go to Church. His staying at home would, until I see why he stays at home, if from vulgar reasons,—it is dulness still. But he falls desperately in love. Ah, ha! does he? now I am wide-awake, this is not conventional, but the great epoch of the revelation of Beauty to his soul. Now let me see every line he writes, every step he makes, every kiss which makes him immortal; let those laugh who never were worthy to love; to me each act of his in these golden hours is holy and beautiful.

Margaret Fuller talking of women, said, Who would be a goody that could be a genius?

When I commended the adroit New York broker to Alcott, he replied that he saw he had more austerity than I, and that he gave his hand with some reluctance to mere merchant or banker. What is so comic, I pray, as the mutual condescension with which Alcott and Colonel Perkins would give the hand to each other?

In conversing with a lady it sometimes seems a bitterness and unnecessary wound to insist, as I incline to, on this self-sufficiency of man. There is no society, say I; there can be none. "Very true, but very mournful," replies my friend. We talk of courses of action. But to women my paths are shut up, and the fine women I think of who have had genius and cultivation, who have not been wives, but muses, have something tragic in their lot and I shun to name them.

It is ignoble to owe our success to the coaxing and clapping of society, to be told by the incapable, "That's capital. Do some more."

I said when I awoke, After some more sleepings and wakings I shall lie on this mattress sick; then, dead; and through my gay entry they will carry these bones. Where shall I be then? I lifted my head and beheld the spotless orange light of the morning beaming up from the dark hills into the wide Universe.

It is very hard to be simple enough to be good.

I find, in town, the Phi Beta Kappa Oration, of which 500 copies were printed, all sold, in just one month.

Tears are never far from a woman's eye. The loveliest maiden on whom every grace sits, who is followed by all eyes, and never knew anything but admiration, weeps much, and, if unexpected changes should blast her hopes, then the tears fall so naturally as nothing but grief seems her native element.

The event of death is always astounding; our philosophy never reaches, never possesses it; we are always at the beginning of our catechism; always the definition is yet to be made. What is death?

Immense curiosity in Boston to see the Delegation of the Sacs and Foxes, of the Sioux and the Ioways. I saw the Sacs and Foxes at the State House on Monday, about thirty in number, so savage in their head-dress and nakedness that it seemed as if the bears and catamounts had sent a deputation. They danced a war dance on the Common, in the centre of the greatest crowd ever seen on that area. The governor cautioned us of the gravity of the tribe, and that we should beware of any expression of the ridiculous, and the people all seemed to treat their guests gingerly, as the keepers of lions and jaguars do those creatures whose taming is not quite yet trustworthy.

I am agitated with curiosity to know the secret of nature. Why cannot geology, why cannot botany speak and tell me what has been, what is, as I run along the forest promontory, and ask when it rose like a blister on heated steel? Then I looked up and saw the sun shining in the vast sky, and heard the wind bellow above and the water glistened in the vale. These were the forces that wrought then and work now. Yes, there they grandly speak to all plainly, in proportion as we are quick to apprehend.

Yesterday to Faneuil Hall where Webster presided at the Caucus, and heard Bell of Tennessee, Graves and Underwood of Kentucky, and Hoffmann of New York. The speaking was slovenly, small, and tiresome, but the crowd exciting, and the sound of the cheering extraordinarily fine. Webster said, when Bell ended, that "it was not a festive occasion, yet he would venture to propose a sentiment to the meeting: The Health of Mr. Bell and the Whigs of Tennessee, and three times three!" Then was heard the splendid voice of four or five thousand men in full cry together. Such voice might well predominate over brute beasts. It was merely a spectacle to me. But the *genius loci* is more commanding at Faneuil Hall than at any other spot in America. The air is electric. Every man thinks he can speak whilst he hears—lifted off his feet oftentimes—the multitude swaying alternately this side and that. In such crowds few old men; mostly young and middle-aged, with shining heads and swollen veins. The mob is all the time interlocutor, and the bucket goes up and down according to the success of the speaker. The pinched, wedged, elbowed, sweltering multitude, as soon as the speaker loses their ear by tameness of his harangue, feel all sorely how ill accommodated they are, and begin to attend only to themselves and the coarse outcries made all around them. Then they push, resist, swear, and fill the hall with cries of tumult. The speaker stops; the moderator persuades, commands, entreats, "Order!" The speaker gets breath, and a new hint, and resumes, goes to the right place, his voice alters, vibrates, pierces the private ear of every one, the mob quiets itself somehow, every one being magnetized, and the hall hangs suspended on the lips of one man. A happy deliverance of common sentiments charms them [the people]. Never the fineness or depth of the thought, but the good saying of the very few and very poor particulars which lie uppermost in every man's mind at the meeting. All appear struck with wonder and delight at this cheap and mediocre faculty, so rarely is it found. If the speaker become dull again, instantly our poor wedges begin to feel their pains and strive and cry.

The self-subsistent shakes like a reed before a sneering paragraph in the newspaper, or even at a difference of opinion, concerning something to be done, expressed in a private letter from just such another shaking bullrush as himself. He sits expecting a dinner-guest with a suspense which paralyses his inventive or his acquiring faculties. He finds the solitude of two or three entire days, when mother, wife and child are gone, tedious and dispiriting. Let him not wrong the truth and his own experience by too stiffly standing on the cold and proud doctrine of self-sufficiency.

Lovejoy* has given his breast to the bullet for his part, and has died when it was better not to live. He is absolved. There are always men enough ready to die for the silliest punctilio; to die like dogs, who fall down under each

---

* An Abolitionist, lynched in Illinois for denouncing slavery.

other's teeth, but I sternly rejoice that one was found to die for humanity and the rights of free speech and opinion.

The fair girl whom I saw in town expressing so decided and proud choice of influences, so careless of pleasing, so wilful and so lofty a will, inspires the wish to come nearer to and speak to this nobleness: so shall we be ennobled also. I wish to say to her, Never strike sail to any. Come into port greatly, or sail with God the seas. Not in vain you live, for the passing stranger is cheered, refined and raised by the vision.

1838

Sleep and Dreams. The landscape and scenery of dreams seem not to fit us, but like a cloak or coat of some other person, to overlap and incumber the wearer. So is the ground, the road, the house, in dreams too long or too short, and, if it serve no other purpose, would at least show us how accurately nature fits man awake.

Five days ago came Carlyle's letter, and has kept me warm ever since with its affection and praise. It seems his friend John Sterling loves Waldo Emerson also, by reason of reading the book *Nature.* I am quite bewitched, maugre all my unamiableness, with so dainty a relation as a friendship for a scholar and poet I have never seen, and he Carlyle's friend.

February 9
In Boston, Wednesday night, I read at the Masonic Temple the tenth and last lecture of my Course on Human Culture.

The pecuniary advantage of the Course has been considerable.

Season tickets sold	319 for	$620.
Single tickets sold	373 for	186.
		$806.
Deduct error somewhere		13
		$793.
Deduct expenses		225
		$568. net profit.

The attendance on this course (adding to the above list 85 tickets distributed by me to friends) will be about 439 persons, on the average, of an evening—and, as it was much larger at the close than at the beginning, I think five hundred persons at the closing lectures.

At the "teachers' meeting" last night, my good Edmund, after disclaiming any wish to difference Jesus from a human mind, suddenly seemed to alter his tone, and said that Jesus made the world and was the Eternal God. Henry Thoreau merely remarked that "Mr. Hosmer had kicked the pail over." I delight much in my young friend [Thoreau], who seems to have as free and erect a mind as any I have ever met. He told as we walked this afternoon a good story about a boy who went to school with him, Wentworth, who resisted the school mistress's command that the children should bow to Dr. Heywood and other gentlemen as they went by, and when Dr. Heywood stood waiting and cleared his throat with a Hem, Wentworth said, "You needn't hem, Doctor. I shan't bow."

My good Henry Thoreau made this else solitary afternoon sunny with his simplicity and clear perception. How comic is simplicity in this double-dealing, quacking world. Every-thing that boy says makes merry with society, though noth-ing can be graver than his meaning.

Solitude is fearsome and heavy-hearted. I have never known a man who had so much good accumulated upon him as I have. Reason, health, wife, child, friends, com-petence, reputation, the power to inspire, and the power to please; yet, leave me alone a few days, and I creep about as if in expectation of a calamity.

Last night a remembering and remembering talk with Li-dian. I went back to the first smile of Ellen on the door-stone at Concord.* I went back to all that delicious rela-tion to feel, as ever, how many shades, how much reproach. Strange is it that I can go back to no part of youth, no past relation, without shrinking and shrinking. Not Ellen, not Edward, not Charles. Infinite compunctions embitter each of these dear names, and all who surrounded them.

I console myself with the thought that if Ellen, if Ed-ward, if Charles, could have read my entire heart, they should have seen nothing but rectitude of purpose and generosity conquering the superficial coldness and pru-dence. But I ask now, Why was not I made like all these beatified mates of mine, *superficially* generous and noble, as well as *internally so?* They never needed to shrink at any remembrance;—and I at so many sad passages that look to me now as if I had been blind and mad. Well, O God, I will try and learn from this sad memory to be brave and circumspect and true henceforth and weave now a web that will not shrink. This is the thorn in the flesh.

* New Hampshire.

They say of Alcott, and I have sometimes assented, that he is one-toned, and hearkens with no interest to books or conversation out of the scope of his one commanding idea. Maybe so, but very different is his centralism from that of vulgar monomaniacs, for he looks with wise love at all real facts, at street faces, at the broad-shouldered, long-haired farmer, at the domestic woman, at the kitchen, at the furniture, at the season as related to man, and so on. He can hear the voice which said to George Fox, "That which others trample on must be thy food."

I have read with astonishment and unabated curiosity and pleasure Carlyle's *Revolution* again, half through the second volume. I cannot help feeling that he squanders his genius. Why should an imagination such as never rejoiced before the face of God, since Shakespeare, be content to play? Why should he trifle and joke? I cannot see; I cannot praise. It seems to me, he should have writ in such deep earnest that he should have trembled to his fingers' ends with the terror and the beauty of his visions.

At church all day, but almost tempted to say I would go no more. Men go where they are wont to go, else had no soul gone this afternoon. Yet no fault in the good man. Evidently he thought himself a faithful, searching preacher,—mentioned that he thought so several times; and seemed to be one of that large class, *sincere persons based on sham; sincere persons who are bred and do live in shams.* . . .

A minister nowadays is plainest prose, the prose of prose. He is a warming-pan, a night-chair at sickbeds and rheumatic souls; and the fire of the minstrel's eye and the vivacity of his word is exchanged for intense, grumbling enunciation of the Cambridge sort, and for Scripture phraseology.

I thought, as I rode to Acton, that we all betray God to the Devil, Being to Negation. I know well the value of a sentiment and of sincerity, yet how easily will any fop, any coat and boots, draw me to an appearance of sympathy with him and to an air of patronizing the sentiments; the commonest person of condition and fashion affects me more than is right, and I am mute, passive, and let their world wag, let them make the world, I being but a block of the same. I ought to go upright and vital and say the truth in all ways.

Consider that it is a refreshment to the eyes to look at a poultry-yard. I hear the hen cluck and see her stepping round with perfect complacency, but if a man goes by, I have a sorrowful feeling.

In conversation, women *run on,* as it is called. A great vice. A fine woman keeps her purpose and maintains her ground with integrity of manner, whilst you censure or rally her. If she is disconcerted or grieved, the game is up and society a gloom.

Preaching, especially false preaching, is for able men a sickly employment. Study of books is also sickly; and the garden and the family, wife, mother, son, and brother are a balsam. There is health in table talk and nursery play. We must wear old shoes and have aunts and cousins.

Last night ill dreams. Dreams are true to nature and, like monstrous formations (e.g. the horse-hoof divided into toes), show the law. Their double consciousness, their sub- and objectiveness is the wonder. I call the phantoms that rise the creation of my fancy, but they act like volunteers, and counteract my inclination. They make me feel that every act, every thought, every cause, is bipolar, and in the act is contained the counter act. If I strike, I am struck. If I chase, I am pursued. If I push, I am resisted.

I have mentioned the fine persons I have seen, but I must add human nature's postscript, that persons, unless they be of commanding excellence, do not rejoice heads as old as mine like thoughts. Persons I labor at, and grope after, and experiment upon, make continual effort at sympathy, which sometimes is found and sometimes is missed; but I tire at last, and the fruit they bring to my intellect or affections is oft small and poor. But a thought has its own proper motion which it communicates to me, not borrows of me, and on its Pegasus back I override and overlook the world.

"Always pay." I am praised by some half-seeing friends for punctuality and common sense. They see not as I see, that for just that seemliness and passableness I fail so much to think and live in the right Olympian loftiness.

Lidian says that when she gives any new direction in the kitchen she feels like a boy who throws a stone and runs.

This tragic Cherokee* business which we stirred at a meeting in the church yesterday will look to me degrading and injurious, do what I can. It is like dead cats around one's

---

* The exile of the Cherokee tribe from their ancestral lands to the Indian Territory.

neck. It is like school committees and Sunday School classes and teachers' meetings and the Warren Street Chapel and all the other holy hurrahs. I stir in it for the sad reason that no other mortal will move, and if I do not, —why it is left undone. The amount of it, be sure, is merely a Scream, but sometimes a scream is better than a thesis.

Yesterday went the letter to Van Buren, a letter hated of me, a deliverance that does not deliver the soul. What I do, be sure, is all that concerns my majesty, and not what men great or small think of it. Yet I accept the Dartmouth College invitation to speak to the boys with great delight. I write my journal, I read my lecture, with joy, but this stirring in the philanthropic mud gives me no peace. I will let the Republic alone until the Republic comes to me. I fully sympathize, be sure, with the sentiment I write, but I accept it rather from my friends than dictate it. It is not my impulse to say it, and therefore my genius deserts me. No muse befriends, no music of thought or of word accompanies. Bah!

As far as I notice what passes in philanthropic meetings and holy hurrahs there is very little depth of interest. The speakers warm each other's skin and lubricate each other's tongue, and the words flow and the superlatives thicken and the lips quiver and the eyes moisten, and an observer new to such scenes would say, Here was true fire; the assembly were all ready to be martyred, and the effect of such a spirit on the community would be irresistible; but they separate and go to the shop, to a dance, to bed, and an hour afterwards they care so little for the matter that on slightest temptation each one would disclaim the meeting. "Yes, he went, but they were for carrying it too far," etc., etc.

The lesson is, to know that men are superficially very

inflammable, but that these fervors do not strike down and reach the action and habit of the man.

Yesterday afternoon I went to the Cliff with Henry Thoreau. Warm, pleasant, misty weather, which the great mountain amphitheatre seemed to drink in with gladness. A crow's voice filled all the miles of air with sound. A bird's voice, even a piping frog, enlivens a solitude and makes world enough for us. At night I went out into the dark and saw a glimmering star and heard a frog, and Nature seemed to say, Well, do not these suffice? Here is a new scene, a new experience. Ponder it, Emerson, and not like the foolish world, hanker after thunders and multitudes and vast landscapes, the sea or Niagara.

Have I said it before in these pages? then I will say it again, that it is a curious commentary on society that the expression of a devout sentiment by any young man who lives in society strikes me with surprise and has all the air and effect of genius.

The poor Pickwick stuff (into which I have only looked and with no wish for more) teaches this, that prose and parlors and shops and city widows, the tradesman's dinner and such matters, are as good materials in a skilful hand for interest and art as palaces and revolutions.

Distinction gives freedom to the wise man. It gives him leave to speak the truth and act with spirit. If people say the spring is beautiful, let him think whether it is or is not, before he ducks to the remark with a paraphrastic yes.

The advantage of the Napoleonic temperament, impassive, unimpressionable by others, is a signal convenience over this other tender one, which every aunt and every gossiping girl can daunt and tether. This weakness, be sure, is merely cutaneous, and the sufferer gets his revenge by the sharpened observation that belongs to such sympathetic fibre, as even in college I was already content to be "screwed" in the recitation room, if, on my return, I could accurately paint the fact in my youthful journal.

How painful to give a gift to any person of sensibility, or of equality! It is next worst to receiving one. The new remembrance of either is a scorpion.

If the splendid function of seeing should lose its interest, I can still flee to the sanctity of my moral nature, and trust, renounce, suffer, bleed.

If Mr. G., that old gander should now stop at my gate, I should duck to him as to an angel, and waste all my time for him, etc., etc., instead of telling him, as truth seems to require, that his visit and his babble was an impertinence, and bidding him Begone. Just so, when Miss X and Mrs. Y and Miss Z come, I straightway sit glued to my chair, all thought, all action, all play, departed and paralyzed, and acquiesce, and become less than they are, instead of nodding slightly to them and treating them like shadows, and persisting in the whim of pathos, or the whim of fun, or the whim of poetry in which they found me, and constraining them to accept the law of this higher thought (also theirs) instead of kneeling to their triviality.

What a satire to behold the man who has been astonishing a company with his assurances of the infinite faculties and destiny of man, nodding in his chair.

Last night the moon rose behind four distinct pine-tree tops in the distant woods and the night at ten was so bright that I walked abroad. But the sublime light of night is unsatisfying, provoking; it astonishes but explains not. Its charm floats, dances, disappears, comes and goes, but palls in five minutes after you have left the house. Come out of your warm, angular house, resounding with few voices, into the chill, grand, instantaneous night, with such a Presence as a full moon in the clouds, and you are struck with poetic wonder. In the instant you leave far behind all human relations, wife, mother and child, and live only with the savages—water, air, light, carbon, lime, and granite. I become a moist, cold element. "Nature grows over me." Frogs pipe; waters far off tinkle; dry leaves hiss; grass bends and rustles, and I have died out of the human world and come to feel a strange, cold, aqueous, terraqueous, aerial, ethereal sympathy and existence. I sow the sun and moon for seeds.

Scorn trifles. Leave to the man-milliners the question of coat and hat and gown, the color of your dress, the mode of riding, of the question of dancing, of parties, and all the jackstraws on which doctors have debated. The sailor "damns the proprieties." It is the only good sense on the subject, though coarse the expression.

Dr. Jackson once said that the laws of disease were as beautiful as the laws of health. Our good Dr. Hurd came to me yesterday before I had yet seen Dr. Ripley (yesterday represented as in a dying condition)—with joy sparkling in his eyes. "And how is the Doctor, Sir?" I said. "I have not seen him to-day," he replied, "but it is the most correct apoplexy I have ever seen, face and hands livid, breathing sonorous, and all the symptoms perfect"; and he rubbed his hands with delight.

I read to-day with wicked pleasure the saying ascribed to Kant, that "detestable was the society of mere literary men." It must be tasted sparingly to keep its gusto. If you do not quit the high chair, lie quite down and roll on the ground a good deal, you become nervous and heavy-hearted. The poverty of topics, the very names of Carlyle, Channing, Cambridge, and the Reviews become presently insupportable. The dog that was fed on sugar died. So all this summer I shall talk of Chenangoes and my new garden spout; have you heard of my pig? I have planted forty-four pine-trees; what will my tax be this year?—and never a word more of Goethe or Tennyson.

At dinner today we wickedly roasted the martyrs. I say that nothing is so disgusting in our day, as nothing is so dog-cheap, as martyrdom. The abolitionist came here to Concord where every third man lectures on Slavery, and being welcomed by some gentleman at the church to Concord, replied, "Yes, we that turn the world upside down have come hither also." It reminds one of a sophomore's exclamation during a college rebellion, "Come, Bowers! let us go join those noble fellows."

A woman's strength is the unresistible might of weakness.

Hostility, bitterness to persons or to the age indicate infirm sense, unacquaintance with men who are really at top selfish, and really at bottom fraternal, alike, identical.

We resent all criticism which denies us anything that lies in our line of advance.

I look with pity upon the young preachers who float into the profession thinking all is safe.

When I told Alcott that I would not criticise his compositions; that it would be as absurd to require them to conform to my way of writing and aiming, as it would be to reject Wordsworth because he was wholly unlike Campbell; that here was a new mind, and it was welcome to a new style;—he replied, well pleased, "That is criticism."

Take care, O ye martyrs! who, like St. Ursula and her choir, number eleven thousand, if, of all, one of you, one single soul is true, take care not to snap in petulance instead of jetting out in spouts of true flame. Reserve your fire. Keep your temper. Render soft answers. Bear and forbear. Do not dream of suffering for ten years yet. Do not let the word *martyrdom* ever escape out of the white fence of your teeth. Be sweet and courtly and merry these many long summers and autumns yet, and husband your strength, so that when an authentic, inevitable crisis comes, and you are fairly driven to the wall, cornered up in your Utica, you may then at last turn fairly round on the baying dogs, all steel—with all Heaven in your eye—and die for love, with all heroes and angels to friend.

I told my friend last night I could think of nothing more deeply satisfactory than to be shut up in a little schooner bound on a voyage of three or four weeks, with a man—an entire stranger—of a great and regular mind, of vast resources in his nature. I would not speak to him, I would not look at him; I would eat my supper; I would pack my trunk; I would read the newspaper; I would roll in my berth; so sure should I be of him, so luxuriously should I

husband my joys that I should steadily hold back all the
time, make no advances, leaving altogether to Fortune for
hours, for days, for weeks even, the manner and degrees
of intercourse. Yet what a proud peace would soothe the
soul to know that—heads and points, as we lie and welter
out at sea, all etiquette impossible, all routine far out of
sight—here close by me was grandeur of mind, grandeur
of character; that here was element wherein all I am, and
more than I am yet, could bathe and dilate; that here by
me was my greater self; he is me, and I am him. Give me,
not a thought, but a magazine of a man.

A good deal of character in our abused age. The rights of
women, the antislavery-, temperance-, peace-, health-, and
money-movements; female speakers, mobs and martyrs,
the paradoxes, the antagonisms of old and new, the anom-
alous church, the daring mysticism and the plain prose,
the uneasy relation of domestics, the struggling toward
better household arrangements,—all indicate life at the
heart, not yet justly organized at the surface.

A man must have aunts and cousins, must buy carrots and
turnips, must have barn and woodshed, must go to market
and to the blacksmith's shop, must saunter and sleep and
be inferior and silly.

I pleased myself in seeing the pictures brought in her portfolio by Margaret Fuller: Guercino, Piranesi, Leyden, etc.
It takes me long to know what to think of them, but I
think I find out at last. I am quite confident in my criticism upon that infernal architecture of Piranesi, and very
delicious it is to me to judge them when at last I begin to
see. The difficulty consists in righting one's self before
them; in arriving at a quite simple conviction that the

sketch appeals to me, and coming at a state of perfect equilibrium, leaving all allowance to spontaneous criticisms. Fear to judge, or haste to judge, alike vitiate the insight. Many good pictures, as much knowledge of the artist and his times as can be; and perfect equilibrium of mind; —are the conditions of right judgment.

Why do we seek this lurking beauty in skies, in poems, in drawings? Ah! because there we are safe, there we neither sicken nor die. I think we fly to Beauty as an asylum from the terrors of finite nature. We are made immortal by this kiss, by the contemplation of beauty.

I delight in our pretty country church music, and to hear that poor slip of a girl without education, without thought, yet show this fine instinct in her singing, so that every note of her song sounds to me like an adventure and a victory in the *ton-welt*, and whilst all the choir beside stay fast by their leader and the bass viol, this angel voice goes choosing, choosing, choosing on, and with the precision of genius keeps its faithful road and floods the house with melody.

Last night, at ten, I left my dreamy journal and went abroad to receive the fair inscriptions of night. The moon was making amber of the world. Every cottage pane glittered into silver. The trees were beautiful, yet ominous with gloom. The meadows sent up the rank smells of all their ferns and grasses and folded flowers into a nocturnal fragrance. The little harlot flies of the lowlands sparkled in the grass and in the air. It is all music. Then we see that the man who has seen the moon break out of clouds at night, arising, has been present, like an archangel, at the creation of light and of the world; and that he who has been in love has assisted at a new and second morning.

Mercury 90° in the shade. Rivers of heat, yea, a circum-ambient sea. Welcome as truly as finer and coarser influences to this mystic, solitary "purple island" that I am! I celebrate the holy hour at church amid these fine creative deluges of light and heat which evoke so many gentle traits,—gentle and bold,—in man and woman. Man in summer is Man intensated. See how truly the human history is written out in the faces around you. The silent assembly thus talks very loud. The old farmer, like Daniel Wood or David Buttrick, carries, as it were palpable in his face, stone walls, rough woodlots, the meadows and the barnyard; the old Doctor is a gallipot; the bookbinder binds books in his face; and the good landlord mixes liquors, yet in motionless pantomime. Beauty, softness, piety and love come there also in female form, and touch the heart. Vices even, in slight degree, improve the expression. Malice and scorn add to beauty. I see eyes set too near, and limited faces,—faces, I mean, of one marked but invariable expression. I wonder how such wear with the husband. They pique, but must tire. I prefer universal faces, countenances of a general humane type which pique less, but to which I can always safely return home. I read plainly in these manifold persons the plain prose of life, timidity, caution, appetite, old houses, musty smells, stationary, retrograde, faculties *puttering round* (to borrow Peter Howe's garden phrase) in paltry routines from January to December.

Private, accidental, confidential conversation breeds thought. Clubs produce oftener words.

Do not speak of God much. After a very little conversation on the highest nature, thought deserts us and we run into formalism.

When I read the *North American Review*, or the *London Quarterly*, I seem to hear the snore of the Muses, not their waking voice.

Read and think. Study now, and now garden. Go alone, then go abroad. Speculate awhile, then work in the world.

Elizabeth Peabody brought me yesterday Hawthorne's *Footprints on the Seashore* to read. I complained that there was no inside to it. Alcott and he together would make a man.

The unbelief of the age is attested by the loud condemnation of trifles. Look at our silly religious papers. Let a minister wear a cane, or a white hat, go to a theatre, or avoid a Sunday School, let a school-book with a Calvinistic sentence or a Sunday School book without one be heard of, and instantly all the old grannies squeak and gibber and do what they call "sounding an alarm," from Bangor to Mobile. Alike nice and squeamish is its ear. You must on no account say "stink" or "Damn."

The art of writing consists in putting two things together that are unlike and that belong together, like a horse and cart.

It will take an imaginative and philosophical writer nearly as long to write the preface to his book—a preface of a page—as the book itself; and an advertisement will pain him for a week, and then cost half a day to execute it.

Have you had doubts? Have you struggled with coldness; with apathy; with self-contempt that made you pale and thin? George Fox perambulated England in his perplexity. In elegant Cambridge have you walked a mile in perturbation of the spirit? Yet somehow you must come to the bottom of those doubts, or the human soul in its great ebbs and flows asking you for its law will call you, Boy! Life, authentic life you must have, or you can teach nothing.

I by no means believe in storms. Quite as much as Lord Byron I hate scenes. I think I have not the common degree of sympathy with dark, turbid, mournful, passionate natures; but in compunction, in a keen resentment of violation, in shame for idleness, in shame at standing still, in remorse for meanness, in remorse for wounded affection, in rolling in the dust and crying, Unclean! Unclean! when we have debased ourselves to appetite, or undone ourselves with injustice,—I believe, I believe. I honor the retirements of men. I love the flush of hope.

You must treat the men and women of one idea, the Abolitionist, the Phrenologist, the Swedenborgian, as insane persons with a continual tenderness and special reference in every remark and action to their known state, which reference presently becomes embarrassing and tedious.

I hate goodies. I hate goodness that preaches. Goodness that preaches undoes itself. A little electricity of virtue lurks here and there in kitchens and among the obscure, chiefly women, that flashes out occasional light and makes the existence of the thing still credible. But one had as lief curse and swear as be guilty of this odious religion that watches the beef and watches the cider in the pitcher at table, that shuts the mouth hard at any remark it cannot twist nor wrench into a sermon, and preaches as long as itself and its hearer is awake. Goodies make us very bad.

We should, if the race should increase, be scarce restrained from calling for bowl and dagger. We will almost sin to spite them.

I woke and watched one night a dull hour on hearing noises, steps below stairs, or creaking of windows or doors. But the love of my spoons shall not again hinder me from sleep.

The moon and Jupiter side by side last night stemmed the sea of clouds and plied their voyage in convoy through the sublime Deep as I walked the old and dusty road. The snow and the enchantment of the moonlight make all landscapes alike, and the road that is so tedious and homely that I never take it by day,—by night is Italy or Palmyra. In these divine pleasures permitted to me of walks in the June night under moon and stars, I can put my life as a fact before me and stand aloof from its honor and shame.

Never compare. God is our name for the last generalization to which we can arrive, and, of course, its sense differs today and tomorrow. But never compare your generalization with your neighbor's. Speak now, and let him hear you and go his way. Tomorrow, or next year, let him speak, and answer thou not. So shall you both speak truth and be of one mind; but insist on comparing your two thoughts; or insist on hearing in order of battle, and instantly you are struck with blindness, and will grope and stagger like a drunken man.

There is a limit to the effect of written eloquence. It may do much, but the miracles of eloquence can only be expected from the man who thinks on his legs. He who thinks may thunder; on him the Holy Ghost may fall, and from him pass.

The price of the picture indicates the common sense of men in regard to the chance there is for the appearance of equal genius. The chances are millions to one that no new Raphael is born today, and therefore pictures as great as the actual Raphael painted express that chance in their nominal value.

Trees look to me like imperfect men. It is the same soul that makes me, which, by a feebler effort, arrives at these graceful portraits of life. I think we all feel so. I think we all feel a certain pity in beholding a tree: rooted there, the would-be-Man is beautiful, but patient and helpless. His boughs and long leaves droop and weep his strait imprisonment.

If that worthy ancient king, in the schoolbooks, who offered a reward to the inventor of a new pleasure could make his proclamation anew, I should put in for the first prize. I would tell him to write an oration, and then print it, and, setting himself diligently to the correction, let him strike out a blunder and insert the right word just ere the press falls, and he shall know a new pleasure.

Sanity is very rare: every man almost, and every woman, has a dash of madness.

Saw beautiful pictures yesterday. Miss Fuller brought with her a portfolio of Sam Ward's, containing a chalk sketch of one of Raphael's Sibyls, of Cardinal Bembo, and the angel in Heliodorus's profanation; and Thorwaldsen's Entry of Alexander, etc., etc. I have said sometimes that it depends little on the object, much on the mood, in art. I have enjoyed more from mediocre pictures, casually seen when the mind was in equilibrium, and have reaped a true benefit of the art of painting,—the stimulus of color, the idealizing of common life into this gentle, elegant, unoffending fairy-land of a picture, than from many masterpieces seen with much expectation and tutoring, and so not with equipoise of mind. The mastery of a great picture comes slowly over the mind. If I see a fine picture with other people, I am driven almost into inevitable affectations. The scanty vocabulary of praise is quickly exhausted, and we lose our common sense, and, much worse, our reason, in our *superlative degrees*.

How much a fine picture seems to say! It knows the whole world. How good an office it performs! What authentic messengers are these of a wise soul, which thus stamped its thought, and sends it out distinct, undecayed, unadulterated to me, at the end of centuries, and at the ends of the earth.

Life is a pretty tragedy, especially for women. On comes a gay dame, of manners and tone so fine and haughty that all defer to her as to a countess, and she seems the dictator of society. Sit down by her, and talk of her own life in earnest, and she is some stricken soul with care and sorrow at her vitals, and wisdom or charity cannot see any way of escape for her from remediless evils. She envies her companion in return, until she also disburdens into her ear the story of *her* misery, as deep and hopeless as her own.

Dr. Ripley prays for rain with great explicitness on Sunday, and on Monday the showers fell. When I spoke of the speed with which his prayers were answered, the good man looked modest.

I think it must be conceded to books that they are grown
so numerous and so valuable that they deserve to have imperfect characters, half-witted persons, and the like persons
who are confessedly incapable of working out their own
salvation, appointed to study these, and render account of
them. For want of a learned class, here, I am in ignorance
where valuable facts and theories are found till years after
their promulgation.

Always that work is the more pleasant to the imagination
which is not now required. Ah! how wistfully, when I
have been going somewhere to preach, I looked upon the
distant hills.

I think myself more a man than some men I know, inasmuch as I see myself to be open to the enjoyment of talents and deeds of other men, as they are not. When a talent comes by, which I cannot appreciate and other men
can, I instantly am inferior. With all my ears I cannot detect
unity or plan in a strain of Beethoven. Here is a man who
draws from it a frank delight. So much is he more a man
than I.

In women, you shall see one whose bonnet and dress are
one thing, and the lady herself quite another and wearing
withal an expression of meek submission to her bonnet and
dress; another whose dress obeys and heightens the expression of her form.

In perfect eloquence, the hearer would lose the sense of
dualism, of hearing from another; would cease to distinguish between the orator and himself; would have the sense
only of high activity and progress.

What makers are our eyes! In yonder boat on the pond the two boys, no doubt, find prose enough. Yet to us, as we sit here on the shore, it is quite another sort of canoe, a piece of fairy timber which the light loves and the wind, and the wave,—a piece of sunshine and beauty.

The address to the Divinity School is published, and they are printing the Dartmouth Oration. The correction of these two pieces for the press has cost me no small labor, now nearly ended. There goes a great deal of work into a correct literary paper, though of few pages. Of course, it cannot be overseen and exhausted except by analysis as faithful as this synthesis. But negligence in the author is inexcusable. I know and will know no such thing as haste in composition.

I decline invitations to evening parties chiefly because, besides the time spent, commonly ill, in the party, the hours preceding and succeeding the visit are lost for any solid use, as I am put out of tune for writing or reading. That makes my objection to many employments that seem trifles to a bystander, as packing a trunk, or any small handiwork, or correcting proof-sheets, that they put me out of tune.

What is more alive among works of art than our plain old wooden church, built a century and a quarter ago, with the ancient New England spire? I pass it at night, and stand and listen to the beats of the clock—like heart-beats; not sounding, as Elizabeth Hoar well observed, so much like tickings, as like a step. It is the step of Time. You catch the sound first by looking up at the clock-face, and then you see this wooden tower rising thus alone, but stable and

aged, towards the midnight stars. It has affiance and privilege with them.

Put three or four educated people together who have not
seen each other for years, and perhaps they shall be unable to converse aloud without force. Each predicts the
opinion of the other, so that talking becomes tedious. All
know what each would say. Why should I officiously and
emphatically offer a pail of water to my neighbor Minot?
He has a well of his own that sucks the same springs at
the same level that mine does. Why should I drum on his
tympanum with my words to convey thoughts to which he
has access equally with me?

How expressive is form! I see by night the shadow of a
poor woman against a window-curtain that instantly tells a
story of so much meekness, affection, and labor, as almost
to draw tears.

Almost every woman described to you by a woman presents a tragic idea, and not an idea of well-being. One most
deserving person whom I commiserated last night with
my friends, has such peculiar and unfortunate habits of
conversation that she can say nothing agreeable to me. Say
what she will,—rare and accomplished person that she is,—
I hear her never, but only *wait* until she is done. I think
with profound pity of her family. Were she my sister, I
should sail for Australasia and put the earth's diameter between us.

The whole History of the negro is tragedy. I think they are
more pitiable when rich than when poor. Of what use are
riches to them? They never go out without being insulted.
Yesterday I saw a family of negroes riding in a coach. How
pathetic!

The meaning of good and bad, of better and worse, is simply helping or hurting. He is great who confers the most benefits. He is base—and that is the one base thing in the universe—to receive favors and render none. In the order of nature we cannot render benefits to those from whom we receive them, or only seldom. But the benefits we receive must be rendered again line for line, deed for deed to somebody.

I dislike to be a clergyman and refuse to be one. Yet how rich a music would be to me a holy clergyman in my town. It seems to me he cannot be a man, quite and whole; yet how plain is the need of one, and how high, yes, highest, is the function. Here is division of labor that I like not. A man must sacrifice his manhood for the social good. Something is wrong, I see not what.

Society has no bribe for me, neither in politics, nor church, nor college, nor city. My resources are far from exhausted. If they will not hear me lecture, I shall have leisure for my book which wants me. Besides it is an universal maxim worthy of all acceptation that a man may have that allowance which he takes. Take the place and attitude to which you see your unquestionable right, and all men acquiesce.

It is one of the blessings of old friends that you can afford to be stupid with them.

I have usually read that a man suffered more from one hard word than he enjoyed from ten good ones. My own experience does not confirm the saying. The censure (I either know or fancy) does not hit me; and the praise is very good.

Is it not better to live in Revolution than to live in dead times? Are we not little and low out of good nature now, when, if our companions were noble, or the crisis fit for heroes, we should be great also?

All that befals me in the way of criticism and extreme blame and praise, drawing me out of equilibrium,—putting me for a time in a false position to people, and disallowing the spontaneous sentiments,—wastes my time, bereaves me of thoughts, and shuts me up within poor personal considerations. Therefore, I hate to be conspicuous for blame or praise. It spoils thought.

How attractive is the book in my friend's house which I should not read in my own!

Fancy relates to color; imagination to form.

Stetson, talking of Webster this morning, says, "He commits great sins sometimes, but without any guilt."

Alcott wants a historical record of conversations holden by you and me and him. I say, how joyful rather is some Montaigne's book which is full of fun, poetry, business, divinity, philosophy, anecdote, smut, which dealing of bone and marrow, of cornbarn and flour barrel, of wife, and friend, and valet, of things nearest and next, never names names, or gives you the glooms of a recent date or relation, but hangs there in the heaven of letters, unrelated, untimed, a joy and a sign, an autumnal star.

A sermon, my own, I read never with joy, though sincerely written; an oration, a poem, another's or my own, I read with joy. Is it that from the first species of writing, we cannot banish tradition, convention, and that the last is more easily genuine? Or is it that the last, being dedicated to Beauty, and the first to Goodness, to Duty, the Spirit flies with hilarity and delight to the last; with domestic obligation and observance only to the first?

It is difficult not to be affected by sour faces. Sympathy is a supporting atmosphere, and in it we unfold easily and well. But climb into this thin, iced, difficult air of Andes of reform, and sympathy leaves you and hatred comes.

Martyrs with thumb-screws, martyrs sawn asunder, martyrs eaten by dogs, may claim with gory stumps a crown. But the martyrs in silk stockings and barouches, with venison and champagne, in ballrooms and picture galleries, make me sick—self-pitying.

After thirty, a man is too sensible of the strait limitations which his physical constitution sets to his activity. The stream feels its banks, which it had forgotten in the run and overflow of the first meadows.

I found in the wood this afternoon the drollest mushroom, tall, stately, pretending, uprearing its vast dome as if to say, "Well I am something! Burst, ye beholders! thou luck-holder! with wonder." Its dome was a deep yellow ground with fantastic, starlike ornaments richly overwrought; so shabby genteel, so negrofine, the St. Peter's of the beetles and pismires. Such ostentation *in petto* I never did see. I touched the white column with my stick,—it nodded like old Troy, and so eagerly recovered the perpendicular as seemed to plead piteously with me not to burst the fabric of its pride. Shall I confess it? I could almost hear my little

Waldo at home begging me, as when I have menaced his little block-house, and the little puff-ball seemed to say, "Don't, Papa, pull it down!" So, after due admiration of this blister, this cupola of midges, I left the little scaramouch alone in its glory. Good-bye, Vanity, good-bye, Nothing! Certainly there is comedy in the Divine Mind when these little vegetable self-conceits front the day as well as Newton or Goethe, with such impressive emptiness.

The greatest expression of limitation in the human frame is in the teeth. "Thus far," says the face; "No farther," say the teeth.

Tennyson is a beautiful half of a poet.

The thermometer, the microscope, the prism are little deists. They stand like pagans, have a very pagan look when the creed and catechism begin; they are little better than profane: and so a doctor of medicine, a chemist, an astronomer do never remind me of St. Athanasius.

Nature is the beautiful asylum to which we look in all the years of striving and conflict as the assured resource when we shall be driven out of society by ennui or chagrin or persecution or defect of character. I say, as I go up the hill and through the wood and see the soliciting plants, I care not for you, mosses and lichens, and for you, fugitive birds, or secular rocks! Grow, fly, or sleep there in your order, which I know is beautiful, though I perceive it not; I am content not to perceive it. Now have I entertainment enough with things nearer, homelier. Things wherein passion enters, and hope and fear have not yet become too dangerous, too insipid, for me to handle. But by and by, if men shall drive me out, if books have become stale, I see gladly that the door of your palace of magic stands ajar.

Nature is no fool. She knows the world. She has calculated the chances of her success, and if her seeds do not vegetate, she will not be chagrined and bereft. She has another arrow left, another card to play, her harvest is insured. From her oak she scatters down a thousand seeds, and if nine hundred rot, the forest is still perpetuated for a century.

In childhood, in youth, each man has had many checks and censures, and thinks modestly enough of his own endowment. When, by and by, he comes to unfold it in propitious circumstance, it fills his eye and it fills the eye of all. It seems the only talent. He is surprised and delighted with his success, and carries that out also into the infinite, as man will, and accounts himself already the fellow of the great. But he goes into company, into a banking house, into a mob, into a mechanic's shop, into a society of scholars, a camp, a ship, a laboratory; and in each new place he is a fool; other talents take place and rule the hour, and his presumption, cowed and whipped, goes back to the timid condition of the boy. For every talent of man runs out to the horizon as well as his.

Our health is our sound relation to external objects; our sympathy with external being. A man wakes in the morning sick with fever; and he perceives at once he has lost his just relation to the world. Every sound in the lower parts of the house, or in the street, falls faint and foreign on his ear.

We are ungrateful creatures. There is nothing we value and hunt and cultivate and strive to draw to us, but in some hour we turn and rend it. We sneer at ignorance and the life of the senses and the ridicule of never thinking, and then goes by a fine girl like M. R., a piece of life, gay because she is happy and making these very commonalities beautiful by the energy and heart with which she does them, and seeing this, straightway we admire and love her and them, say, "Lo! a genuine creature of the fair earth, not *blasé*, not *flétri* by books, philosophy, religion or care"; insinuating by these very words a treachery and contempt for all that we had so long loved and wrought in ourselves and others.

I hate to be defended in a newspaper. As long as all that is said is said *against* me, I feel a certain sublime assurance of success, but as soon as honied words of praise are spoken for me, I feel as one that lies unprotected before his enemies.

I, as always, venerate the oracular nature of woman. The sentiment which the man thinks he came unto gradually through the events of years, to his surprise he finds woman dwelling there in the same, as in her native home.

Every vice is only an exaggeration of a necessary and virtuous function.

Every man's idea of God is the last or most comprehensive generalization at which he has arrived.

I do not gladly utter any deep conviction of the soul in any company where I think it will be contested, no, nor unless I think it will be welcome. Truth has already ceased to be itself if polemically said.

The aid we can give each other is only incidental, lateral, and sympathetic.

Once I thought it a defect peculiar to me, that I was confounded by interrogatories and when put on my wits for a definition was unable to reply without injuring my own truth: but now, I believe it proper to man to be unable to answer in terms the great problems put by his fellow: it is enough if he can live his own definitions. A problem appears to me. I cannot solve it with all my wits: but leave it there; let it lie awhile: I can by patient, faithful truth lift at last its uttermost darkness into light.

How soon the sunk spirits rise again, how quick the little wounds of fortune skin over and are forgotten. I am sensitive as a leaf to impressions from abroad, and under this night's beautiful heaven I have forgotten that ever I was reviewed. It is strange how superficial are our views of these matters, seeing we are all writers and philosophers. A man thinks it of importance what the great sheet or pamphlet of to-day proclaims of him to all the reading town; and if he sees graceful compliments, he relishes his dinner; and if he sees threatening paragraphs and odious nicknames, it becomes a solemn, depressing fact and sables his whole thought until bedtime.

I passed by the shop and saw my spruce neighbor, the dictator of our rural Jacobins, teaching his little circle of villagers their political lessons. And here, thought I, is one who loves what I hate: here is one wholly reversing my code. I hate persons who are nothing but persons. I hate numbers. He cares for nothing but numbers and persons. All the qualities of man, all his accomplishments, affections, enterprises, except solely the ticket he votes for, are nothing to this philosopher. Numbers of majorities are all he sees in the newspaper. All of North or South, all in Georgia,

Alabama, Pennsylvania or New England that this man considers is, What is the relation of Mr. Clay, or of Mr. Van Buren, to those mighty mountain chains, those vast, fruitful champaigns, those expanding nations of men. What an existence is this, to have no home, no heart, but to feed on the very refuse and old straw and chaff of man,—the numbers and names of voters.

A man writes a book which displeases somebody, who writes an angry paragraph about it in the next newspaper. That solitary paragraph, whilst it stands unanswered, seems the voice of the world. Hundreds of passive readers read it with such passiveness that it becomes their voice. The man that made the book and his friends are superstitious about it. They cannot put it out of their heads. Their entire relations to society seem changed. What was yesterday a warm, convenient, hospitable world, soliciting all the talents of all its children, looks bleak and hostile, and our native tendency to complete any view we take carries the imagination out at once to images of persecution, hatred and want.

In debate, the last speaker always carries with him such a prevailing air that all seems to be over and the question settled when he concludes; so that, if a new man arise and state with nonchalance a new and opposite view, we draw our breath freely and hear with a marked surprise this suspension of fate.

If a man live in the saddle, the saddle somehow will come to live in him. Tick, tack.

It is a beautiful fact that every spot of earth, every dog, pebble, and ash-heap, as well as every palace and every man, is whirled round in turn to the meridian.

It seems not unfit that the scholar should deal plainly with society and tell them that he saw well enough before he spoke the consequence of his speaking; that up there in his silent study, by his dim lamp, he fore-heard this Babel of outcries. The nature of man he knew, the insanity that comes of inaction and tradition, and knew well that when their dream and routine were disturbed, like bats and owls and nocturnal beasts they would howl and shriek and fly at the torch-bearer. But he saw plainly that under this their distressing disguise of birdform and beast form, the divine features of man were hidden, and he felt that he would dare to be so much their friend as to do them this violence to drag them to the day and to the healthy air and water of God, that the unclean spirits that had possessed them might be exorcised and depart. The taunts and cries of hatred and anger, the very epithets you bestow on me, are so familiar long ago in my reading that they sound to me ridiculously old and stale. The same thing has happened so many times over (that is, with the appearance of every original observer) that, if people were not very ignorant of literary history, they would be struck with the exact coincidence. I, whilst I see this, that you must have been shocked and must cry out at what I have said, I see too that we cannot easily be reconciled, for I have a great deal more to say that will shock you out of all patience.

The physician tends always to invert man, to look upon the body as the cause of the soul, to look upon man as tyrannized over by his members.

Do not be a night-chair, a warming-pan, at sick-beds and rheumatic souls. Do not let them make a convenience of you. Do not be a pastry-cook either and give parties.

Here came on Sunday morning Edward Palmer and departed today, a gentle, faithful, sensible, well-balanced man for an enthusiast. He has renounced, since a year ago last April, the use of money. When he travels, he stops at night at a house and asks if it would give them any satisfaction to lodge a traveller without money or price. If they do not give him a hospitable answer, he goes on, but generally finds the country people free and willing. When he goes away, he gives them his papers or tracts.

It is a poor-spirited age. The great army of cowards who bellow and bully from their bed-chamber windows have no confidence in truth or God. Truth will not maintain itself, they fancy, unless they bolster it up, and whip and stone the assailants; and the religion of God, the being of God, they seem to think dependent on what we say of it. The feminine vehemence with which the Daily Advertiser beseeches the dear people to whip that naughty heretic is the natural feeling in the mind whose religion is external. It cannot subsist; it suffers shipwreck if its faith is not confirmed by all surrounding persons. A believer, a mind whose faith is consciousness, is never disturbed because other persons do not yet see the fact which he sees.

Steady, steady! When this fog of good and evil affections falls, it is hard to see and walk straight.

What said my brave Asia* concerning the paragraph writers, today? that "this whole practice of self-justification and recrimination betwixt literary men seemed every whit as low as the quarrels of the Paddies."

---

* Emerson's pet name for his wife.

Then said I, "But what will you say, excellent Asia, when my smart article comes out in the paper, in reply to Mr. A. and Dr. B.?"—"Why, then," answered she, "I shall feel the first emotion of fear and sorrow on your account."—"But do you know," I asked, "how many fine things I have thought of to say to these fighters? They are too good to be lost."—"Then," rejoined the queen, "there is some merit in being silent."

It is plain from all the noise that there is atheism some-where; the only question is now, Which is the atheist?

I, for my part, am very well pleased to see the variety and velocity of the movements that all over our broad land, in spots and corners, agitate society. War, slavery, alcohol, animal food, domestic hired service, colleges, creeds, and now at last money, also, have their spirited and unwearia-ble assailants, and must pass out of use or must learn a law.

Mine Asia says, A human being should beware how he laughs, for then he shows all his faults.

Edward Palmer asked me if I liked two services in a Sab-bath. I told him, Not very well. If the sermon was good I wished to think of it; if it was bad, one was enough.

If one of these monotones, whereof, as my friends think, I have a savage society, like a menagerie of monsters, come to you, receive him. For the partial action of his mind in one direction is a telescope for the objects on which it is pointed.

Ignorant people think a foreigner speaking a foreign tongue a formidable, odious nature, alien to the backbone. So is it with our brothers. Our journey, the journey of the soul, is through different regions of thought, and to each its own vocabulary. As soon as we hear a new vocabulary from our own, at once we exaggerate the alarming differences,— account the man suspicious, a thief, a pagan, and set no bounds to our disgust or hatred, and, late in life, perhaps too late, we find he was loving and hating, doing and thinking the same *things* as we, under his own vocabulary.

Every word, every striking word that occurs in the pages of an original genius, will provoke attack and be the subject of twenty pamphlets and a hundred paragraphs. Should he be so duped as to stop and listen? Rather, let him know that the page he writes today will contain a new subject for the pamphleteers, and that which he writes tomorrow, more. Let him not be misled to give it any more than the notice due from him, viz., just that which it had in his first page, before the controversy. The exaggeration of the notice is right for them, false for him. Every word that he quite naturally writes is as prodigious and offensive. So write on, and, by and by, will come a reader and an age that will justify all your contest. Do not even look behind. Leave that bone for them to pick and welcome.

Let me study and work contentedly and faithfully; I do not remember my critics. I forget them,—I depart from them by every step I take. If I think then of them, it is a bad sign.

In my weak hours I look fondly to Europe and think how gladly I would live in Florence and Rome. In my manly hours, I defy these leanings, these lingering looks *behind*, these flesh-pots of Egypt, and feel that my duty is my place and that the merrymen of circumstance should follow as they might.

Sincerity is the highest compliment you can pay. Jones Very* charmed us all by telling us he hated us all.

There is no terror like that of being known. The world lies in night of sin. It hears not the cock crowing: it sees not the grey streak in the East. At the first entering ray of light, society is shaken with fear and anger from side to side. Who opened that shutter? they cry, Wo to him! They belie it, they call it darkness that comes in, affirming that they were in light before. Before the man who has spoken to them the dread word, they tremble and flee. They flee to new topics, to their learning, to the solid institutions about them, to their great men, to their windows, and look-out on the road and passengers, to their very furniture, and meats, and drinks,—anywhere, anyhow to escape the apparition. The wild horse has heard the whisper of the tamer: the maniac has caught the glance of the keeper. They try to forget the memory of the speaker, to put him down into the same obscure place he occupied in their minds before he spake to them. It is all in vain. They even flatter themselves that they have killed and buried the enemy, when they have magisterially denied and denounced him. But vain, vain, all vain. It was but the first mutter of the distant storm they heard,—it was the first cry of the Revolution,— it was the touch, the palpitation that goes before the earthquake. Even now society is shaken because a thought or two have been thrown into the midst. The sects, the colleges, the church, the statesmen all have forebodings. It now works only in a handful. What does State Street and Wall Street and the Royal Exchange and the Bourse at Paris care for these few thoughts and these few men? Very little; truly; most truly. But the doom of State Street, and

* A friend of Emerson; a poet and mystic.

Wall Street, of London, and France, of the whole world, is advertised by those thoughts; is in the procession of the Soul which comes after those few thoughts.

There are some men above grief and some men below it.

When I look at life, and see the patches of thought, the gleams of goodness here and there amid the wide and wild madness, I seem to be a god dreaming; and when shall I awake and dissipate these fumes and phantoms?

We owe a good many valuable observations to people who are not very acute or profound, and who say things without effort which we want and have been long toiling for in vain. This, and that other fact, that we kindle each other's interest so fast in what happens to be our present studies, and the rapid communication of results that is obviously possible between scholars of various pursuit,—lead me to think that acquisition would be increased by literary society: that I could read more, learn faster, by association with good scholars, than I do or can alone.

There are few scholars. The mob of so-called scholars are unapt peasants caught late, coated over merely with a thin varnish of Latin and reading-room literature, but unlearned and unintelligent: they sleep in the afternoons, read little, and cannot be said to have faith or hope.

I should not dare to tell all my story. A great deal of it I do not yet understand. How much of it is incomplete. In my strait and decorous way of living, native to my family and to my country, and more strictly proper to me, is nothing extravagant or flowing. I content myself with moderate, languid actions, and never transgress the staidness of village manners. Herein I consult the poorness of my powers. More culture would come out of great virtues and vices perhaps, but I am not up to that. Should I obey an irregular impulse, and establish every new relation that my fancy prompted with the men and women I see, I should not be followed by my faculties; they would play me false in making good their very suggestions. They delight in inceptions, but they warrant nothing else.

I told Jones Very that I had never suffered, that I could scarce bring myself to feel a concern for the safety and life of my nearest friends that would satisfy them; that I saw clearly that if my wife, my child, my mother, should be taken from me, I should still remain whole, with the same capacity of cheap enjoyment from all things. I should not grieve enough, although I love them.

A woman should always challenge our respect, and never move our compassion.

In an evening party you have no variety of persons, but only one person. For, say what you will, and to whom you will, —they shall all render one and the same answer, without thought, without heart,—a conversation of the lips.

I am very sensible to beauty in the human form, in children, in boys, in girls, in old men, and old women. No trait of beauty I think escapes me. So am I to beauty in nature: a clump of flags in a stream, a hill, a wood, a path running into the woods, captivate me as I pass.

I hear occasionally young people dwelling with emphasis on beauties of nature, which may be there or may not, but which I do not catch, and blind, at the same time, to the objects which give me most pleasure. I am quite unable to tell the difference, only I see that they are less easily satisfied than I; that they talk where I would be silent, and clamorously demand my delight where it is not spontaneous. I fancy the love of nature of such persons is rhetorical.

I will, I think, no longer do things unfit for me. Why should I act the part of the silly women who send out invitations to many persons, and receive each billet of acceptance as if it were a pistol shot? Why should I read lectures with care and pain and afflict myself with all the meanness of ticket-mongering, when I might sit, as God in his goodness has enabled me, a free, poor man with wholesome bread and warm clothes, though without cakes or gew-gaws, and write and speak the beautiful and formidable words of a free man? If you cannot be free, be as free as you can.

I have said on a former page that natural science always stands open to us as any asylum, and that, in the conflict with the common cares, we throw an occasional affectionate glance at lichen and fungus, barometer and microscope, as cities of refuge to which we can one day flee, if the worst come to the worst. Another asylum is in the exercise of the fancy. Puck and Oberon, Tam O'Shanter and Lili's Park, the Troubadours and old ballads are bowers of joy that beguile us of our woes, catch us up into short heavens and drown all remembrance, and that too without a death-tramp of Eumenides being heard close behind, as behind other revels. Better still it is to soar into the heaven of invention, and coin fancies of our own,—weave a web of dreams as gay and beautiful as any of these our brothers have done, and learn by bold attempt our own riches.

So is music an asylum. It takes us out of the actual and whispers to us dim secrets that startle our wonder as to who we are, and for what, whence, and whereto. All the great interrogatories, like questioning angels, float in on its waves of sound.

We read Lear and hate the unkind daughters. But meantime perhaps our fathers and mothers find *us* hard and forgetful. We swell the cry of horror at the slave-holder, and we treat our laborer or grocer or farmer as a thing, and so hold slaves ourselves.

Let me never fall into the vulgar mistake of dreaming that I am persecuted whenever I am contradicted. No man, I think, had ever a greater well-being with a less desert than I. I can very well afford to be accounted bad or foolish by a few dozen or a few hundred persons,—I who see myself greeted by the good expectation of so many friends far beyond any power of thought or communication of thought residing in me. Besides, I own, I am often inclined to take part with those who say I am bad or foolish, for I fear I am both.

I find no good lives. I would live well, I seem to be free to do so, yet I think with very little respect of my way of living; it is weak, partial, not full and not progressive. But I do not see any other that suits me better. The scholars are shiftless and the merchants are dull.

My brave Henry Thoreau walked with me to Walden this afternoon and complained of the proprietors who compelled him, to whom, as much as to any, the whole world belonged, to walk in a strip of road and crowded him out of all the rest of God's earth. I begged him, having this maggot of Freedom and Humanity in his brain, to write it out into good poetry and so clear himself of it.

I could forgive your want of faith if you had any knowledge of the uttermost that man could be and do, if arithmetic could predict the last possibilities of instinct. But men are not made like boxes, a hundred or thousand to order, and all exactly alike, of known dimension, and all their properties known; but no, they come into nature through a nine months' astonishment, and of a character, each one, incalculable, and of extravagant possibilities. Out of darkness and out of the awful Cause they come to be caught up into this vision of a seeing, partaking, acting and suffering life, not foreknown, not fore-estimable, but slowly or speedily they unfold new, unknown, mighty traits: not boxes, but these machines are alive, agitated, fearing, sorrowing.

I like the rare, extravagant spirits who disclose to me new facts in nature.

"Fire," Aunt Mary said, "was a great deal of company"; and so is there company, I find, in water. It animates the solitude. Then somewhat nearer to human society is in the hermit birds that harbor in the wood. I can do well for weeks with no other society than the partridge and the jay, my daily company.

What is the hardest task in the world? To think.

In the presence of a man or woman of elegance and fashionable manners, you do not play a quite manly part. Where is your wisdom? Why falters the word of truth on your tongue, and comes so lamely and inarticulately off? Why do you defer to such persons? Have you not been taught of God that all things are yours? Why should you decline from the state of truth, and vail your manly supremacy to a woman or a fine gentleman? It is in vain these questions are asked: you have asked them yourself. You cannot do otherwise. Admit your weakness. Do not be disturbed by it. Keep your will true and erect, and, by and by, this rebellious blood, this painful suppleness, this epilepsy of the wit, will pass away imperceptibly, and the whole man shall be the faithful organ of the wisdom which is no respecter of persons.

I remember that when I preached my first sermon in Concord, "On Showing Piety at Home," Dr. Ripley remarked on the frequent occurrence of the word *Virtue* in it, and said his people would not understand it, for the largest part of them, when Virtue was spoken of, understood *Chastity*.

A man of letters who goes into fashionable society on their terms and not on his own makes a fool of himself. Why I should be given up to that shame so many times after so much considered experience, I cannot tell. Heaven has good purposes in these often mortifications, perchance.

It is strange to me how sensible I am to circumstances. I know not how it is, but in the streets I feel mean. If a man should accost me in Washington Street and call me base fellow! I should not be sure that I could make him feel by my answer and behaviour that my ends were worthy and noble. If the same thing should occur in the country I should feel no doubt at all that I could justify myself to his conscience.

The strong bent of nature is very prettily seen in the winning, half-artful, half-artless ways of young girls in the middle classes who go into the shops to buy a skein of silk or a sheet of paper and talk half an hour about nothing with the broad-faced, good-natured shop-boy. . . .

We put our love where we have put our labor.

I had rather hear a round volley of Ann Street oaths than the affectation of that which is divine on the foolish lips of coxcombs.

The test of a religion or philosophy is the number of things it can explain: so true is it. But the religion of our churches explains neither art nor society nor history, but itself needs explanation.

Races pass and perish; cities rise and fall, like the perpetual succession of shells on the beach; and the sound of the waters and the colors of the flower, cloud, and the voice of man are as new and affecting today as at any moment in the vast Past.

PART III

1839-1841

"I am, as usual, neither sick nor well," wrote Emerson in 1839. "I do not write much and writing is always my meter of health." Nevertheless, during the year he continued his course of winter lectures in Boston and began work on the first volume of *Essays*. This also was the birth year of his first daughter, Ellen.

During 1840 Emerson's health gradually improved. He again gave his course of lectures in Boston, and spent much time and thought on *The Dial*, which was started that year with Margaret Fuller as editor.

In 1841 the first volume of the *Essays* was published; Henry Thoreau, then twenty-four years old, came to live with the Emersons and stayed for two years; and a second daughter, Edith, was born.

During these years the spiritual awakening that came to be known as Transcendentalism, and the ferment of reform so characteristic of the period, impinged with increasing force on the serenity of life in Concord.

1839

The drunkard retires on a keg and locks himself up for a three days' debauch. When I am sick, I please myself not less in retiring on a Salamander stove, heaping the chamber with fuel, and inundating lungs, liver, head and feet with floods of caloric, heats on heats. It is dainty to be sick, if you have leisure and convenience for it. How bland the aspect of all things! One sees the colors of the carpet and the paper-hangings. All the housemates have a softer, fainter look to the debilitated retina.

As soon as a child has left the room his strewn toys become affecting.

In the morning a man walks with his whole body; in the evening, only with his legs; the trunk is carried along almost motionless.

Ellen was never alone. I could not imagine her poor and solitary. She was like a tree in flower, so much soft, budding, informing beauty was society for itself, and she taught the eye that beheld her why Beauty was ever painted with loves and graces attending her steps.

Yesterday morning, 24 February at 8 o'clock, a daughter was born to me, a soft, quiet, swarthy little creature, apparently perfect and healthy. Lidian, who magnanimously makes my gods her gods, calls the babe Ellen. I can hardly ask more for thee, my babe, than that name implies. Be that vision, and remain with us, and after us.

A fine voice in a choir seems to inundate the house with spouts and jets and streams of sound, and to float the old hulk of the choir itself, insinuating itself under all the droning groans and shrill screams and hurrying them all away, the spoils of its own stream.

We all wish to be of importance in one way or another. The child coughs with might and main, since it has no other claims on the company.

Byron says of Jack Bunting, "He knew not what to say, and so he swore." I may say it of our preposterous use of books, He knew not what to do, and so *he read*.

Do not be so troublesome modest, you vain fellow. Real modesty still puts the thing forward and postpones the person, nor worries me with endless apologies.

I like the silent church before the service begins better than any preaching.

The office of conversation is to give me self-possession. I lie torpid as a clod—Virtue, wisdom, sound to me fabulous,—all cant. I am an unbeliever. Then comes by a safe and gentle spirit who spreads out in order before me his own life and aims, not as experience, but as the good and desirable. Straightway I feel the presence of a new and yet old, a genial, a native element. I am like a Southerner, who, having spent the winter in a polar climate, feels at last the south wind blow, the rigid fibres relax, and his whole frame expands to the welcome heats. In this bland, flowing atmosphere, I regain, one by one, my faculties, my organs; life returns to a finger, a hand, a foot. A new nimbleness,—almost wings, unfold at my side,—and I see my right to the heaven as well as to the farthest fields of the earth. The effect of the conversation resembles the effect of a beautiful voice in a church choir as I have noted it above, which insinuates itself as water into all chinks and cracks and presently floats the whole discordant choir and holds it in solution in its melody. Well, I too am a ship aground, and the bard directs a river to my shoals, relieves me of these perilous rubs and strains, and at last fairly uplifts me on the waters, and I put forth my sails, and turn my head to the sea. Alcott is the only majestic converser I now meet. He gives me leave to be, more than all others. Alcott is so apprehensive that he does not need to be learned.

Popularity is for dolls; a hero cannot be popular.

"*It is in bad taste*," is the most formidable word an Englishman can pronounce.

I see my thought standing, growing, walking, working, out there in nature. Look where I will, I see it. Yet when I seek to say it, all men say, "No: it is not. These are whimsies and dreams!" Then I think they look at one thing, and I at others. My thoughts, though not false, are far, as yet, from simple truth, and I am rebuked by their disapprobation, nor think of questioning it. Society is yet too great for me.

Would it not dissipate the maiden's romance if she foresaw, in the hour of wedding, the arrival of young cousins three, four years hence at her door, without any work in their hands, or word in their mouths, dropped out of the stage-coach like eggs not yet alive, to spend a fortnight?

The pulpit concedes that judgment is not executed in this world; that the wicked are successful; that the good are miserable; that is to say, these last are to have their full swing of wine and peaches another day. You sin now, we shall sin by and by. Or we would sin now if we could; not being successful, we expect our revenge tomorrow.

Heaven proceeds forever *from* me outward to all things, and not *to* me from coffee and custard.

Unroof any house, and you must find there confusion. Order is too precious and divine a thing to dwell with such fools and sinners as we all are. Incredible is it to me that in any family the work can be despatched from Monday to Monday again, all the year round, with sense and system. On the whole, I am sure there is no house well kept: there go too many things to it.

The whole world seems to be in conspiracy to invade you, to vanquish you with emphatic details, to break you into crumbs, to fritter your time. Friend, wife, child, mother, fear, want, charity, all knock at the student's door at the critical moment, ring larums in his ear, scare away the Muse, and spoil the poem.

The simple knot of Now and Then will give an immeasurable value to any sort of catalogue or journal kept with common sense for a year or two. See in the merchant's counting-room, for his peddling of cotton and indigo, the value that comes to be attached to any Blotting book or Ledger; and if your aims and deeds are superior, how can any record of yours (suppose, of the books you wish to read, of the pictures you would see, of the facts you would scrutinize), any record that you are genuinely moved to begin and continue, not have a value proportionately superior? It converts the heights you have reached into table-land. That book or literary fact which had the whole emphasis of attention a month ago stands here along with one which was as important in preceding months, and with that of yesterday; and, next month, there will be another. Here they all occupy but four lines, and I cannot read these together without juster views of each than when I read them singly.

In life it is a great matter to live with the people you are used to. Go where there is real affinity and the highest relations for you, and it serves very well for the short time that thought and poetry flow, but as soon as the tea-tray comes in, we feel the yoke of foreigners, and wish we were at home with our stupid familiars.

How great it is to do a little, as, for instance, to deserve the praise of good nature, or of humility, or of punctuality; but to say, This was a man; he lived wisely; he lived well,—outgoes all probability. I dare not believe it of my fellow.

I think I gain more from one picture than from a gallery. One picture gives me, in the first place, all the agreeable stimulus of color,—itself a tonic,—that a gallery can. This makes me brisk, gay, and thoughtful. Then, I see freely the forms, and dream pleasantly of what they would say;—I carry the picture out far and wide on every side, and I highly enjoy the unity of the hour: for the picture, of course, excludes all other things; and for a long time afterwards I can well remember the day. I conspire with the painter, lend myself willingly to him, see more than he has done, see what he meant to do. But the gallery will not permit this. The eye glances from picture to picture. Each interferes with the other. Each can only now stand for what it really is, no more. And the artist is lowered, not exalted, by the beholder.

It is somewhat so with men. They are less together than they are apart. They are somewhat wronged, discrowned and disgraced by being put many together in one apartment.

The poor mind does not seem to itself to be anything unless it have an outside oddity, some Graham diet, or Quaker coat, or Calvinistic prayer-meeting, or Abolition effort, or anyhow some wild, contrasting action, to testify that it is somewhat. The rich mind lies in the sun and sleeps.

Our people are timid, desponding, recreant whimperers. If they fail in their first enterprises they lose all heart. If the young merchant fails, men say he is RUINED.

My brave Henry [Thoreau] here who is content to live now, and feels no shame in not studying any profession, for he does not postpone his life, but lives, already,—pours contempt on these crybabies of routine and Boston. He has not one chance but a hundred chances.

There is no history; only biography.

How can I hope for a friend to me who have never been one.

The Sabbath is painfully consecrated because the other days are not, and we make prayers in the morning because we sin all day.

My life is a May game, I will live as I like. I defy your strait-laced, weary social ways and modes. Blue is the sky; green the fields and groves, fresh the springs, glad the rivers, and hospitable the splendor of sun and star. I will play my game out.

Love is thaumaturgic. It converts a chair, a box, a scrap of paper, or a line carelessly drawn on it, a lock of hair, a faded weed, into amulets worth the world's fee. If we see out of what straws and nothings he builds his Elysium, we shall read nothing miraculous in the New Testament.

At Dartmouth College, last July, was a good sheriff-like gentleman with a loud voice, a pompous air, and a fine coat, whose aid, it seemed, the College annually called in, to marshal their procession. He was in his element; he commanded us all with such despotic condescension, as put all dignities and talents but his own quite aside. He marched before, the College followed him like a tame dog.

I know no means of calming the fret and perturbation into which too much sitting, too much talking, brings me, so perfect as labor. I have no animal spirits; therefore, when surprised by company and kept in a chair for many hours, my heart sinks, my brow is clouded and I think I will run for Acton woods, and live with the squirrels henceforward. But my garden is nearer, and my good hoe, as it bites the ground, revenges my wrongs, and I have less lust to bite my enemies. I confess I work at first with a little venom, lay to a little unnecessary strength. But by smoothing the rough hillocks, I smooth my temper; by extracting the long roots of the pipergrass, I draw out my own splinters; and in a short time I can hear the bobolink's song and see the blessed deluge of light and colour that rolls around me.

The man I saw believed that his suspenders would hold up his pantaloons and that his straps would hold them down. His creed went little farther.

All the objections to the great projects of philanthropy are met and answered by a deep and universal reform. Our doctrine is that the labor of society ought to be shared by all, and that in a community where labor was the point of honor, the coxcombs would labor; that a mountain of chagrins, inconveniences, diseases and sins would sink into the sea with the uprise of this one doctrine of Labor. Domestic hired service would go over the dam. Slavery would fall into the pit. Dyspepsia would die out. Morning calls would end.

It is proposed to form a very large society to devise and execute means for propping in some secure and permanent manner this planet. It has long filled the minds of the benevolent and anxious part of the community with lively emotion, the consideration of the exposed state of the globe;

the danger of its falling and being swamped in absolute space; the danger of its being drawn too near the sun and roasting the race of mankind, and the daily danger of its being overturned, and, if a stage-coach overset costs valuable lives, what will not ensue on the upset of this omnibus? It has been thought that by a strenuous and very extensive concert aided by a committee of masterbuilders and blacksmiths, a system of booms and chains might be set round the exterior surface and that it might be underpinned in such a manner as to enable the aged and women and children to sleep and eat with greater security henceforward. It is true that there is not a perfect unanimity on this subject at present, and it is much to be regretted. A pert and flippant orator remarked to the meeting last Sunday that the world could stand without linch-pins, and that even if you should cut all the ropes and knock away the whole underpinning, it would swing and poise perfectly, for the poise was in the globe itself. But this is Transcendentalism.

I owe much to these beneficent reformers of all colors and qualities. Each one shows me that there is somewhat I can spare. Shows me thus how rich I am. Within my trench there is a wall; if the town be taken, there is yet a citadel. If the tower be stormed, there is still the invincible me.

A lecture is a new literature, which leaves aside all tradition, time, place, circumstance, and addresses an assembly as mere human beings, no more. It has never yet been done well. It is an organ of sublime power, a panharmonicon for variety of note. But only then is the orator successful when he is himself agitated, and is as much a hearer as any of the assembly. In that office you may and shall (please God!) yet see the electricity part from the cloud and shine from one part of heaven to the other.

Men are made as drunk by party as by rum. In this county they have let a proven defaulter be chosen to Congress over an affectionate, honest, able gentleman, because, as the lovely philanthropists say, the only question they ask is, "What is his relation to the slave?" Thus you cease to be a man that you may be an Abolitionist.

Be hospitable to the soul as well as to the body of thy guest, thou tart hater.

When I walk in Walden wood, as on 4 July, I seem to myself an inexhaustible poet, if only I could once break through the fence of silence, and vent myself in adequate rhyme.

Nature delights in punishing stupid people. The very strawberry vines are more than a match for them with all their appetites, and all their fumbling fingers. The little, defenceless vine coolly hides the best berry, now under this leaf, then under that, and keeps the treasure for yonder darling boy with the bright eyes when Booby is gone.

The "*abandon*" of a scatter-brain, the "*abandon*" of a woman, are no better than calculation; but the "*abandon*" of a self-commanding and reserved mind is like the fire of troops when the enemy is at the end of the bayonet.

Last night came to me a beautiful poem from Henry Thoreau, "Sympathy." The purest strain, and the loftiest, I think, that has yet pealed from this unpoetic American forest.

I have no right of nomination in the choice of my friends. Sir, I should be happy to oblige you, but my friends must elect themselves.

It is the peculiarity of Truth that it must *live* every moment in the beginning, in the middle, and onward forever in every stage of statement. I cannot accept without qualification the most indisputable of your axioms. I see that they are not quite true.

Manners need somewhat negligent and even slow in the perceptions, as Business requires quick perceptions. Manners must have an ignoring eye, a languid, graceful hand; a sluggard knight who does not see the annoyances, inconveniences, shifts, that cloud the brow and smother the voice of the sensitive. The popular men and women are often externally sluggish, lazy natures, not using superlatives, nor staking their all on every peppercorn.

We are shut up in schools and college recitation rooms for ten or fifteen years, and come out at last with a bellyful of words and do not know a thing. We cannot use our hands, or our legs, or our eyes, or our arms. We do not know an edible root in the woods. We cannot tell our course by the stars, nor the hour of the day by the sun. It is well if we can swim and skate. We are afraid of a horse, of a cow, of a dog, of a cat, of a spider. Far better was the Roman rule to teach a boy nothing that he could not learn standing.

Now here are my wise young neighbors* who, instead of getting, like the woodmen, into a railroad-car, where they have not even the activity of holding the reins, have got into a boat which they have built with their own hands,

* John and Henry Thoreau.

with sails which they have contrived to serve as a tent by
night, and gone up the Merrimack to live by their wits on
the fish of the stream and the berries of the wood. My
worthy neighbor Dr. Bartlett expressed a true parental instinct when he desired to send his boy with them to learn
something. The farm, the farm, is the right school. The reason of my deep respect for the farmer is that he is a realist,
and not a dictionary. The farm is a piece of the world, the
school-house is not.

I hate preaching, whether in pulpits or in teachers' meetings. Preaching is a pledge, and I wish to say what I think
and feel today, with the proviso that tomorrow perhaps I
shall contradict it all. Freedom boundless I wish. I will not
pledge myself not to drink wine, not to drink ink, not to lie,
and not to commit adultery, lest I hanker tomorrow to do
these very things by reason of my having tied my hands.
Besides, man is so poor he cannot afford to part with any
advantages, or bereave himself of the functions even of one
hair. I do not like to speak to the Peace Society, if so I am
to restrain me in so extreme a privilege as the use of the
sword and bullet. For the peace of the man who has for-
sworn the use of the bullet seems to me not quite peace,
but a canting impotence.

The mob are always interesting. We hate editors, preachers
and all manner of scholars, and fashionists. A blacksmith, a truckman, a farmer, we follow into the bar-room
and watch with eagerness what they shall say, for such as
they do not speak because they are expected to, but because they have something to say.

How sad a spectacle, so frequent nowadays, to see a young
man after ten years of college education come out, ready

for his voyage of life,—and to see that the entire ship is made of rotten timber, of rotten, honeycombed, traditional timber without so much as an inch of new plank in the hull.

It seems as if the present age of words should naturally be followed by an age of silence, when men shall speak only through facts, and so regain their health. We die of words. We are hanged, drawn and quartered by dictionaries. We walk in the vale of shadows. It is an age of hobgoblins.

With the Past, as past, I have nothing to do; nor with the Future as future. I live now, and will verify all past history in my own moments.

All conversation among literary men is muddy. I derive from literary meetings no satisfaction. Yet it is pity that meetings for conversation should end as quickly as they ordinarily do. They end as soon as the blood is up, and we are about to say daring and extraordinary things. They adjourn for a fortnight, and when we are reassembled we have forgot all we had to say.

In Massachusetts a number of young and adult persons are at this moment the subject of a revolution. They are not organized into any conspiracy: they do not vote, or print, or meet together. They do not know each other's faces or names. They are united only in a common love of truth and love of its work. They are of all conditions and natures. They are, some of them, mean in attire, and some mean in station, and some mean in body, having inherited from their parents faces and forms scrawled with the traits of every vice. Not in churches, or in courts, or in large assemblies; not in solemn holidays, where men were met in festal dress, have these pledged themselves to new life, but in lonely and obscure places, in servitude, in solitude, in solitary compunctions and shames and fears, in disappointments, in diseases, trudging beside the team in the dusty road, or drudging, a hireling in other men's cornfields, schoolmasters who teach a few children rudiments for a pittance, ministers of small parishes of the obscurer sects, lone women in dependent condition, matrons and young maidens, rich and poor, beautiful and hard-favoured, without conceit or proclamation of any kind, have silently given in their adherence to a new hope.

Children are all foreigners. We treat them as such. We cannot understand their speech or the mode of life, and so our Education is remote and accidental and not closely applied to the facts.

I have read *Oliver Twist* in obedience to the opinions of so many intelligent people as have praised it. The author has an acute eye for costume; he sees the expression of dress, of form, of gait, of personal deformities; of furniture, of the outside and inside of houses; but his eye rests always on surfaces; he has no insight into character. For want of key to the moral powers the author is fain to strain all his stage trick of grimace, of bodily terror, of murder, and the most approved performances of Remorse. It all avails nothing, there is nothing memorable in the book except the *flash*, which is got at a police office, and the dancing of the madman which strikes a momentary terror. Like Cooper and Hawthorne he has no dramatic talent. The moment he attempts dialogue the improbability of life hardens to wood and stone. And the book begins and ends without a poetic ray, and so perishes in the reading.

I love the Sunday morning. I hail it from afar. I walk with gladness and a holiday feeling always on that day. The church is ever my desk. If I did not go thither I should not write so many of these wayward pages. The better place, the better deed.

I hate to hear a singer who is learning, let her voice be never so sweet. I wish not to be asked in every note whether I will allow it. I wish every note to command me with sweet yet perfect empire. Also I hate Early Poems.

I can be wise very well for myself, but not for another, nor among others. I smile and ignore wo, and if that which they call wo shall come to me I hope and doubt not to smile still. They smile never and think joy amiss. All their facts are tinged with gloom, and all my pains are edged with pleasure. But if I intermeddle, if I quit my divine island and seek to right them in particulars, if I look upon them as corrigible individuals and their fortunes curable, I grow giddy and skeptical presently in their company. Old age is a sad riddle which this stony Sphinx reads us. How base to live, as the old, when now their period of outdoor activity is over, in their sensations; to exist to trifles; to have the palate and the eye and ear and skin so ignominiously wise and knowing; to be a taster, and an inexhaustible quiddle; to sell the sweet and noble human soul to all the imps of spite and gloom on the cause of an ill-done omelet, heavy cakes, or a draught of air. I can only solve this sad problem by esteeming it a slide in my lamp. It is a shade which adds splendor to the lights. But if I intermeddle, if I esteem it an entity,—already my own hair grizzles.

The Power that deals with us, the Power which we study and which we are to inherit as fast as we learn to use it, is, in sum, dazzling, terrific, inaccessible. It now benignly shows us in parts and atoms some arc of its magnificent circle, elements which are radically ours.

A walk in the woods is only an exalted dream.

Some faces turn on the pivot of the collar-bone, with eyes that are shallow beads—no more: and some on a pivot at least as deep as the orbit of the sphere, so slow and lazily and great they move.

In every house there is a good deal of false hospitality. Relatives come thither of all the degrees of cousindom and family acquaintances, who, like cats, frequent the place and not the man. The hero meets with content all this claim on time and labor and takes care that his "hospitality run fine to the last," as Lamb finely said. But not so the saint. He is so much the servant of absolute goodness, that he feels the falsehood of merely feeding and amusing these butterflies and beetles, and austerely tells them so.

When I was thirteen years old, my Uncle Samuel Ripley one day asked me, "How is it, Ralph, that all the boys dislike you and quarrel with you, whilst the grown people are fond of you?" Now am I thirty-six and the fact is reversed, —the old people suspect and dislike me, and the young love me.

The little bigots of each town and neighborhood seek to subdue the manly and free-born. But, for this poor, dependent fraction of a life, they bereave me of that magnificent destiny which the young soul has embraced with auguries of immeasurable hope. I turn my back on these insane usurpers. The soul always believes in itself.

I must not bait my hook to draw men to me. I must angle with myself and use no lower means.

It is strange how long our noviciate lasts; that the period of our mastership still loiters, that as long as we remain growing, and do not inveterate, we are always subject to circumstances and do not control them. All the chemical agents act with energy on us, and we come, greenhorns, to every conversation. The young, the knowing, the fashionable, the practical, the political, the belle, the Pharisee and the Sadducee, all overact on us, and make us dumb.

Society in our bright hours seems not to claim equality, but ought to be treated like children to whom we administer camomile and magnesia on our own judgment, without consultation. What we can do is law enough for them. But when our own light beams less steadily and flickers in the socket, the pupil seems suddenly riper and more froward, and even assumes the mien of a patron whom we must court.

The best effect of fine persons is felt after we have left their presence.

How we hate this solemn Ego that accompanies the learned, like a double, wherever he goes.

Only this strip of paper remains to me to record my introduction to Anna Barker last Friday at Jamaica Plains. A new person is to me ever a great event, and few days of my quiet life are so illustrated and cheered as were these two in which I enjoyed the frank and generous confidence of a being so lovely, so fortunate, and so remote from my own experiences. She seemed to me a woman singularly healthful and entire. She had no detached parts or powers. She had not talents, or affections or accomplishments, or single features of conspicuous beauty, but was a unit and whole, so that whatsoever she did became her, whether she walked or sat or spoke. She had an instinctive elegance. She had too much warmth and sympathy and desire to please than that you could say her manners were marked with dignity, yet no princess could surpass her clear and erect demeanor on each occasion. She is not an intellectual beauty, but is of that class which in society is designated as having a great deal of Soul, that is, the predominant character of her nature is not thought, but emotion or sympathy, and of course she is not of my class, does not resemble the women I have most admired and loved, but she is so perfect in her own nature as to meet these by the fulness of her heart, and does not distance me, as I believe all others of that cast of character do. She does not sit at home in her mind, as my angels are wont to do, but instantly goes abroad into the minds of others, takes possession of society and warms it with noble sentiments. Her simple faith seemed to be, that by dealing nobly with all, all would show themselves noble, and so her conversation is the frankest I ever heard. She can afford to be sincere. The wind is not purer than she is.

Lyceum.—Here is all the true orator will ask, for here is a convertible audience, and here are no stiff conventions that prescribe a method, a style, a limited quotation of books and an exact respect to certain books, persons or opinions.

No, here everything is admissible, philosophy, ethics, divinity, criticism, poetry, humor, fun, mimicry, anecdotes, jokes, ventriloquism, all the breadth and versatility of the most liberal conversation; highest, lowest, personal, local topics, all are permitted, and all may be combined in one speech;—it is a panharmonicon,—every note on the longest gamut, from the explosion of cannon, to the tinkle of guitar. Let us try if Folly, Custom, Convention and Phlegm cannot hear our sharp artillery. Here is a pulpit that makes other pulpits tame and ineffectual—with their cold, mechanical preparation for a delivery the most decorous,— fine things, pretty things, wise things, but no arrows, no axes, no nectar, no growling, no transpiercing, no loving, no enchantment.

Here he may lay himself out utterly, large, enormous, prodigal, on the subject of the hour. Here he may dare to hope for ecstasy and eloquence.

We sing as we are bid. Our inspirations are very manageable and tame. Death and Sin have whispered in the ear of our wild horses and they are become drays and hacks.

A question which well deserves examination now is the Dangers of Commerce. This invasion of Nature by Trade with its Money, its Credit, its Steam, its Railroad, threatens to upset the balance of man, and establish a new, universal Monarchy more tyrannical than Babylon or Rome. Very faint and few are the poets or men of God. Those who remain are so antagonistic to this tyranny that they appear mad or morbid, and are treated as such. Sensible of this extreme unfitness they suspect themselves. And all of us apologize when we ought not, and congratulate ourselves when we ought not.

For the five last years I have read each winter a new course of lectures in Boston, and each was my creed and confession of faith. Each told all I thought of the past, the present and the future. Once more I must renew my work, and I think only once in the same form, though I see that he who thinks he does something for the last time ought not to do it at all. Yet my objection is not to the thing, but with the form: and the concatenation of errors called *society* to which I still consent, until my plumes be grown, makes even a duty of this concession also. So I submit to sell tickets again.

But the form is neither here nor there. What shall be the substance of my shrift? Adam in the garden, I am to new name all the beasts in the field and all the gods in the sky. I am to invite men drenched in Time to recover themselves and come out of time, and taste their native immortal air. I am to fire with what skill I can the artillery of sympathy and emotion. I am to indicate constantly, though all unworthy, the Ideal and Holy Life, the life within life, the Forgotten Good, the Unknown Cause in which we sprawl and sin. I am to try the magic of sincerity, that luxury permitted only to kings and poets. I am to celebrate the spiritual powers in their infinite contrast to the mechanical powers and the mechanical philosophy of this time. I am to console the brave sufferers under evils whose end they cannot see by appeals to the great optimism, self-affirmed in all bosoms.

Think, and you annihilate the times. Drink of the cup which God proffers to your lips and these storming, anxious, contradicting, threatening crowds which surround you, mad with debt and credit, with banks and politics, with books and churches and meats and drinks, shall all flee away like ghosts from the new-born soul.

Another day; the old game; up again, this wonderful but unhandsome machine, with thy hopes and shames; poor boasting augur, who sufferest as many misgivings on the edge of success as on the brink of failure, and tremblest with as many hopes on the eve of misfortune as on thy best day.

Who can blame men for seeking excitement? They are polar, and would you have them sleep in a dull eternity of equilibrium? Religion, love, ambition, money, war, brandy —some fierce antagonism must break the round of perfect circulation or no spark, no joy, no event can be.

How can I not record, though now with sleepy eye and flagging spirits, so fair a fact as the visit of Alcott and Margaret Fuller, who came hither yesterday and departed this morning? Very friendly influences these, each and both. Cold as I am, they are almost dear. I shall not, however, fill my page with the gifts or merits of either. They brought nothing but good spirits and good tidings with them of new literary plans here, and good fellowship and recognition abroad. And then to my private ear a chronicle of sweet romance, of love and nobleness which have inspired the beautiful and brave. What is good to make me happy is not however good to make me write. Life too near paralyses art. Long these things refuse to be recorded except in the invisible colors of memory.

See a knot of country people working out their road tax or laying a new bridge. How close are they to their work.

How they sympathize with every log, and foreknow its every nod and stir with chain and crowbar, and seem to see through the ground all the accidents of preservation and decay.

I hate the giving of the hand unless the whole man accompanies it. I hate giving seven pounds of rice or sugar to a poor person whose whole character is disagreeable to me.

Men are multiplex. The good offices they do are not their genuine aim, the mere flower and perfume of their nature, but are a compliance and a compliment, and contradicted by other actions on the same day. Their temperance is a plume, a feather in the cap, this ostentatious glass of cold water and dry, raw, vegetable diet that makes your blood run cold to see, is not the joyful sign that they have ceased to care for food in nobler cares, but no, they peak and pine and know all they renounce. Temperance when it is only the sign of intrinsic virtue is graceful as the bloom on the cheek that betokens health, but temperance that is nothing else but temperance is phlegm or conceit. Is it not better they should do bad offices and be intemperate so long as that is their ruling love? So at least they should not be hypocrites.

There are facts which turn curled heads round at church and send wonderful eyebeams across assemblies, from one to one, never missing in the thickest crowd, which it behooves the philosopher to remember.

Don't seek to vamp and abut principles. They were before you were born, and will be when you are rotten. You might as well paint the sky blue with a bluebag.

The old thought which I loved in my youth when the roar of politics fell harshest on my ear, that presently government would cease to be sought by gentlemen and would be despatched by a few clerks, is now embodied, and, as far as I heard last night, very ably and truly preached by the Non-Resistants with Garrison at their head, a man of great ability in conversation, of a certain longsightedness in debate which is a great excellence, a tenacity of his proposition which no accidents or ramblings in the conversation can divert, a calmness and method in unfolding the details of his argument, and an eloquence of illustration, which contents the ear and the mind,—thus armed with all the weapons of a great apostle—no, not yet, until I have remembered his religion, which is manifest, his religious trust in his principles, and his clearness from any taint of private end. And yet the man teases me by his continual wearisome trick of quoting texts of Scripture and his Judaical Christianity, and then by the continual eye to numbers, to societies. Himself is not enough for him.

We should never cumber ourselves with maintaining either popular religion or popular Sabbaths or popular Laws, if we do not want them ourselves. Are they now maintained by [us] because the world needs them? Let the world maintain them. And you shall find, if the deacons and the priests all fail, the bank presidents and the chambers of commerce, yea, the very inn-holders and democrats of the county would muster with fury to their support.

In our modern reforms there's a little too much commentary on the movement by the mover.

I have conceived more highly of the possibilities of the art sometimes in looking at weather-stains on a wall, or fantastic shapes which the eye makes out of shadows by lamp-light, than from really majestic and finished pictures.

In the afternoon I visited Alcott and in the evening Ward came to see me, and the next morning again brought me Raphael's designs to show me that Raphael was greater than Angelo, great as Shakspear. But in making this scale we must be very passive. The gods and demigods must seat themselves without seneschal in our Olympus, and as they can instal themselves by seniority divine, so will I worship them, and not otherwise. I had told Alcott that my First Class stood, for today, perhaps thus: Phidias, Jesus, Angelo, Shakspear; or if I must sift more sternly still, —Jesus and Shakspear were two men of genius.

It is the condition of inspiration—Marry Nature, and not use her for pleasure.

Teeth in the physiognomy express limitation.

A great man stands on God. A small man stands on a great man.

The book that alarms one man, threatening the disorganization of society, is heard of by one of higher principle with no more emotion than the cheeping of a mouse in the wall.

It is very hard to find an ideal in history. By courtesy we call saints and heroes such, but they are very defective characters. I cannot easily find a man I would be.

Fear when your friends say to you what you have done well, and say it through. But when they cannot say it, when they stand beside you with uncertain, timid looks of respect and yet half dislike, inclined to suspend their judgment of you for years to come, then you may begin to hope and to trust.

Alcott seems to need a pure success. If the men and women whose opinion is fame could see him as he is and could express heartily as these English correspondents their joy in his genius, I think his genius would be exalted and relieved of some spots, with which a sense of injustice and loneliness has shaded it.

No great man will ever drill. None will ever solve the problem of his character according to our preconceived notions or wishes, but only in his own high, unprecedented way.

As the wandering sea-bird which, crossing the ocean, alights on some rock or islet to rest for a moment its wings and to look back on the wilderness of waves behind and forward to the wilderness of waters before, so stand we perched on this rock or shoal of Time arrived out of the Immensity of the Past and bound and road-ready to plunge into immensity again.

I thought it a good remark which somebody repeated here from S. S., that I "always seemed to be on stilts." It is even so. Most of the persons whom I see in my own house I see across a gulf. I cannot go to them nor they come to me. Nothing can exceed the frigidity and labor of my speech with such. You might turn a yoke of oxen between every pair of words; and the behavior is as awkward and proud. I see the ludicrousness of the plight as well as they. But, having never found any remedy, I am very patient with this folly or shame, patient of my churl's mask, in the belief that this privation has certain rich compensations, inasmuch as it makes my solitude dearer, and the impersonal God is shed abroad in my heart more richly, and more lowly welcome for this porcupine impossibility of contact with men. And yet in one who sets his mark so high, who presumes so vast an elevation as the birthright of man, is it not a little sad to be a mere mill or pump yielding one wholesome product at the mouth in one particular mode, but as impertinent and worthless in any other place or purpose as a pump or a coffee-mill would be in a parlor or a chapel? I made rockets; must I therefore be a good senator?

I need hardly say to anyone acquainted with my thoughts that I have no System. When I was quite young, I fancied that by keeping a manuscript Journal by me, over whose pages I wrote a list of the great topics of human study, as, *Religion, Poetry, Politics, Love,* etc., in the course of a few years I should be able to complete a sort of encyclopaedia containing the net value of all the definitions at which the world had yet arrived. But at the end of a couple of years, my Cabinet Cyclopaedia, though much enlarged, was no nearer to a completeness than on its first day. Nay, somehow the whole plan of it needed alteration, nor did the following months promise any speedier term to it than the foregoing. At last I discovered that my curve was a parabola whose arcs would never meet, and came to acquiesce in the perception that, although no diligence can rebuild the universe in a model by the best accumulation of disposition of details, yet does the world reproduce itself in miniature in every event that transpires, so that all the laws of nature may be read in the smallest fact. So that the truth-speaker may dismiss all solicitude as to the proportion and congruency of the aggregate of his thoughts, so long as he is a faithful reporter of particular impressions.

Those eclectics are doomed to an agreeable surprise who have fancied the Creator so poor in invention that he can produce but three or four Ages or Schools of thought, and having run through so short a gamut, must needs repeat the old tune to infinity.

The real danger of American scholars is not analysis, but sleep.

Man exists for his own sake and not to add a laborer to the State. Therefore, I never can forgive a great man who succumbs so far to the mere forms of his day as to peril his integrity for the sake of adding to the weight of his personal character the authority of office, or making a real government titular. Adams, Clay and Webster electioneer. And Nature does not forgive them, for thus they compromise their proper majesty, and are farther than ever from obtaining the adventitious.

Our life is infested by unjust persons, by fools, by paltry fellows who win a political importance—by all these tormentors who exercise a power of annoyance sadly disproportioned to the shortness of the term in which we converse with the Ideas of Religion, Wisdom and Society. Yet the power to annoy which is given to these agents for a season, we give. It is merely an outward or reflex exhibition of our defects.

Why should they call me good-natured? I too, like puss, have a retractile claw.

Men kill themselves. And run the risk of great absurdity; for our faculties fail us here to say what is the amount of this freedom, this only door left open in all the padlocked secrets of nature, this main entry and royal staircase admitting apparently to the Presence-Chamber, yet so designedly it seems left wide. It may be that he who sheathes his knife in his own heart does an act of grand issues, and it may be a preposterous one. I think I would not try it until I had first satisfied myself that I did not baulk and fool myself. The question is whether it is the way *out*, or the way *in*.

L.C.B. went to board in the country, and complained that she got bad air, bad light, bad water, bad fire, bad sound, bad food, and bad company. The house shook with rats and mice, smelt of onions, the oil in the lamp would not burn, the water was foul, the wood on the fire was soggy and made no flame, the children stunned her, the table was poverty itself, and the people vulgar and knavish, and when she would walk abroad she could not draw the bolt.

Who argues so sourly for beef and mutton against the man of herbs and grains? The fat and ruddy eater who hath just wiped his lips from feeding on a sirloin, whose blood is spouting in his veins, and whose strength kindles that evil fire in his eye. It is not then the voice of man that I hear, but it is the beef and brandy that roar and rail for beef and brandy. But shall these play the judge in their own cause?

Literary accomplishments, skill in grammar, logic and rhetoric can never countervail the want of things that demand voice. Literature is but a poor trick when it busies itself to make words pass for things.

Women see better than men. Men see lazily, if they do not expect to act. Women see quite without any wish to act. Men of genius are said to partake of the masculine and feminine traits. They have this feminine eye, a function so rich that it contents itself without asking any aid of the hand.

O Lord! unhappy is the man whom man can make unhappy.

This country is not an aristocracy, but a cacocracy rather. This town is governed in Wesson's bar-room; and the Country in bar-rooms.

When once and again the regard and friendship of the noble-minded is offered me, I am made sensible of my disunion with myself. The head is of gold, the feet are of clay. In my *worthiness* I have such confidence, that I can court solitude. I know that if my aspirations should demonstrate themselves, angels would not disdain me. Of my *unworthiness*, the first person I meet shall apprize me. I shall have so little presence, such pitiful, gingerbread considerations, so many calculations, and such unconcealable weariness of my company,—that in my heart I beseech them begone, and I flee to the secretest hemlock shade in Walden woods to recover my self-respect. *Patimur quisque suos manes!* But when I have shriven myself to the partridges, I am gay again and content to be alone. Then I am let into the secret, daily history of others to whom that grace and conversation I covet is given, and find such savage melancholy, such passion, discontent and despair, that suddenly I count myself the happiest of men, and will know the sweetness of bread and water, and live with the jays and sparrows still.

Poetry makes its own pertinence, and a single stanza outweighs a book of prose. I do not wish to read the verses of a poetic mind, but only of a poet. I do not wish to be shown early poems, or any steps of progress. I wish my poet to be born adult. I do not find youth or age in Shakespear, Milton, Herbert, and I dread minors.

Did you ever eat the poorest rye or oatcake with a beautiful maiden in the wilderness? and did you not find that the mixture of sun and sky with your bread gave it a certain mundane savour and comeliness?

In taking, this afternoon, farewell looks at the sibyls and prophets of Michel Angelo, I fancied that they all looked not free, but necessitated; ridden by a superior will, by an Idea which they could not shake off. It sits in their life. The heads of Raphael look freer certainly, but this obedience of Michel's figures contrasts strangely with the living forms of this age. These old giants are still under the grasp of that terrific Jewish Idea before which ages were driven like sifted snow, which all the literatures of the world—Latin, Spanish, Italian, French, English—tingle with; but we sleek, dapper men have quite got free of that old reverence, have heard new facts on metaphysics, and they are quite ready to join any new church. We are travellers, and not responsible.

"*Society*," like wealth, is good for those who understand it. It is a foolish waste of time for any who do not. It seems impossible for anyone to expand in the crowd to his natural dimensions. It seems vain to expect any sentiment, any truth and human encouragement. All character seems to fade away from all the accomplices. Every woman seems to be suffering for a chair, and you accuse yourself and commiserate those you talk to. . . . He must be rich, and of a commanding constitution, who can stand this malaria. It spoils the best persons for me.

I woke this morn with devout thanksgiving for my friends, the old and the new. I think no man in the planet has a circle more noble. They have come to me unsought: the great God gave them to me. Will they separate themselves from me again, or some of them? I know not, but I fear it not, for my relation to them is so pure that we hold by simple affinity; and the Genius of my life being thus social, the same affinity will exert its energy on whosoever is as noble as these men and women, wherever I may be.

I say how the world looks to me without reference to Blair's Rhetoric or Johnson's Lives. And I call my thoughts The Present Age, because I use no will in the matter, but honestly record such impressions as things make. So transform I myself into a dial, and my shadow will tell where the sun is.

It seemed, as I mused in the street in Boston on the unpropitious effect of the town on my humor, that there needs a certain deliberation and tenacity in the entertainment of a thought,—a certain longanimity to make that confidence and stability which can meet the demand others make on us. I am too quick-eyed and unstable. My thoughts are too short, as they say my sentences are. I step along from stone to stone over the Lethe which gurgles around my path, but the odds are that my companion encounters me just as I leave one stone and before my foot has well reached the other, and down I tumble into Lethe water. But the man of long wind, the man who receives his thought with a certain phlegmatic entertainment and unites himself to it for the time, as a sailor to his boat, has a better principle of poise and is not easily moved from the perpendicular.

In my dream I saw a man reading in the Library at Cambridge, and one who stood by said, "He readeth advertisements," meaning that he read for the market only, and not for truth. Then I said, Do I read advertisements?

If you would write a code, or logarithms, or a cookbook, you cannot spare the poetic impulse. We must not only have hydrogen in balloons, and steel springs under coaches, but we must have fire under the Andes at the core of the world.

Love is only the reflection of a man's own worthiness from other men.

Some books leave us free and some books make us free.

All life is a compromise. We are haunted by an ambition of a celestial greatness, and baulked of it by all manner of paltry impediments.

I have heard that it is not usually beauty which inspires the strongest passion. I can even believe that Aspasia was not beautiful, seen *tête-à-tête*, but almost plain and homely, yet in a circle of dames in a gallery or across the apartment, hers was the only face on which the eye would fix, and when all were gone, the only one whose form and behaviour the heart would remember.

Pleasant these jets of affection that relume a young world for me again. Delicious is a just and firm encounter of two in a thought, in a feeling. But we must be tormented presently by baffled blows, by sudden unseasonable apathies, by epilepsies of wit and of animal spirits in the heyday of friendship and thought. Our faculties do not play us true.

1840

Guy* wished all his friends dead on very slight occasion. Whoever was privy to one of his gaucheries had the honour of this Stygian optation. Had Jove heard all his prayers, the planet would soon have been unpeopled. At last it occurred to Guy that, instead of wringing this hecatomb of friends' necks every morning, he would dine better if he gave as much life as he now took. He found to his astonishment the embryos of a thousand friends hid under his own heart, and that for every offence he forgave, and for every great choice he made, suddenly from afar a noble stranger knocked at his street gate.

If Russia is a scarecrow, that fact at least tells somewhat of them whom it scares.

February 19

I closed last Wednesday my course of lectures in Boston, on "The Present Age." The average audience at a lecture consisted of about 400 persons. 256 course tickets were sold and 305 evening tickets or passes. I distributed about 110 to 120 course tickets.

These lectures give me little pleasure. I have not done

* Emerson occasionally jotted down half-humorous, half-idealized character sketches of himself under various assumed names.

what I hoped when I said, I will try it once more. I have not once transcended the coldest self-possession. I said I will agitate others, being agitated myself, I dared to hope for ecstasy and eloquence. A new theatre, a new art, I said, is mine. Let us see if philosophy, if ethics, if chiromancy, if the discovery of the divine in the house and the barn, in all works and all plays, cannot make the cheek blush, the lips quiver, and the tear start. I will not waste myself. On the strength of Things I will be borne, and try if Folly, Custom, Convention, and Phlegm cannot be made to hear our sharp artillery. Alas! alas! I have not the recollection of one strong moment. A cold mechanical preparation for a delivery as decorous,—fine things, pretty things, wise things,—but no arrows, no axes, no nectar, no growling, no transpiercing, no loving, no enchantment.

And why?

I seem to lack constitutional vigor to attempt each topic as I ought. I ought to seek to lay myself out utterly,— large, enormous, prodigal, upon the subject of the week. But a hateful experience has taught me that I can only expend, say, twenty-one hours on each lecture, if I would also be ready and able for the next. Of course, I spend myself prudently; I economize; I cheapen; whereof nothing grand ever grew. Could I spend sixty hours on each, or, what is better, had I such energy that I could rally the lights and mights of sixty hours into twenty, I should hate myself less, I should help my friend.

I saw a maiden, the other day, dressed so prettily and fancifully that she gave the eye the same sort of pleasure that a gem does,—a fine opal, or the coloured stones.

I like manners and their aristocracy better than the *morgue* of wealth. It is a gay chivalry, a merit, and indicates certainly the presence of a sense of beauty. I am always a fool to these mannered men at the first encounter. The Southerner holds me at arm's length; he will not let me measure him, and after twenty-four hours my opinion shall still not be worth the telling,—such a cloak is his *politesse*.

Ah, my poor countrymen! Yankees and Dollars have such inextricable association that the words ought to rhyme. In New York, in Boston, in Providence, you cannot pass two men in the street without the word escaping them in the very moment of encounter, "dollars," "two and a half per cent," "three per cent."

We walked this afternoon to Edmund Hosmer's and Walden Pond. The South wind blew and filled with bland and warm light the dry sunny woods. The last year's leaves flew like birds through the air. As I sat on the bank of the Drop, or God's Pond, and saw the amplitude of the little water, what space, what verge, the little scudding fleets of ripples found to scatter and spread from side to side and take so much time to cross the pond, and saw how the water seemed made for the wind, and the wind for the water, dear playfellows for each other,—I said to my companion, I declare this world is so beautiful that I can hardly believe it exists.

There are, no doubt, many dogs barking at the moon, and many owls hooting in this Saturday night of the world, but the fair moon knows nothing of either.

In conversation, Alcott will meet no man who will take a superior tone. Let the other party say what he will, Alcott unerringly takes the highest moral ground and commands the other's position, and cannot be outgeneralled. And this because, whilst he lives in his moral perception, his sympathies with the present company are not troublesome to him, never embarrass for a moment his perception. He is cool, bland, urbane, yet with his eye fixed on the highest fact. With me it is not so. In all companies I sympathize too much. If they are ordinary and mean, I am. If the company were great, I should soar: in all mere mortal parties, I take the contagion of their views and lose my own. I cannot out-see them, or correct, or raise them. As soon as they are gone, the Muse returns; I see the facts as all cultivated men always have seen them, and am a great man alone.

Every man supposes himself not to be fully understood or appreciated.

Strange how hard it is for cultivated men to free themselves from the optical illusion by which a great man appears an institution.

If you have no talent for scolding, do not scold; if none for explaining, do not explain; if none for giving parties, do not give parties, however graceful or needful these acts may appear in others.

If a man knows the law, he may settle himself in a shanty in the pine forest, and men will and must find their way to him as readily as if he lived in the City Hall.

I begin to dislike animal food. I had whimsies yesterday after dinner which disgusted me somewhat. The man will not be much better than the beast he eats.

Suppose you have reformed, and live on grains and black-birch bark and muddy water, that you may have leisure.

Well, what then? What will you do with the long day? Think? What! All day? Do you not see that instantly taste and arithmetic and power will plan plantations and build summer-houses and carve gods?

Conformity is the ape of harmony.

Beware when the great God lets loose a new thinker on this planet.

An apple-tree near at hand is a great awkward flower, but seen at some distance it gives a wonderful softness to the landscape.

How few cosmogonies have we. A few have got a kind of classical character, and we let them stand, for a world-builder is a rare man. And yet what ghosts and hollow, formless, dream-gear these theories are; how crass and inapplicable; how little they explain; what a poor handfull of facts in this plentiful universe they touch. Let me see.— Moses, Hesiod, Egyptian lore of Isis and Osiris, Zoroaster, Menu—with these few rude poems, or extracts from rude poems, the nations have been content when any clever boy, black or white, has anywhere interrupted the stupid uproar by a sharp question, "Would any one please tell me whence I came hither?" To be sure that question is contrary to the rules of good society in all countries. For society is always secondary, not primary, and delights in secondaries. It is gregarious and parasitic and loves to lay its egg like the cow-troopial in a nest which other birds have built, and to build no nest itself. Absolute truths, previous questions, primary natures, Society loathes the sound of and the name of. "Can you not as well say Christ as say truth?" it asks. "Who are you, child, that you must needs ask so many questions? See what a vast procession of your uncles and aunts who never asked any. Can't you eat your dinner and read in the books? besides, I hate conversation, it makes my head ache." But if the urchin has wild eyes, and can neither be coaxed nor chidden into silence, and cares not a pin for the Greeks and Romans, for art or antiquity, for Bible or Government, for politics or money, and keeps knocking soundly all night at the gate, then at last the good world condescends to unroll for him these solemn scrolls as the reports of the Commissioners from the East, from the South, from the North and the West, to whom his question had been formerly referred. If the poor lad got no answer before, he has got none now.

I went to the circus. One horse brought a basket in his teeth, picked up a cap, and selected a card out of four. All wonder comes of showing an effect at two or three removes from the cause. Show us the two or three steps by which the horse was brought to fetch the basket, and the wonder would cease. But I and Waldo were of one mind when he said, "It makes me want to go home."

A pleasant walk and sail this fine afternoon with George Bradford. I threatened by way of earnest-penny in this absorbing Reform to renounce beef and the Daily Advertiser. There is ever a slight suspicion of the burlesque about earnest, good men. It is very strange, but we flee to the speculative reformer to escape that same slight ridicule.

I think it ought to be remembered in every essay after the Absolute Criticism that one circumstance goes to modify every work of literature, this, namely, that books are written generally by the unmagnetic class of mankind, by those who have not the active faculties, and who describe what they have never done. This circumstance must certainly color what they say of character and action.

Sad spectacle that a man should live and be fed that he may fill a paragraph every year in the newspapers for his wonderful age, as we record the weight and girth of the Big Ox or Mammoth Girl. We do not count a man's years until he has nothing else to count.

What can we do in dark hours? We can abstain. In the bright hours we can impart.

The books of men of genius are divers or dippers. When they alight on the water, they soon disappear, but after some space they emerge again. Other books are land-birds which, falling in the water, know well that their own safety is in keeping at the top. They flutter and chirp and scream, but if they once get their heads under they are drowned forever.

My cow milks me.

I finish this morning transcribing my old essay on Love, but I see well its inadequateness. I, cold because I am hot, —cold at the surface only as a sort of guard and compensation for the fluid tenderness of the core,—have much more experience than I have written there, more than I will, more than I can write. In silence we must wrap much of our life, because it is too fine for speech, because also we cannot explain it to others, and because somewhat we cannot yet understand. That which passes for love in the world gets official, and instead of embracing, hates all the divine traits that dare to appear in other persons. A better and holier society will mend this selfish cowardice, and we shall have brave ties of affection, not petrified by law, not dated or ordained by law to last for one year, for five years, or for life; but drawing their date, like all friendship, from itself only; brave as I said, because innocent, and religiously abstinent from the connubial endearments, being a higher league on a purely spiritual basis. This nobody believes possible who is not good. The good know it is possible. Cows and bulls and peacocks think it nonsense.

Our countrymen love intoxication of some sort. One is drunk with whiskey, and one with party, and one with music, and one with temper. Many of them fling themselves into the excitement of business until their heads whirl and they become insane. But ambition is for strong heads, not for weak ones.

I like Henry Thoreau's statement on Diet: "If a man does not believe that he can thrive on board nails, I will not talk with him."

I, who suffer from excess of sympathy, proclaim always the merits of self-reliance.

Once I was in love, and whenever I thought of what should happen to me and the maiden, we were always travelling; I could not think of her otherwise. Again I was in love, and I always painted this maiden at home.

Talent without character is friskiness.

The language of the street is always strong. What can describe the folly and emptiness of scolding like the word *jawing?* I feel too the force of the double negative, though

clean contrary to our grammar rules. And I confess to some pleasure from the stinging rhetoric of a rattling oath in the mouth of truckmen and teamsters. How laconic and brisk it is by the side of a page of the *North American Review*. Cut these words and they would bleed; they are vascular and alive; they walk and run. Moreover they who speak them have this elegancy, that they do not trip in their speech. It is a shower of bullets, whilst Cambridge men and Yale men correct themselves and begin again at every half sentence.

I know nobody among my contemporaries except Carlyle who writes with any sinew and vivacity comparable to Plutarch and Montaigne. Yet always this profane swearing and bar-room wit has salt and fire in it.

The pastures are full of ghosts for me, the morning woods full of angels. Now and then they give me a broad hint.

Let my friend come and say that he has to say, and go his way. Otherwise we live for show. That happens continually in my house, that I am expected to play tame lion by readings and talkings to the friends. The rich live for show: I will not.

A month ago, I met myself, as I was speeding away from some trifle to chase a new one, and knew that I had eaten lotus and been a stranger from my home all this time. And now I see that, with the word and thought in my mind, another wave took me and washed my remembrance away, and only now I regain myself a little and turn in my sleep.

Our expense is almost all for conformity. It is for cake that we all run in debt.

Men of genius, being apart, half snore and spend their time in girding at society for not thinking as they do, but do nothing to convert it. But these hermits, when brought near and acting directly on each other, shall sleep no more, but be put on their mettle.

When I have talked of myself, I am presently punished by a sense of emptiness, and, as it were, flatulency, that I have lost all the solemnity and majesty of being.

Osman* was a poor and simple man and was neglected in his youth, being esteemed a person of narrow intellect, whilst his brothers were able and ambitious men. His features were mean and irregular, his form was unproportioned, his movement was awkward and he had a bass, unmusical voice. He was, therefore, never instructed in any trade or art, but was put to household chares, and later, to aid a small farmer in his husbandry. Not until he reached the middle age was he at all remarked, but left in obscurity, served last, and no notice taken of what he said. Osman thought no more of himself than others thought of him, but acquiesced in this low and menial place which was assigned to him, and with great respect to others who, he doubted not, had superior parts, and with great good humor, did all that was required of him. Much serving made him very meek and very useful. He could turn his hand to any ordinary work, and do it well. As there was no one to serve him, he learned to serve himself, and, as happens where a man waits on his own wants, he made them very few. He was social and affectionate in his nature as a dog, and readily talked with all who availed themselves of

* Emerson is referring to himself.

his hands to end some odd piece of work. Nobody dreamed of being either civil or of assuming any airs before poor Osman, so that he knew everybody for just what they were, as they all knew him. Although affable enough, he really spoke little during the day, and was of a grave, quiet deportment. In his youth he had been sickly, but these long habits of light daily work established his constitution, and when he had counted thirty-five years he began to be much considered for his probity and his wisdom. Everybody who knew him liked him, as if he had been their brother. The farmers said he worked like the rain or the wind, which need nobody's aid, but do their charity themselves. He had a strong memory, and having neither selfishness nor learning to cloud it, it might be depended on like a thermometer or a sun-dial. He was temperate in his diet, and, on account of his ill-health in childhood, had been bred to prefer a vegetable nutriment.

All diseases run into one, Old Age. We grizzle every day.

The common man has no time. One circumstance delivers him over to another. Now he cannot be, for he is travelling. Then he cannot be, for he has arrived in a new place; now, because he labors, then because he rests.

I like to see a man or a woman who does not palter or dodge, whose eyes look straight forward, and who throws the wisdom he or she has attained into the address and demeanor.

I weep with the weepers and fear with the fearers and am not a tower of defence, but a foolish sympathy.

I cannot visit any one with advantage for a longer time than one or two hours.

A newspaper in Providence contains some notice of Transcendentalism, and deplores Mr. Emerson's doctrine that the argument for immortality betrays weakness. The piece seems to be written by a woman. It begins with round sentences, but ends in Ohs and Ahs.

Love makes us little children. We never attain a perfect sincerity in our speech except we feel a degree of tenderness. And lovers use the monosyllables and short and pretty speech of children.

Do not *say* things. What you *are* stands over you the while and thunders so that I cannot hear what you say to the contrary.

Margaret [Fuller] taxed me, as often before, so now more explicitly, with inhospitality of soul. She and C. would gladly be my friends, yet our intercourse is not friendship, but literary gossip. I count and weigh, but do not love. They make no progress with me, but however often we have met, we still meet as strangers. They feel wronged in such relation and do not wish to be catechised and criticised. I thought of my experience with several persons which resembled this: and confessed that I would not converse with the divinest person more than one week. M. insisted that it was no friendship which was thus so soon exhausted, and that I ought to know how to be silent and companionable at the same moment. She would surprise me,—she would have me say and do what surprised myself. I confess to all this charge with humility unfeigned. I can better converse with George Bradford than with any other. Elizabeth Hoar and I have a beautiful relation, not however quite free from the same hardness and fences.

Yet would nothing be so grateful to me as to melt once for all these icy barriers, and unite with these lovers. Great is the law. But this survey of my experience taught me anew that no friend I have surprises, none exalts me. This then is to be set down, is it not? to the requirements we make of the friend, that he shall constrain us to sincerity, and put under contribution all our faculties.

And now I think that our *Dial* ought not to be a mere literary journal, but that the times demand of us all a more earnest aim. It ought to contain the best advice on the topics of Government, Temperance, Abolition, Trade, and Domestic Life. It might well add to such compositions such poetry and sentiment as now will constitute its best merit. Yet it ought to go straight into life with the devoted wisdom of the best men and women in the land. It should—should it not?—be a degree nearer to the hodiurnal facts than my writings are. I wish to write pure mathematics, and not a culinary almanac, or application of science to the arts.

One fact the fine conversation of the last week—now already fast fading into oblivion—revealed to me, not without a certain shudder of joy, that I must thank what I am, and not what I do, for the love my friends bear me. I, conscious all the time of the shortcoming of my hands, haunted ever with a sense of beauty which makes all I do and say pitiful to me, and the occasion of perpetual apologies, assure myself to disgust those whom I admire,—and now suddenly it comes out that they have been loving me all this time, not at all thinking of my hands or my words, but only of that love of something more beautiful than the world, which, it seems, being in my heart, overflowed through my eyes or the tones of my speech.

Granted that my theory of the world born out of the side of
man is a false one, and that it is pedantry in us helpless
and ignorant people to make this vast pretension, when we
do not want a dollar the less, not a yard of cloth, not a loaf
of bread less than other people who do not talk of their relations to the universe. Well, you do not talk of such things,
but only of stocks and streets, the Cunard boats, and the
politics of the new administration. Well, it is just as much
pedantry in you not to talk of that which really is there,
and makes the dignity of politics and trade, viz., your relation to the world. Each was a half view; granted. But one
half view was nobler, and therefore truer, than the other.

A sleeping child gives me the impression of a traveller in a
very far country.

I am only an experimenter. Do not, I pray you, set the least
value on what I do, or the least discredit on what I do not,
as if I had settled anything as true or false. I unsettle all
things. No facts are to me sacred, none are profane; I
simply experiment, an endless seeker, with no past at my
back.

Every hour has its morning, noon, and night.

Alcott said, "Who are these people? there is not one of
them whom I cannot offend in any moment." Ah vast
Spirit! I weary of these egotisms. I see well how puny and
limitary they are.

Can we not trust ourselves? Must we be such coxcombs as
to keep watch and ward over our noblest sentiments even,
lest they also betray us, and God prove a little too divine?

You would have me love you. What shall I love? Your body? The supposition disgusts you. What you have thought and said? Well, whilst you were thinking and saying them, but not now. I see no possibility of loving anything but what now is, and is becoming.

The life of man is the true romance which, when it is valiantly conducted and all the stops of the instrument opened, will go nigh to craze the reader with anxiety, wonder and love.

When I write a letter to anyone whom I love, I have no lack of words or thoughts. I am wiser than myself and read my paper with the pleasure of one who receives a letter, but what I write to fill up the gaps of a chapter is hard and cold, is grammar and logic; there is no magic in it; I do not wish to see it again.

You think it is because I have an income which exempts me from your day-labor, that I waste (as you call it) my time in sun-gazing and star-gazing. You do not know me. If my debts, as they threaten, should consume what money I have, I should live just as I do now: I should eat worse food, and wear a coarser coat, and should wander in a potato patch instead of in the wood,—but it is I, and not my twelve hundred dollars a year, that love God.

Yesterday George and Sophia Ripley, Margaret Fuller and Alcott discussed here the Social Plans.* I wished to be convinced, to be thawed, to be made nobly mad by the kindlings before my eye of a new dawn of human piety. But

---

* The Brook Farm Community.

this scheme was arithmetic and comfort: this was a hint borrowed from the Tremont House and United States Hotel; a rage in our poverty and politics to live rich and gentlemanlike, an anchor to leeward against a change of weather; a prudent forecast on the probable issue of the great questions of Pauperism and Poverty. And not once could I be inflamed, but sat aloof and thoughtless; my voice faltered and fell. It was not the cave of persecution which is the palace of spiritual power, but only a room in the Astor House hired for the Transcendentalists. I do not wish to remove from my present prison to a prison a little larger. I wish to break all prisons. I have not yet conquered my own house. It irks and repents me. Shall I raise the siege of this hencoop, and march baffled away to a pretended siege of Babylon? It seems to me that so to do were to dodge the problem I am set to solve, and to hide my impotency in the thick of a crowd. I can see too, afar— that I should not find myself more than now,—no, not so much, in that select, but not by me selected, fraternity.

Society, when I rarely enter the company of my well-dressed and well-bred fellow creatures, seems for the time to bereave me of organs, or perhaps only to acquaint me with my want of them.

I love spring water and wild air, and not the manufacture of the chemist's shop. I see in a moment, on looking into our new *Dial*, which is the wild poetry, and which the tame, and see that one wild line out of a private heart saves the whole book.

What a pity that we cannot curse and swear in good society! Cannot the stinging dialect of the sailors be domesticated? It is the best rhetoric, and for a hundred occasions those forbidden words are the only good ones. My page about "Consistency" would be better written thus: Damn Consistency!

Every new thought which makes day in our souls has its long morning twilight to announce its coming.

I dreamed that I floated at will in the great Ether, and I saw this world floating also not far off, but diminished to the size of an apple. Then an angel took it in his hand and brought it to me and said, "This must thou eat." And I ate the world.

It is not irregular hours or irregular diet that make the romantic life.

Calmness is fabulous. The most iron men give to the spiritual eye the impression of leaning, mendicant manners. Calmness is always Godlike.

In Boston, at Dr. Jackson's, I saw five or six persons take the nitrous-oxide gas. It looked very much as if the bladder was full of opinions.

I hear much that is ridiculous in music. You would laugh to know all that passes through my head in hearing a concert. Not having an ear for music, I speculate on the song and guess what it is saying to other people; what it should say to me. It is Universal and seems to hint at communication more general than speech, more general than music also. What mystic obscurities in every breast do these lovesongs accost?

How fast these wrinkles come!

Beauty can never be clutched.

I shed all influences. A.* is a tedious archangel.

People are uneasy because the philosopher seems to compromise their personal immortality. Mr. Quin thinks that to affirm the eternity of God and not to affirm the reappearance of Mr. Quin, bodily and mentally with all the appearances and recollections of Mr. Quin, excepting of course his green surtout and bank-stock scrip, is to give up the whole ship. But Mr. Quin is a sick God.

If you do not see your right to all, and your being reflected to you from all things, then the world may easily seem to you a hoax, and man the dupe. Yet the little fellow takes it so innocently, works in it so earnest and believing, blushes and turns pale, talks and sweats, is born red and dies grey, thinking himself an adjunct to the world which exists from him, that, until he is explained to himself, he may well look on himself as the most wronged of victims.

Genius always finds itself a century too early.

A droll dream last night, whereat I ghastly laughed. A congregation assembled, like some of our late conventions, to debate the institution of Marriage; and grave and alarming objections stated on all hands to the usage; when one speaker at last rose and began to reply to the arguments, but suddenly extended his hand and turned on the audience the spout of an engine which was copiously supplied from within the wall with water, and whisking it vigor-

* Bronson Alcott.

ously about, up, down, right, and left, he drove all the company in crowds hither and thither and out of the house. Whilst I stood watching, astonished and amused at the malice and vigor of the orator, I saw the spout lengthened by a supply of hose behind, and the man suddenly brought it round a corner and drenched me as I gazed. I woke up relieved to find myself quite dry, and well convinced that the institution of marriage was safe for tonight.

1841

To find a story which I thought I remembered in *Quentin Durward*, I turned over the volume until I was fairly caught in the old foolish trap and read and read to the end of the novel. Then, as often before, I feel indignant to have been duped and dragged after a foolish boy and girl, to see them at last married and portioned, and I instantly turned out of doors like a beggar that has followed a gay procession into the castle.

As the drunkard who cannot walk can run, so I can speak my oration to an assembly, when I cannot without pain answer a question in the parlor.

I am not sick that I know, yet the names and projects of my friends sound far off and faint and unaffecting to my ear, as do, when I am sick, the voices of persons and the sounds of labor which I overhear in my solitary bed. A puny, limitary creature am I, with only a small annuity of vital force to expend, which if I squander in a few feast-days, I must feed on water and moss the rest of the time.

If I judge from my own experience I should unsay all my fine things, I fear, concerning the manual labor of literary men. They ought to be released from every species of public or private responsibility. To them the grasshopper is a burden. I guard my moods as anxiously as a miser his money; for company, business, my own household chares, untune and disqualify me for writing. I think then the writer ought not to be married; ought not to have a family. I think the Roman Church with its celibate clergy and its monastic cells was right. If he must marry, perhaps he should be regarded happiest who has a shrew for a wife, a sharp-tongued notable dame who can and will assume the total economy of the house, and, having some sense that her philosopher is best in his study, suffers him not to intermeddle with her thrift. He shall be master but not mistress, as Elizabeth Hoar said.

If the world would only wait one moment, if a day could now and then be intercalated, which should be no time, but pause and landing-place, a vacation during which sun and star, old age and decay, debts and interest of money, claims and duties, should all intermit and be suspended for the halcyon trance, so that poor man and woman could throw off the harness and take a long breath and consider what was to be done, without being fretted by the knowledge that new duties are gathering for them in the moment when they are considering the too much accumulated old duties! But this on, on, forever onward, wears out adamant. All families live in a perpetual hurry. Every rational thing gets still postponed and is at last slurred and ill-done or huddled out of sight and memory.

There is no deeper dissembler than the sincerest man. Do not trust his blushes, for he blushes not at his affection, but at your suspicion. Do not trust his actions, for they are expiations and fines often, with which he has amerced himself, and not the indications of his desire. Do not conclude his ignorance or his indifference from his silence. Do not think you have his thought, when you have heard his speech to the end. Do not judge him worldly and vulgar, because he respects the rich and the well-bred, for to him the glittering symbol has a surpassing beauty which it has not to other eyes, and fills his eye, and his heart dances with delight in which no envy and no meanness are mixed.

The poet who is paralysed in the company of the young and beautiful, where he would so gladly shine, revenges himself by satire and taxing that with emptiness and display.

I am tempted lately to wish, for the benefit of our literary society, that we had the friendly institution of the *Café*. How much better than Munroe's bookshop would be a coffee-room wherein one was sure at one o'clock to find what scholars were abroad taking their walks after the morning studies were ended.

We assume a certain air of holiness when we go to deal with our children, and appeal at that moment to a principle to which we do not appeal at other times. Of course, we do not succeed: the child feels the fraud.

The great men bequeath never their projects to their sons to finish: these eat too much pound cake.

The most interesting class of people are those who have genius by accident and are powerful obliquely.

Pirates do not live on nuts and herbs.

I frequently find the best part of my ride in the Concord Coach from my house to Winthrop Place to be in Prince Street, Charter Street, Ann Street, and the like places at the North End of Boston. The dishabille of both men and women, their unrestrained attitudes and manners, make pictures greatly more interesting than the clean-shaved and silk-robed procession in Washington and Tremont streets.

Aunt Mary, whose letters I read all yesterday afternoon, is Genius always new, subtle, frolicksome, musical, unpredictable. Her wit is the wild horse of the desert, who snuffs the sirocco and scours the palm-grove without having learned his paces in the Stadium or at Tattersall's.

In reading these letters of M.M.E. I acknowledge (with surprise that I could ever forget it) the debt of myself and my brothers to that old religion which, in those years, still dwelt like a Sabbath peace in the country population of New England, which taught privation, self-denial, and sorrow. A man was born, not for prosperity, but to suffer for the benefit of others, like the noble rock-maple tree which all around the villages bleeds for the service of man.

I feel suddenly that my life is frivolous and public; I am as one turned out of doors, I live in a balcony, or on the street; I would fain quit my present companions as if they were thieves or pot-companions, and betake myself to some Thebais, some Mount Athos, in the depths of New Hampshire or Maine, to bewail my innocency and to recover it. The genius of that woman, the key to her life is in the conflict of the new and the old ideas in New England. The heir of whatever was rich and profound and efficient in thought and emotion in the old religion which planted and peopled this land. She strangely united to this passionate piety the fatal gifts of penetration, a love of philosophy, an impatience of words, and was thus a religious skeptic. She hated the poor, low, thin, unprofitable, unpoetical Humanitarians as the devastators of the Church and robbers of the soul, and never wearies with piling on them new terms of slight and weariness. "Ah!" she said, "what a poet would Byron have been, if he had been born and bred a Calvinist."

The troops of guests who succeed each other as inmates of our houses and messmates at our tables, week after week, are recording angels who inspect and report our domestic behaviour, our temperance, our conversation, and manners.

I am continually tempted to sacrifice genius to talent, the hope and promise of insight (through the sole door of better being) to the lust of a freer play and demonstration of those gifts I have. We seek that pleasurable excitement which unbinds our faculties and gives us every advantage for the display of that skill we possess, and we buy this freedom to glitter by the loss of general health.

Coffee is good for talent, but genius wants prayer.

The good river-god has taken the form of my valiant Henry Thoreau here and introduced me to the riches of his shadowy, starlit, moonlit stream, a lovely new world lying as close and yet as unknown to this vulgar trite one of streets and shops as death to life, or poetry to prose. Through one field only we went to the boat and then left all time, all science, all history, behind us, and entered into Nature with one stroke of a paddle.

We are too civil to books. For a few golden sentences we will turn over and actually read a volume of four or five hundred pages.

I value my welfare too much to pay you any longer the compliment of attentions. I shall not draw the thinnest veil over my defects, but if you are here, you shall see me as I am. You will then see that, though I am full of tenderness, and born with as large hunger to love and to be loved as any man can be, yet its demonstrations are not active and bold, but are passive and tenacious. My love has no flood and no ebb, but is always there under my silence, under displeasure, under cold, arid, and even weak behavior.

Ah, ye old ghosts! Ye builders of dungeons in the air! Why do I ever allow you to encroach on me a moment; a moment, to win me to your hapless company? In every week there is some hour when I read my commission in every cipher of Nature, and know that I was made for another office, a professor of the Joyous Science, a detector and delineator of occult harmonies and unpublished beauties, a herald of civility, nobility, learning, and wisdom; an affirmer of the One Law, yet as one who should affirm it in music or dancing.

If I were a preacher, I should carry straight to church the remark Lidian made today, that "she had been more troubled by piety in her help than with any other fault." The girls that are not pious, she finds kind and sensible, but the church members are scorpions, too religious to do their duties, and full of wrath and horror at her if she does them.

If I should or could record the true experience of my late years, I should have to say that I skulk and play a mean, shiftless, subaltern part much the largest part of the time. Things are to be done which I have no skill to do, or are to be said which others can say better, and I lie by, or occupy my hands with something which is only an apology for idleness, until my hour comes again.

The Church aërates my good neighbors and serves them as a somewhat stricter and finer ablution than a clean shirt or a bath or a shampooing. The minister is a functionary and the meeting-house a functionary: they are one and, when they have spent all their week in private and selfish action, the Sunday reminds them of a need they have to stand again in social and public and ideal relations beyond neighborhood,—higher than the town-meeting—to their fellow men.

Shall I write a sincerity or two?—I, who never write anything else, except dullness? I think no persons whom I know could afford to live together on their merits. Some of us, or of them, could much better than others live together, but not by their power to command respect, but because of their easy, genial ways: that is, could live together by aid of their weakness and inferiority.

The world is a Dancer; it is a Rosary; it is a Torrent; it is a Boat; a Mist; a Spider's Snare; it is what you will; and the metaphor will hold, and it will give the imagination keen pleasure. Swifter than light the world converts itself into that thing you name, and all things find their right place under this new and capricious classification. Must I call the heaven and the earth a maypole and country fair with booths, or an anthill, or an old coat, in order to give you the shock of pleasure which the imagination loves and the sense of spiritual greatness? Call it a blossom, a rod, a wreath of parsley, a tamarisk-crown, a cock, a sparrow, the ear instantly hears and the spirit leaps to the trope.

The doctrine of Necessity or Destiny is the doctrine of Toleration, but every moment, whilst we think of this offending person that he is ridden by a devil and go to pity him, comes in our sensibility to persuade us that the person is the devil, then the poison works, the devil jumps on our neck, and back again wilder on the other: jumps from neck to neck, and the kingdom of hell comes in.

I will add to the portrait of Osman that he was never interrupted by success: he had never to look after his fame and his compliments, his claps and editions.

When I was praised I lost my time, for instantly I turned round to look at the work I had thought slightly of, and that day I made nothing new.

I do not wish to appear at one time great, at another small, but to be of a stellar and undiminishable light.

Genius unsettles everything. Make a new rule, and tomorrow Genius shall stamp on it with his starry sandal.

The turnip grows in the same soil with the strawberry; knows all the nourishment that it gets, and feeds on the very same itself, yet is a turnip still.

I remember, when a child, in the pew on Sundays amusing myself with saying over common words as "black," "white," "board," etc., twenty or thirty times, until the word lost all meaning and fixedness, and I began to doubt which was the right name for the thing, when I saw that neither had any natural relation, but all were arbitrary. It was a child's first lesson in Idealism.

How noble in secret are the men who have never stooped nor betrayed their faith! The two or three rusty, perchance wearisome, souls, who could never bring themselves to the smallest composition with society, rise with grandeur in the background like statues of the gods, whilst we listen in the dusty crowd to the adroit flattery and literary politics of those who stoop a little.

In regard to H——I suppose we all feel alike that we care very little what he says, provided only that he says it well. What he establishes with so much ingenuity to-day, we know he will demolish with equal ingenuity to-morrow, not valuing any position or any principle, but only the tactics or method of the fight. Intellectual play is his delight, the question is indifferent. He is a warrior, and so only there be war, he is not scrupulous on which side his aid is wanted.

Long ago I said, I have every inch of my merits allowed me, and was sad because my success was more than I deserved,—sad for others who had less. Now the beam trembles, and I see with some bitterness the slender claims I can make on fortune and the inevitable parsimony with which they will be answered.

There are some public persons born not for privacy, but for publicity, who are dull and even silly in a *tête-à-tête*, but the moment they are called to preside, the form dilates, the senatorial teeth appear, the eye brightens, a certain majesty sits on the shoulders, and they have a wit and happy deliverance you should never have found in them in the closet.

When we quarrel, O then we wish we had always kept our appetites in rein, that we might speak so coolly and majestically from unquestionable heights of character.

I had occasion, in 1835, to inquire for the facts that befel on the Nineteenth April, 1775. Doctor Ripley carried me to Abel Davis and Jonas Buttrick and Master Blood. The Doctor carried in his mind what he wished them to testify, and extorted, where he could, their assent to his forewritten History. I, who had no theory, was anxious to get at their recollections, but could learn little. Blood's impression plainly was that there was no great courage exhibited, except by a few.

At Cambridge, the last Wednesday, I met twenty members of my college class and spent the day with them. It was strange how fast the company returned to their old relation, and the whole mass of college nonsense came back in a flood. They all associated perfectly, were an unit for the day—men who now never meet. Each resumed his old place. The change in them was really very little in twenty years, although every man present was married, and all but one fathers. I too resumed my old place and found myself as of old a spectator rather than a fellow. I drank a great deal of wine (for me) with the wish to raise my spirits to the pitch of good fellowship, but wine produced on me its old effect, and I grew graver with every glass. Indignation and eloquence will excite me, but wine does not.

Almost all these were prosperous men, but there was something sad and affecting in their prosperity. Very easy

it was to see that each owed his success to some one trait
or talent not supported by his other properties.

There is this pleasure in a class meeting. Each has been
thoroughly measured and known to the other as a boy,
and they are not to be imposed upon by later circumstances and acquisitions. One is a governor of a state, one
is a president of a college, one is president of a senate, two
or three are bank presidents. They have removed from
New Hampshire or from Massachusetts or from Vermont
into the state where they live. Well, all these are imposing
facts in the new neighborhood, in the imaginations of the
young men among whom they come; but not for us. When
they come into the presence of either of their old mates,
off goes every disguise, and the boy meets the boy as of
old.

I see the law of Nature equally exemplified in bar-room
and in a saloon of philosophers. I get instruction and the
opportunities of my genius indifferently in all places, companies and pursuits, so only that there be antagonism. Yet
there would be the greatest practical inconvenience, if,
because the same law appears indifferently in all, we
should bring the philosophers of the bar-room and of the
saloon together. Like to like.

A poet is very rare. I spoke the other day to Ellery's*
ambition and said, Think that in so many millions, perhaps
there is not another one whose thought can flow into
music. Will you not do what you are created to do? But
Ellery, though he has fine glances and a poetry that is
like an exquisite nerve communicating by thrills, yet is a
very imperfect artist, and, as it now seems, will never

* Ellery Channing, Emerson's friend and neighbor.

finish anything. He does not even like to distinguish between what is good and what is not, in his verses, would fain have it all pass for good,—for the best,—and claim inspiration for the worst lines. But he is very good company, with his taste, and his cool, hard, sensible behavior, yet with the capacity of melting to emotion, or of awakening to the most genial mirth. It is no affectation in him to talk of politics, of knives and forks, or of sanded floors, if you will; indeed, the conversation always begins low down, and, at the least faltering or excess on the high keys, instantly returns to the weather, the Concord Reading Room, and Mr. Rice's shop. Now and then something appears that gives you to pause and think. But his feeling, as his poetry, only runs in veins, and he is, much of the time, a very common and unedifying sort of person.

Osman said that when he went a-berrying the devil got into the blueberries and tempted him to eat a bellyful, but if he came to a spring of water he would wash his hands and mouth and promise himself that he would eat no more. Instantly the devil would come to him again in the shape of larger and fairer berries than any he had yet found, and if he still passed them by, he would bring him blackberries, and if that would not serve, then grapes. He said, of one thing he was persuaded, that wisdom and berries grew on the same bushes, but that only one could ever be plucked at one time.

I sympathize with all the sad angels who on this planet of ours are shirking work and crying, O for something worthy to do. It does not seem worth our while to toil for anything so pitiful as skill to do one of the little feats we magnify so much, when presently the dream will scatter and we shall burst into universal power. The reason of all idleness and of all crime is the same. Whilst we are waiting, we beguile the time, one with jokes, one with sleep, one with eating, one with crimes.

Dr. Ripley died this morning. The fall of this oak of ninety years makes some sensation in the forest, old and doomed as it was. He has identified himself with the forms at least of the old church of the New England Puritans, his nature was eminently loyal, not in the least adventurous or democratical; and his whole being leaned backward on the departed, so that he seemed one of the rear-guard of this great camp and army which have filled the world with fame, and with him passes out of sight almost the last banner and guidon flag of a mighty epoch. For these Puritans, however in our last days they have declined into ritualists, solemnized the heyday of their strength by the planting and the liberating of America.

Great, grim, earnest men, I belong by natural affinity to other thoughts and schools than yours, but my affection hovers respectfully about your retiring footprints, your unpainted churches, strict platforms, and sad offices; the iron-gray deacon and the wearisome prayer rich with the diction of ages.

I stood one day in the Court House talking with Luther Lawrence when the sheriff introduced through the crowd a number of women who were witnesses in the trial that was pending. As they filed rapidly through the crowd, Mr. Lawrence said, "There go the light troops!" Neither Plato, Mahomet, nor Goethe have said a severer thing on our fair Eve. Yet the old lawyer did not mean to be satanic. The ridicule lies in the misplacement of our good Angel, in the violence of direction with which this string of maids and matrons are coming with hot heads to testify what gossip they know about Mr. Gulliver or Mrs. Veal, —being quite dislodged from that shrine of sanctity, sentiment, and solitude in which they make courts and forums appear absurd.

The Whig party in the Universe concedes that the Radical enunciates the primal law, but makes no allowance for friction, and this omission makes their whole doctrine impertinent. The Whig assumes sickness, and his social frame is a hospital, his total legislation is for the present distress, —a universe in slippers and flannels, with bib and pap-spoon, swallowing pills and herb-tea.

The merchant will not allow a book in the counting-house, suspects every taste and tendency but that for goods, has no conversation, no thought but cotton, qualities of cotton, and its advance or fall a penny or a farthing. What a cramping of the form in wooden cap, wooden belt, and wooden shoes, is this, and how should not the negro be more a man than one of these victims?—the negro, who, if low and imperfect in organization, is yet no wooden sink, but a wild cedar swamp, rich with all vegetation of grass and moss and confervæ and ferns and flags, with rains and sunshine; mists and moonlight, birds and insects filling its wilderness with life and promise.

G. W. *Tyler* came here with all his rattle. The attributes of God, he said were two, power and risibility. It was the duty of every pious man, he said, to keep up the hoax the best he could, and so to patronize Whiggism, Piety, and Providence, and wherever he saw anything that would help keep the people in order, schools or churches, or poetry, or what-not, he must cry Hist-a-boy! and urge the game on. He sleeps four hours, from three to seven. He outwitted

Mr. Greenleaf in the courts. He practised medicine somewhere in the barracks, and, at St. Johns, having in a freak called himself a Free-will Baptist, he was immediately carried off to preach at a meeting, which he did for fifty-five minutes, and left the audience in tears, and got up a revival. A pound and a half of coffee to a pint of water, he drinks every night, of the thickness of molasses, and when he had headache, he piled a peck of ice on his head, by means of an iron hoop.

This hold we have on the selfish man, that he always values consequences, reputation, or afterclap of some sort; but the benevolent man never looks so far. Let the self-seeker be never so sharp, this unlucky trick of Nature is sharper than he, and has him on the hip.

The philosopher sat with his face to the East until cobwebs were spun over the brim of his pot of porridge. Intemperance is the only vulgarity.

I can forgive anything to a deep nature, for they outlive all their foibles and pedantries, and are just as good ten years hence and much better. Strange it is so hard to find good ones: the profound nature will have a savage rudeness, the delicate one will be shallow or have a great crack running through it, and so every piece has a flaw.

We cannot rectify marriage, because it would introduce such carnage into our social relations. Woman hides her form from the eyes of men in our world: they cannot, she rightly thinks, be trusted. In a right state the love of one, which each man carries in his heart, should protect all women from his eyes as by an impenetrable veil of indifference. The love of one should make him indifferent to all others, or rather their protector and saintly friend, as if for her sake. But now there is in the eyes of all men a certain evil light, a vague desire which attaches them to the forms of many women, whilst their affections fasten on some one. Their natural eye is not fixed into coincidence with their spiritual eye.

Why do I write another line since my best friends assure me that in every line I repeat myself? Yet the God must be obeyed even to ridicule. The criticism of the public is, as I have often noted, much in advance of its invention. The ear is not to be cheated. A continuous effect cannot be produced by discontinuous thought, and when the eye cannot detect the juncture of the skillful mosaic, the spirit is apprised of disunion simply by the failure to affect the spirit. This other thing I will also concede,—that the man Fingal* is rather too swiftly plastic, or, shall I say, works more in the spirit of a cabinetmaker, than of an architect. The thought which strikes him as great and Dantesque, and opens an abyss, he instantly presents to another transformed into a chamber or a neat parlor, and degrades ideas.

I told Henry Thoreau that his freedom is in the form, but he does not disclose new matter. I am very familiar with all his thoughts,—they are my own quite originally drest. But if the question be, what new ideas has he thrown into circulation, he has not yet told what that is which he was created to say. I said to him what I often feel, I only knew three persons who seem to me fully to see this law of reciprocity or compensation,—himself, Alcott, and myself: and 't is odd that we should all be neighbors, for in the

---

* Emerson is probably referring to himself.

wide land or the wide earth I do not know another who seems to have it as deeply and originally as these three Gothamites.

Of poetry I would say, that when I go out into the fields in a still sultry day, in a still sultry humor, I do perceive that the finest rhythms and cadences of poetry are yet unfound, and that in that purer state which glimmers before us, rhythms of a faery and dream-like music shall enchant us, compared with which the finest measures of English poetry are psalm-tunes. I think now that the very finest and sweetest closes and falls are not in our metres, but in the measures of eloquence, which have greater variety and richness than verse. Now, alas, we know something too much about our poetry,—we are not part and parcel of it: it does not descend like a foreign conqueror from an unexpected quarter of the horizon upon us, carry us away with our flocks and herds into a strange and appalling captivity, to make us, at a later period, adopted children of the Great King, and, in the end, to disclose to us that he was our real parent, and this realm and palace is really our native country. Yet I please myself with thinking that there may yet be somewhere such elation of heart, such continuity of thought, that a man shall see the little sun and moon whisk about, making day and night, making month and month, without heed, in the grandeur of his absorption. Now we know not only when it is day, and when night, but we hear the dinner-bell ring with the most laudable punctuality. I am not such a fool but that I taste the joy which comes from a new and prodigious person, from Dante, from Rabelais, from Piranesi, flinging wide to me the doors of new modes of existence, and even if I should intimate by a premature nod my too economical perception of the old thrum, that the basis of this joy is at last the instinct that I am only let into my own estate, that the poet and his book and his story are only fictions and semblances in which my thought is pleased to dress itself, I do not the least yield myself to the keen delight of difference and newness.

Margaret Fuller talked of ballads, and our love for them: strange that we should so value the wild man, the Ishmael-ite, and his slogan, claymore, and tomahawk rhymes, and yet every step we take, everything we do, is to tame him. Margaret does not think, she says, in the woods, only "finds herself expressed."

Of the best jokes of these days is that told of poor Bokum, that when he went to hire a horse and chaise at a stable in Cambridge, and the man inquired whether he should put in a buffalo?* "My God! no," cried the astonished German, "put in a horse!"

When I was in college John L. Gardiner said one day that "he had serious thoughts of becoming religious next week, but perhaps he should join the Porcellians." It is no joke: I have often thought the same thing.

If life is sad and do not content us, if the heavens are brass, and rain no sweet thoughts on us, and especially we have nothing to say to shipwrecked and self-tormenting and young-old people, let us hold our tongues. Patience and truth, patience with our own frosts and negations, and few words must serve. . . .

The view taken of Transcendentalism in State Street is that it threatens to invalidate contracts.

* Meaning, of course, a buffalo robe.

Hippomachus knew a good wrestler by his gait in the street, and an old stager like myself will recognize the subtle Harlequin in his most uncouth frocks, in an Olmsted stove, in a horned ox, in a parliamentary speech, or a bushel of cranberries.

Hurrah for the camera obscura! the less we are, the better we look.

Books,—yes, if worst comes to worst: but not yet. A cup of tea, or a cup of wrath, or a good book will kindle the tinderbox. The poultry must have gravel or egg shells, the swallow and bluebird must have a thread or a wisp of straw for his nest. Have you got the whole beaver, before you have seen his amphibious house? The man is only half himself. Let me see the other half, namely, his expression. Strange, strange, we value this half the most. We worship expressors; we forgive every crime to them. Full expression is very rare. Music, sculpture, painting, poetry, speech, action, war, trade, manufacture is expression. A portrait is this translation of the thing into a new language. What passion all men have to see it done for themselves or others. Now see how small is the list of memorable expressions by book, picture, house, or institution, after so many millions have panted under the Idea!

Elizabeth Hoar consecrates. I have no friend whom I more wish to be immortal than she, an influence I cannot spare, but must always have at hand for recourse. When Margaret mentioned "an expression of unbroken purity," I said, "That is hers." M. replied, "Yes, but she knows." I answer, —Know or know not, the impression she makes is that her part is taken, she has joined herself irrevocably to the sanctities,—to the Muses, and the Gods. Others suggest often that they still balance; their genius draws them to happiness; they contemplate experiment; they have not abdicated the power of election. Opium and honey, the dagger and madness, they like should still lie there in the background, as shadows and possibilities. But Elizabeth's mind is made up, and she has soared into another firmament, and these exist not for her. Bonaparte did not like ideologists: Elizabeth is no poet, but her holiness is substantive and must be felt, like the heat of a stove or the gravity of a stone: and Bonaparte would respect her.

People say law but they mean wealth.

I would have my book read as I have read my favorite books, not with explosion and astonishment, a marvel and a rocket, but a friendly and agreeable influence stealing like the scent of a flower, or the sight of a new landscape on a traveller. I neither wish to be hated and defied by such as I startle, nor to be kissed and hugged by the young whose thoughts I stimulate.

I would that I could, I know afar off that I cannot, give the lights and shades, the hopes and outlooks that come to me in these strange, cold-warm, attractive-repelling conversations with Margaret, whom I always admire, most revere when I nearest see, and sometimes love,—yet whom I freeze, and who freezes me to silence, when we seem to promise to come nearest.

I saw in Boston Fanny Elssler in the ballet of Nathalie. She must show, I suppose, the whole compass of her instrument, and add to her softest graces of motion or "the wisdom of her feet," the feats of the rope-dancer and tumbler: and perhaps on the whole the beauty of the exhibition is enhanced by this that is strong and strange, as when she stands erect on the extremity of her toes or on one toe, or "performs the impossible" in attitude. But the chief beauty is in the extreme grace of her movements, the variety and nature of her attitude, the winning fun and spirit of all her little coquetries, the beautiful erectness of her body, and the freedom and determination which she can so easily assume, and, what struck me much, the air of perfect sympathy with the house, and the mixture of deference and conscious superiority which puts her in perfect spirits and equality to her part.

As for the morals, as it is called, of this exhibition, that lies wholly with the spectator. I should not think of danger to young women stepping with their father or brother out of happy and guarded parlors into this theatre to return in a few hours to the same; but I can easily suppose that it is not the safest resort for college boys who have left metaphysics, conic sections, or Tacitus to see those tripping satin slippers, and they may not forget this graceful, silvery swimmer when they have retreated again to their baccalaureate cells.

Part of the reason why Elssler is so bewitching to the gay people is, that they are pinched and restrained by the decorums of city life, and she shows them freedom.

I saw Webster on the street,—but he was changed since I saw him last,—black as a thunder-cloud, and careworn; the anxiety that withers this generation among the young and thinking class had crept up also into the great lawyer's chair, and too plainly, too plainly he was one of us. I did not wonder that he depressed his eyes when he saw me, and would not meet my face. The cankerworms have crawled to the topmost bough of the wild elm and swing down from that. No wonder the elm is a little uneasy.

Yet is it not ridiculous, this that we do in this languid idle trick that we have gradually fallen into of writing and writing without end? After a day of humiliation and stripes, if I can write it down, I am straightway relieved and can sleep well. After a day of joy, the beating heart is calmed again by the diary. If grace is given me by all angels and I pray, if then I can catch one ejaculation of humility or hope and set it down in syllables, devotion is at an end.

Fashion is a large region and reaches from the precincts of Heaven to the purlieus of Hell. Mr. Philip Sidney is the presiding deity.

Margaret [Fuller] is "a being of unsettled rank in the universe." So proud and presumptuous, yet so meek; so worldly and artificial and with keenest sense and taste for all pleasures of luxurious society, yet living more than any other for long periods in a trance of religious sentiment; a person who, according to her own account of herself, expects everything for herself from the Universe.

A good indignation brings out all one's powers.

Everybody, old men, young women, boys, play the doctor with me and prescribe for me. They always did so.

It seems to every meeting of readers and writers as if it were intolerable that Broad Street Paddies and bar-room politicians, the sots and loafers and all manner of ragged and unclean and foul-mouthed persons without a dollar in their pocket should control the property of the country and make the lawgiver and the law. But is that any more than their share whilst you hold property selfishly? They are opposed to you: yes, but first you are opposed to them: they, to be sure, malevolently, menacingly, with songs and rowdies and mobs; you cunningly, plausibly, and well-bred; you cheat and they strike; you sleep and eat at their expense; they vote and threaten and sometimes throw stones, at yours.

Were you ever daguerrotyped, O immortal man? And did you look with all vigor at the lens of the camera, or rather, by the direction of the operator, at the brass peg a little below it, to give the picture the full benefit of your expanded and flashing eye? and in your zeal not to blur the image, did you keep every finger in its place with such energy that your hands became clenched as for fight or despair, and in your resolution to keep your face still, did you feel every muscle becoming every moment more rigid; the brows contracted into a Tartarean frown, and the eyes fixed as they are fixed in a fit, in madness, or in death? And when, at last you are relieved of your dismal duties, did you find the curtain drawn perfectly, and the coat perfectly, and the hands true, clenched for combat, and the shape of the face and head?—but, unhappily, the total expression escaped from the face and the portrait of a mask instead of a man? Could you not by grasping it very tight hold the stream of a river, or of a small brook, and prevent it from flowing?

I told Garrison that I thought he must be a very young man, or his time hang very heavy on his hands, who can afford to think much and talk much about the foibles of his neighbors, or "*denounce*," and play "the son of thunder" as he called it. I am one who believe all times to be pretty much alike, and yet I sympathize so keenly with this. We want to be expressed, yet you take from us war, that great opportunity which allowed the accumulations of electricity to stream off from both poles, the positive and the negative, —well, now you take from us our cup of alcohol, as before you took our cup of wrath. We had become canting moths of peace, our helm was a skillet, and now we must become temperance water-sops. You take away, but what do you give? Mr. Jefts has been preached into tipping up his barrel of rum into the brook, but day after to-morrow when he wakes up cold and poor, will he feel that he has somewhat for somewhat! No, this is mere thieving. . . . If I could lift him by happy violence into a religious beatitude, or into a Socratic trance and imparadise him in ideas, or into the pursuit of human beauty, a divine lover, then should I have greatly more than indemnified him for what I have taken. I should not take; he would put away, or rather ascend out of this litter and sty, in which he had rolled, to go up clothed and in his right mind into the assembly and conversation of men. I fight in my fashion, but you, O Paddies and roarers, must not fight in yours. I drink my tea and coffee, but as for you and your cups, here is the pledge and the Temperance Society. I walk on Sundays, and read Aristophanes and Rabelais in church hours: but for you, Go to church. Good vent or bad we must have for our nature. . . . Make love a crime, and we shall have lust. If you cannot contrive to raise us up to the love of science and make brute matter our antagonist which we shall have joy in handling, mastering, penetrating, condensing to adamant, dissolving to light, then we must brawl, carouse, gamble, or go to bull-fights. If we can get no full demonstration of our heart and mind, we feel wronged and incarcerated: the philosophers and divines we shall hate most, as the upper turn-keys. We wish to take the gas which allows us to break through your wearisome proprieties, to plant the foot, to set the teeth, to fling abroad the arms, and dance and sing.

"What are you doing, Zeke?" said Judge Webster to his eldest boy.

"Nothing."

"What are you doing, Daniel?"

"Helping Zeke."

A tolerably correct account of most of our activity to-day.

It seems to me sometimes that we get our education ended a little too quick in this country. As soon as we have learned to read and write and cipher, we are dismissed from school and we set up for ourselves. We are writers and leaders of opinion and we write away without check of any kind, play whatsoever mad prank, indulge whatever spleen, or oddity, or obstinacy, comes into our dear head, and even feed our complacency thereon, and thus fine wits come to nothing, as good horses spoil themselves by running away and straining themselves. Now, if a man can write a paragraph for a newspaper, next year he writes what he calls a history, and reckons himself a classic incontinently, nor will his contemporaries in critical Journal or Review question his claims.

As Charles said, we have one set. It takes time to learn their names and allow for their humors so as to draw the most advantage from them. We all know the same stories, have read the same books, know the same politics, churches, geniuses, felons, bores, hoaxes, gossip, so that there is nothing to explain, but we can fall into conversation very quickly and get and give such information by the road as we want without needing to collect lexicons and dragomans when we wish to ask the way to the next village.

We are very near to greatness: one step and we are safe:
can we not take the leap?

'T is certain that the Daguerreotype is the true Republican
style of painting. The artist stands aside and lets you paint
yourself. If you make an ill head, not he but yourself are
responsible, and so people who go Daguerreotyping have a
pretty solemn time. They come home confessing and la-
menting their sins. A Daguerreotype Institute is as good as
a national Fast.

There are three wants which can never be satisfied: that of
the traveller, who says, "*Anywhere but here*"; that of the
rich who wants *something more;* and that of the sick who
wants *something different.*

October 30

On this wonderful day when Heaven and Earth seem to
glow with magnificence, and all the wealth of all the elements is put under contribution to make the world fine, as
if Nature would indulge her offspring, it seemed ungrateful to hide in the house. Are there not dull days enough in
the year for you to write and read in, that you should waste
this glittering season when Florida and Cuba seem to have
left their seats and come to visit us, with all their shining
Hours, and almost we expect to see the jasmine and the
cactus burst from the ground instead of these last gentians
and asters which have loitered to attend this latter glory of
the year? All insects are out, all birds come forth,—the very
cattle that lie on the ground seem to have great thoughts,
and Egypt and India look from their eyes.

Alas, that this awe which the writers inspire should prove
at last to be so ill-founded! They ought to inspire most

reverence when seen, and when they can thunder so loud at a distance not cheep so small in the chamber.

Skepticism esteems ignorance organic and irremovable, believes in the existence of pure malignity, believes in a poor decayed God who does what he can to keep down the nuisances, and to keep the world going for our day. It believes the actual to be necessary; it argues habitually from the exception instead of the rule; and, if it went to the legitimate extreme, the earth would smell with suicide.

To believe in luck, if it were not a solecism so to use the word *believe*, is skepticism.

Our contemporaries do not always contemporize us, but now one is continually surprised to find some stranger, who has been educated in the most different manner, dreaming the same dream.

We like all the better to see some graceful youth, free and beautiful as a palm or a pine tree, who hears with curiosity and intelligence our theory of the world and has his own, and does not hiss with our hiss, but only has the same mother-tongue.

Great causes are never tried, assaulted, or defended on their merits: they need so long perspective, and the habits of the race are marked with so strong a tendency to particulars. The stake is Europe or Asia, and the battle is for some contemptible village or dog-hutch. A man shares the new light that irradiates the world and promises the establishment of the Kingdom of Heaven,—and ends with champing unleavened bread or devoting himself to the nourishment of a beard, or making a fool of himself about his hat or his shoes. A man is furnished with this superb case of instruments, the senses, and perceptive and executive faculties, and they betray him every day. He transfers his allegiance from Instinct and God to this adroit little committee. A man is an exaggerator. In every conversation see how the main end is still lost sight of by all but the best, and with slight apology or none, a digression made to a creaking door or a buzzing fly. What heavenly eloquence could hold the ear of an audience if a child cried! A man with a truth to express is caught by the beauty of his own words and ends with being a rhymester or critic. And Genius is sacrificed to talent every day.

The great majority of men grow up and grow old in seeming and following; and when they die they occupy themselves to the last with what others will think, and whether Mr. A and Mr. B will go to their funeral.

In every moment and action and passion, you must be a man, must be a whole Olympus of gods. I surprised you, O Waldo Emerson, yesterday eve hurrying up one page and down another of a little book of some Menzel, panting and straining after the sense of some mob, better or worse, of German authors. I thought you had known better. Adhere, sit fast, lie low.

All writing is by the grace of God. People do not deserve to have good writing, they are so pleased with bad. In these sentences that you show me. I can find no beauty, for I see death in every clause. Give me initiative, spermatic, prophesying, man-making words.

It is never worth while to worry people with your contritions. We shed our follies and absurdities as fast as the rosebugs drop off in July and leave the apple tree which they so threatened. Nothing dies so fast as a fault and the memory of a fault. I am awkward, sour, saturnine, lumpish, pedantic, and thoroughly disagreeable and oppressive to the people around me. Yet if I am born to write a few good sentences or verses, these shall endure, and my disgraces utterly perish out of memory.

Woman is the requiring genius.

We cannot forgive another for not being ourselves.

The Universe does not jest with us, but is in earnest.

If I should go out of church whenever I hear a false sentiment, I could never stay there five minutes.

When, in our discontent with the pedantry of scholars, we prefer farmers, and when, suspecting their conservatism, we hearken after the hard words of drovers and Irishmen, this is only subjective or relative criticism, this is alkali to our acid, or shade to our too much sunshine; but abide with these, and you will presently find they are the same men you left. A coat has cheated you.

PART IV

1842-1844

Early in 1842 Emerson's beloved son died of scarlet fever at the age of five. Lectures in New York and the task of editing *The Dial*, which he took over from Margaret Fuller, were fortunate distractions. In the spring, his friend, Bronson Alcott, visited England, returning with H. G. Wright and Charles Lane, two idealistic Englishmen who battered Emerson with their high-flown theories.

In 1843 Emerson lectured in New York, Philadelphia, Baltimore, and Washington. There are many references to Daniel Webster, an idol soon to be overthrown. This was the year of the disastrous experiment of Fruitlands, a New Eden founded by Alcott and his English friends at Harvard, Mass., as a practical demonstration of their theories, including a belief that the enslavement, robbery, and murder of animals was abhorrent, or even the use of animal manure for enrichment of the soil.

The Dial, which Emerson had been painfully editing with the help of Henry Thoreau, expired in 1844; a son, Edward Waldo, was born; and the Second Series of *Essays* was published.

1842

January 28

Yesterday night, at fifteen minutes after eight, my little Waldo ended his life.

January 30

What he looked upon is better; what he looked not upon is insignificant. The morning of Friday, I woke at three o'clock, and every cock in every barnyard was shrilling with the most unnecessary noise. The sun went up the morning sky with all his light, but the landscape was dishonored by this loss. For this boy, in whose remembrance I have both slept and waked so oft, decorated for me the morning star, the evening cloud, how much more all the particulars of daily economy; for he had touched with his lively curiosity every trivial fact and circumstance in the household.

A boy of early wisdom, of a grave and even majestic deportment, of a perfect gentleness.

Every tramper that ever tramped is abroad, but the little feet are still.

He gave up his little innocent breath like a bird.

Sorrow makes us all children again,—destroys all differences of intellect. The wisest knows nothing.

I feel in reference to all great masters, that they are chiefly distinguished by the power of adding a second, a third, and perhaps a fourth step in a continuous line. Many a man had taken their first step. With every additional step you enhance immensely the value of your first. It is like the price which is sometimes set on a horse by jockeys; a price is agreed upon in the stall, and then he is turned into a pasture and allowed to roll, and for every time he shall roll himself over, ten dollars are added to the price.

Bores are good, too. They may help you to a good indignation, if not to a sympathy. Long Beard and Short Beard, who came hither the other day with intent as it seemed to make Artesian Wells of us, taught me something.

Home from New York, where I read six lectures on the Times, viz., Introductory; The Poet; The Conservative; The Transcendentalist; Manners; Prospects. They were read in the "Society Library," were attended by three or four hundred persons, and after all expenses were paid yielded me about two hundred dollars.

My lectures had about the same reception there as elsewhere: very fine and poetical, but a little puzzling. One thought it "as good as a kaleidoscope." Another, a good Staten Islander, would go hear, "for he had heard I was a rattler."

The *Dial* is to be sustained or ended, and I must settle the question, it seems, of its life or death. I wish it to live, but do not wish to be of the Humanity and Reform Men, because they trample on letters and poetry; nor in the hands of the Scholars, for they are dead and dry.

In New York lately, as in cities generally, one seems to lose all substance, and become surface in a world of surfaces. Everything is external, and I remember my hat and coat, and all my other surfaces, and nothing else. If suddenly a reasonable question is addressed to me, what refreshment and relief! I visited twice and parted with a most polite lady without giving her reason to believe that she had met any other in me than a worshipper of surfaces, like all Broadway. It stings me yet.

Hell is better than Heaven, if the man in Hell knows his place, and the man in Heaven does not.

Here prepares now the good Alcott to go to England, after so long and strict acquaintance as I have had with him for seven years. I saw him for the first time in Boston in 1835.

What shall we say of him to the wise Englishman?

He is a man of ideas, a man of faith. Expect contempt for all usages which are simply such. His social nature and his taste for beauty and magnificence will betray him into tolerance and indulgence, even, to men and to magnificence, but a statute or a practice he is condemned to measure by its essential wisdom or folly.

He delights in speculation, in nothing so much, and is very well endowed and weaponed for that work with a copious, accurate and elegant vocabulary; I may say poetic; so that I know of no man who speaks such good English as he, and is so inventive withal. Yet he knows only this one language. He hardly needs an antagonist,—he needs only an intelligent ear. Where he is greeted by loving and intelligent persons, his discourse soars to a wonderful height, so regular, so lucid, so playful, so new and distainful of all boundaries of tradition and experience, that the hearers seem no longer to have bodies or material gravity, but almost they can mount into the air at pleasure, or leap at one bound out of this poor solar system. I say this of his speech exclusively, for when he attempts to write, he loses, in my judgment, all his power, and I derive more pain than pleasure from the perusal. The *Post* expresses the feeling of most readers in its rude joke, when it said of his *Orphic Sayings* that they "resembled a train of fifteen railroad cars with one passenger." He has moreover the greatest possession both of mind and of temper in his discourse, so that the mastery and moderation and foresight, and yet felicity, with which he unfolds his thought, are not to be surpassed. This is of importance to such a broacher of novelties as he is, and to one baited, as he is very apt to be, by the sticklers for old books or old institutions. He takes such delight in the exercise of this faculty that he will willingly talk the whole of a day, and most part of the night, and then again tomorrow, for days successively, and if I, who am impatient of much speaking, draw him out to walk in the woods or fields, he will stop at the first fence and very soon propose either to sit down or to return. He seems to think society exists for this function, and that all literature is good or bad as it approaches colloquy, which is its perfection. Poems and histories may be good, but only as adumbrations of this; and the only true manner of writing the literature of a nation would be to convene the best heads in the community, set them talking, and then introduce stenographers to record what they say. He so swiftly and naturally plants himself on the moral sentiment in any conversation that no man will ever get any advantage of him, unless he be a saint, as Jones Very was. Every one else Alcott will put in the wrong.

It must be conceded that it is speculation which he loves, and not action. Therefore he dissatisfies everybody and disgusts many. When the conversation is ended all is over. He lives to-morrow, as he lived to-day, for further discourse, not to begin, as he seemed pledged to do, a new celestial life. The ladies fancied that he loved cake; very likely; most people do. Yet in the last two years he has changed his way of living, which was perhaps a little too easy and self-indulgent for such a Zeno, so far as to become ascetically temperate. He has no vocation to labor, and, although he strenuously preached it for a time, and made some efforts to practice it, he soon found he had no genius for it, and that it was a cruel waste of his time. It depressed his spirits even to tears.

He is very noble in his carriage to all men, of a serene and lofty aspect and deportment in the street and in the house. Of simple but graceful and majestic manners, having a great sense of his own worth, so that not willingly will he give his hand to a merchant though he be never so rich,—yet with a strong love of men, and an insatiable curiosity concerning all who were distinguished either by their intellect or by their character. He is the most generous and hospitable of men, so that he has been as munificent in his long poverty as Mr. Perkins in his wealth, or I should say much more munificent. And for his hospitality, every thing in the form of man that entered his door as a suppliant would be made master of all the house contained. Moreover, every man who converses with him is presently made sensible that, although this person has no faculty or patience for our trivial hodiernal labors, yet if there were a great courage, a great sacrifice, a self-immolation to be made, this and no other is the man for a crisis,—and with such grandeur, yet with such temperance in his mien.

Such a man, with no talent for household uses, none for action, and whose taste is for precisely that which is most rare and unattainable, could not be popular,—he could never be a doll, nor a beau, nor a bestower of money or presents, nor even a model of good daily life to propose to virtuous young persons. His greatness consists in his attitude merely; of course he found very few to relish or appreciate him; and very many to dispraise him. Somebody called him a "moral Sam Patch." *

Another circumstance marks this extreme love of speculation. He carries all his opinions and all his condition and manner of life in his hand, and, whilst you talk with him, it is plain he has put out no roots, but is an air-plant which can readily and without any ill consequences be transported to any place. He is quite ready at any moment to abandon his present residence and employment, his country, nay, his wife and children, on very short notice, to put any new dream into practice which has bubbled up in the effervescence of discourse. If it is so with his way of living, much more so is it with his opinions. He never remembers. He never affirms anything today because he has affirmed it before. You are rather astonished, by having left him in the morning with one set of opinions, to find him in the eve-

* Patch was a daredevil acrobat of the period.

ning totally escaped from all recollection of them, as confident of a new line of conduct and heedless of his old advocacy.

Another effect of this speculation is that he is preternaturally acute and ingenious to the extent sometimes of a little jesuitry in his action. He condemns the facts so far that his poetic representations have the effect of a falsehood, and those who are deceived by them ascribe the falsehood to him: and sometimes he plays with actions unimportant to him in a manner not justifyable to any observers but those who are competent to do justice to his real magnanimity and conscience.

Like all virtuous persons he is destitute of the appearance of virtue, and so shocks all persons of decorum by the imprudence of his behavior and the enormity of his expressions. . . .

This man entertained in his spirit all vast and magnificent problems. None came to him so much recommended as the most universal. He delighted in the fable of Prometheus; in all the dim, gigantic pictures of the most ancient mythology; in the Indian and Egyptian traditions; in the history of magic, of palmistry, of temperaments, of astrology, of whatever showed any impatience of custom and limits, any impulse to dare the solution of the total problem of man's nature, finding in every such experiment an implied pledge and prophecy of worlds of science and power yet unknown to us. He seems often to realize the pictures of the old alchemists: for he stood brooding on the edge of discovery of the Absolute from month to month, ever and anon affirming that it was within his reach, and nowise discomfited by uniform shortcomings.

The other tendency of his mind was to realize a reform in the Life of Man. This was the steadily returning, the monotonous topic of years of conversation. This drew him to a constant intercourse with the projectors and saints of all shades, who preached or practiced any part or particle of reform, and to a continual coldness, quarrel, and non-intercourse with the scholars and men of refinement who are usually found in the ranks of conservatism. Very soon the Reformers whom he had joined would disappoint him; they were pitiful persons, and, in their coarseness and ignorance, he began to pine again for literary society. In these oscillations from the Scholars to the Reformers, and back again, he spent his days.

His vice, an intellectual vice, grew out of this constitution, and was that to which almost all spiritualists have been liable,—a certain brooding on the private thought which produces monotony in the conversation, and egotism in the character. Steadily subjective himself, the variety of facts which seem necessary to the health of most minds, yielded him no variety of meaning, and he quickly quitted the play on objects, to come to *the Subject,* which was always the same, viz., *Alcott in reference to the World of Today.*

From a stray leaf I copy this:—Alcott sees the law of man truer and farther than anyone ever did. Unhappily, his conversation never loses sight of his own personality. He never quotes; he never refers; his only illustration is his own biography. His topic yesterday is Alcott on the 17th October; to-day, Alcott on the 18th October; to-morrow, on the 19th. So will it be always. The poet, rapt into future times or into deeps of nature admired for themselves, lost in their law, cheers us with a lively charm; but this noble genius discredits genius to me. I do not want any more such persons to exist.

What for the visions of the night? Our life is so safe and regular that we hardly know the emotion of terror. Neither public nor private violence, neither natural catastrophes, as earthquake, volcano, or deluge; nor the expectation of supernatural agents in the form of ghosts, or of purgatory and devils and hell fire, disturb the sleepy circulations of our blood in these calm, well-spoken days. And yet dreams acquaint us with what the day omits. Eat a hearty supper, tuck up your bed tightly, put an additional bedspread over your three blankets, and lie on your back, and you may, in the course of an hour or two, have this neglected part of your education in some measure supplied. Let me consider: I found myself in a garret disturbed by the noise of some one sawing wood. On walking towards the sound, I saw lying in a crib an insane person whom I very well knew, and the noise instantly stopped: there was no saw, a mere stirring among several trumpery matters, fur muffs and empty baskets that lay on the floor. As I tried to approach, the muffs swelled themselves a little, as with wind, and whirled off into a corner of the garret, as if alive, and a kind of animation appeared in all the objects in that corner. Seeing this, and instantly aware that here was Witchcraft, that here was a devilish Will which signified itself plainly enough in the stir and the sound of the wind, I was unable to move; my limbs were frozen with fear; I was bold and would go forward, but my limbs I could not move; I mowed the defiance I could not articulate, and woke with the ugly sound I made. After I woke and recalled the impressions, my brain tingled with repeated vibrations of terror; and yet was the sensation pleasing, as it was a sort of rehearsal of a Tragedy.

Are you not scared by seeing that the Gypsies are more attractive to us than the Apostles? For though we love goodness and not stealing, yet also we love freedom and not preaching.

I like a meeting of gentlemen; for they also bring each one a certain cumulative result. From every company they have visited, from every business they have transacted, they have brought away something which they wear as a certain complexion or permanent coat, and their manners are a certificate, a trophy of their culture.

I ought to be obeyed. The reason I am not is because I am not real. Let me be a lover, and no man can resist me. I am not united, I am not friendly to myself, I bite and tear myself. I am ashamed of myself. When will the day dawn, of peace and reconcilement, when, self-united and friendly, I shall display one heart and energy to the world?

If I should write an honest diary, what should I say? Alas, that life has halfness, shallowness. I have almost completed thirty-nine years, and I have not yet adjusted my relations to my fellows on the planet, or to my own work. Always too young or too old, I do not justify myself; how can I satisfy others?

Dull, cheerless business this of playing lion and talking down to people.

We look wishfully to emergencies, to eventful revolutionary times from the desart of our ennui, and think how easy to have taken our part when the drum was rolling and the house was burning over our heads.

When I saw the sylvan youth, I said, "Very good promise, but I cannot now watch any more buds: like the good Grandfather when they brought him the twentieth babe, he declined the dandling, he had said 'Kitty, Kitty' long enough."

Here is a proposition for the formation of a good neighborhood: Hedge shall live at Concord, and Mr. Hawthorne; George Bradford shall come then; and Mrs. Ripley afterward. Who knows but Margaret Fuller and Charles Newcomb would presently be added? These, if added to our present kings and queens, would make a rare, an unrivalled company. If these all had their hearth and home here, we might have a solid social satisfaction, instead of the disgust and depression of visitation.

Our poetry reminds me of the catbird, who sings so affectedly and vaingloriously to me near Walden. Very sweet and musical! very various! fine execution! but so conscious, and *such a performer!* not a note is his own, except at last, *Miou, miou.*

A highly endowed man with good intellect and good conscience is a Man-woman and does not so much need the complement of woman to his being as another. Hence his relations to the sex are somewhat dislocated and unsatisfactory. He asks in woman sometimes the woman, sometimes the man.

In Boston I saw the new second volume of Tennyson's *Poems.* It had many merits, but the question might remain whether it has *the* merit. In reading aloud, you soon become sensible of a monotony of elegance. It wants a little northwest wind, or a northeast storm; it is a lady's bower —garden-spot; or a lord's conservatory, aviary, apiary, and musky greenhouse.

One seems in debate to play a foolish game for mastery, so inconvertible men are.

Of all the ministers to luxury these novelwrights are the best. It is a trick, a juggle. We are cheated into laughter or wonder by feats which only oddly combine acts that we do every day. There is no new element, no power, no furtherance. It is only confectionery, not the raising of new corn; and being such, there is no limit to its extension and multiplication. Mr. Babbage will presently invent a Novel-writing machine. The old machinery cannot be disguised, however gaily vamped. Money and killing and the Wandering Jew, these are the mainsprings still; new names, but no new qualities in the *dramatis personæ*. Italics and capitals are the stale substitutes for natural epigram and the revelations of loving speech. Therefore the vain endeavor to keep any bit of this fairy gold which has rolled like a brook through our hands. A thousand thoughts awoke, great rainbows seemed to span the sky. A morning among the mountains; but as we close the book, we end the remembrance, nothing survives, not a ray. The power to excite which the page for moments possessed is derived from you.

Some play at chess, some at cards, some at the Stock Exchange. I prefer to play at Cause and Effect.

We need in these twilights of the gods all the conventions of the most regulated life to crutch our lame and indigent loves. The least departure from the usage of marriage would bring too strong a tide against us for so weak a reed as modern love to withstand. Its frigidities, its ebbs already need all the protection and humoring they can get from the forms and manners.

Last night a walk to the river with Margaret, and saw the moon broken in the water, interrogating, interrogating.

Thence followed the history of the surrounding minds. Margaret said she felt herself amidst Tendencies: did not regret life, nor accuse the imperfections of her own or their performance whilst these strong native Tendencies so appeared, and in the children of all of us will be ripened. I told her that I could not discern the least difference between the first experience and the latest in my own case. I had never been otherwise than indolent, never strained a muscle, and only saw a difference in the circumstance, not in the man; at first a circle of boys—my brothers at home, with aunt and cousins, or the schoolroom; all agreed that my verses were obscure nonsense; and now a larger public say the same thing, "obscure nonsense," and yet both conceded that the boy had wit. A little more excitement now, but the fact identical, both in my consciousness and in my relations.

Margaret would beat with the beating heart of Nature; I feel that underneath the greatest life, though it were Jove's or Jehovah's, must lie an astonishment that embosoms both action and thought.

Oaths never go out of fashion, but are always beautiful and thrilling; but the sham of them, which is called profane swearing, is rightly voted a bore. Sham damns we do not like.

Nathaniel Hawthorne's reputation as a writer is a very pleasing fact, because his writing is not good for anything, and this is a tribute to the man.

Sam Ward says, "I like women, they are so finished."

There are two choices for one who is unhappy in an evening party: one, to go no more into such companies, which is flight; the other, to frequent them until their law is wholly learned and they become indifferent, which is conquest. O fine victim, martyr-child! clowns and scullions are content with themselves, and thou art not.

Alas, my friend, you have no generosity; you cannot give yourself away. I see the law of all your friendships. It is a bargain. You tell your things, your friend tells his things, and as soon as the inventory is complete, you take your hats.

How slowly, how slowly we learn that witchcraft and ghost-craft, palmistry and magic, and all the other so-called super-stitions, which, with so much police, boastful skepticism, and scientific committees, we had finally dismissed to the moon as nonsense, are really no nonsense at all, but subtle and valid influences, always starting up, mowing, mutter-ing in our path, and shading our day. The things are real, only they have shed their skin which with much insult we have gibbeted and buried.

Edward Everett. There was an influence on the young peo-ple from Everett's genius which was almost comparable to that of Pericles in Athens. That man had an inspiration that did not go beyond his head, but which made him the gen-ius of elegance. He had a radiant beauty of person, of a classic style, a heavy, large eye, marble lids, which gave the impression of mass which the slightness of his form needed, sculptured lips, a voice of such rich tones, such pre-cise and perfect utterance that, although slightly nasal, it was the most mellow and beautiful and correct of all the instruments of the time. The word that he spoke, in the manner in which he spoke it, became current and classical in New England.

All this was a pure triumph of Rhetoric. This man had

neither intellectual nor moral principles to teach. He had no thoughts. It was early asked, when Massachusetts was full of his fame, what truths he had thrown into circulation, and how he had enriched the general mind, and agreed that only in graces of manner, only in a new perception of Grecian beauty, had he opened our eyes. It was early observed that he had no warm personal friends. Yet his genius made every youth his defender and boys filled their mouths with arguments to prove that the orator had a heart.

Well, this bright morning had a short continuance. Mr. Everett was soon attracted by the vulgar prizes of politics, and quit coldly the splendid career which opened before him (and which, not circumstances, but his own genius had made) for the road to Washington, where it is said he has had the usual fortune of flattery and mortification, but is wholly lost to any real and manly usefulness.

September 27 was a fine day, and Hawthorne and I set forth on a walk. We went first to the Factory where Mr. Damon makes Domett cloths, but his mills were standing still, his houses empty. Nothing so small but comes to honor and has its shining moment somewhere; and so was it here with our little Assabet or North Branch; it was falling over the rocks into silver, and above was expanded into this tranquil lake. After looking about us a few moments, we took the road to Stow. The day was full of sunshine, and it was a luxury to walk in the midst of all this warm and colored light. The days of September are so rich that it seems natural to walk to the end of one's strength, and then fall prostrate, saturated with the fine floods, and cry, *Nunc dimittis me*. Fringed gentians, a thornbush with red fruit, wild apple trees whose fruit hung like berries, and grapevines were the decorations of the path. We scarcely encountered man or boy in our road nor saw any in the fields. This depopulation lasted all day. But the outlines of the landscape were so gentle that it seemed as if we were in a very cultivated country, and elegant persons must be living just over yonder hills.

Our walk had no incidents. It needed none, for we were in excellent spirits, and had much conversation, for we were both old collectors who had never had an opportunity before to show each other our cabinets, so that we could have filled with matter much longer days. We agreed that it needed a little dash of humor or extravagance in the traveller to give occasion to incident in his journey. Here we sober men, easily pleased, kept on the outside of the land and did not by so much as a request for a cup of milk creep into any farmhouse. Then again the opportunities which the taverns once offered the traveller, of witnessing and even sharing in the joke and the politics of the teamster and farmers on the road, are now no more. The Temperance Society emptied the bar-room. It is a cold place. Hawthorne tried to smoke a cigar, but I observed he was soon out on the piazza. After noon we reached Stow, and dined, and then continued our journey towards Harvard, making our day's walk, according to our best computation, about twenty miles.

Next morning we began our walk at 6.30 o'clock for the Shaker Village, distant three and a half miles. Whilst the good Sisters were getting ready our breakfast, we had a conversation with Seth Blanchard and Cloutman of the Brethren, who gave an honest account, by yea and by nay, of their faith and practice. They were not stupid, like some whom I have seen of their Society, and not worldly like others. The conversation on both parts was frank enough; with the downright I will be downright, thought I, and Seth showed some humor. I doubt not we should have had our own way with them to a good extent if we could have stayed twenty-four hours; although my powers of persuasion were crippled by a disgraceful barking cold, and Hawthorne was inclined to play Jove more than Mercurius. From the Shaker Village we came to Littleton and thence to Acton, still in the same redundance of splendor. It was like a day of July, and from Acton we sauntered leisurely homeward, to finish the nineteen miles of our second day before four in the afternoon.

In a town which you enter for the first time at late sunset, the trees and houses look pictorial in the twilight, but you can never play tricks with old acquaintances.

There is something very agreeable in fatigue. I am willinger to die, having had my swing of the fair day; and seven times in his life, I suppose, every man sings, Now, Lord, let thy servant depart.

Landor, though like other poets he has not been happy in love, has written admirable sentences on the passion. Perhaps, said Hawthorne, their disappointment taught them to write these things. Well, it is probable. One of Landor's sentences was worth a divorce; "Those to whom love is a secondary thing love more than those to whom it is a primary."

We have our culture from Europe, and are Europeans. Perhaps we must be content with this and thank God for Europe for a while yet, and there shall be no great Yankee, until, in the unfolding of our population and power, England kicks the beam, and English authors write to America; which must happen ere long.

Avarice, ambition, almost all talents, are restless and vagrant; they go up to the cities; but Religion is a good rooter.

Young preachers are but chipping birds, who chirp now on the bushes, now on the ground, but do not mean anything by their chirping. He must be very green who would go to infer anything in respect to their character from what they say.

At the Shakers' house in Harvard I found a spirit-level on the window-seat, a very good emblem for the Society; but unfortunately, neither the table nor the shelf nor the window-seat were plumb.

The sons of great men should be great; if they are little, it is because they eat too much pound cake, which is an accident; or, because their fathers married dolls.

I woke with a regret that I had made a bargain at B. and had not rather thrown myself wholly on their sense of justice. The Olympian must be Olympian in carriage and deeds wherever he can be symmetrically, not rudely,—and he must dare a little, and try Olympian experiments. Well, courage, and do better again.

When the friend has newly died, the survivor has not yet grief, but the expectation of grief. He has not long enough been deprived of his society to feel yet the want of it. He is surprised, and is now under a certain intellectual excitement, being occupied and in a manner amused by the novelty of the event, and is exploring his changed condition. This defends him from sorrow. It is not until the funeral procession has departed from his doors, and the mourners have all returned to their ordinary pursuits, and forgotten the deceased, that the grief of the friend begins.

Margaret [Fuller] described E. as hobgoblin nature and full of indirections. But he is a good vagabond and knows how to take a walk. The gipsy talent is inestimable in the country, and so rare. In a woman it would be bewitching. Margaret Fuller has not a particle, and only the possibility. And yet this is a relative talent, and to each there doubtless exists a gipsy-maker. I told Hawthorne yesterday that I think every young man at some time inclines to make the experiment of a dare-God and dare-devil originality like that of Rabelais. He would jump on the top of the nearest fence and crow. He makes the experiment, but it proves like the flight of pig-lead into the air, which cannot cope with the poorest hen. Irresistible custom brings him plump down, and he finds himself, instead of odes, writing gazettes and leases.

It is only a young man who supposes there is anything new in Wall Street. The merchant who figures there, so much to his own satisfaction and to the admiration or fear or hatred of the younger or weaker competitors, is a very old business. You shall find him, his way, that is, of thinking concerning the world and men and property and eating and drinking and marriage and education and religion and government,—the whole concatenation of his opinions, the very shade of their color, the same laughter, the same knowingness, the same unbelief, and the same ability and taste, in Rabelais and Aristophanes. Panurge was good Wall Street.

"My evening visitors," said that excellent Professor Fortinbras, "if they cannot see the clock should find the time in my face. As soon as it is nine, I begin to curse them with internal execrations that are minute-guns." And yet, he added, "The devil take half-hospitalities, this self-protecting civility whose invitations to dinner are determined exclusions from the heart of the inviter, as if he said, 'I invite you to eat, because I will not converse with you.'"

You shall have joy, or you shall have power, said God; you shall not have both.

Our fine cousin reminded us of a fierce terrier who conceives it a duty for a dog of honor to bark at every passer-by, whether poet or reformer, and do the honors of the house by barking him out of sight.

Here is Tennyson, a man of subtle and progressive mind, a perfect music-box for all manner of delicate tones and rhythms, to whom the language seems plastic, so superior and forceful in his thought.—But is he a poet? We read Burns and said, He is a poet. We read Tennyson and do him the indignity of asking the question, Is he poet? I feel in him the misfortune of the time. He is a strict contemporary, not Eternal Man. The particular which under this generality deserves most notice is this (and it is a black ingratitude to receive it so), that the argument of the poem is secondary, the finish of the verses primary. It is the splendor of the versification that draws me to the sense, and not the reverse.

It is the merit of a poet to be unanalyzable.

Alcott is a singular person, a natural Levite, a priest forever after the order of Melchizedek, whom all good persons would readily combine, one would say, to maintain as a priest by voluntary contribution to live in his own cottage, literary, spiritual, and choosing his own methods of teaching and action. But for a founder of a family or institution, I would as soon exert myself to collect money for a madman.

Could they* not die? or succeed? or help themselves? or draw others? in any manner, I care not how, could they not be disposed of, and cease to hang there in the horizon an unsettled appearance, too great to be neglected, and not great enough to be of any aid or comfort to this great craving humanity?

Oh, if they could take a second step, and a third! The reformer is so confident, that all are erect whilst he puts the finger on your special abuse, and tells you your great want in America. I tell him, yea, but not in America only, but in the Universe ever since it was known, just this defect has appeared. But when he has anatomized the evil, he will be called out of the room, or have got something else in his head. Remedied it never will be.

If a man will kick a fact out of the window, when he comes back he finds it again in the chimney corner.

Do not gloze and prate and mystify. Here is our dear, grand Alcott says, You shall dig in my field for a day and I will give you a dollar when it is done, and it shall not be a business transaction! It makes me sick. Whilst money is the measure *really* adopted by us all as the most convenient measure of all material values, let us not affectedly disuse the name, and mystify ourselves and others; let us not "say no, and take it." We may very well and honestly have theoretical and practical objections to it; if they are fatal to the use of money and barter, let us disuse them; if they are less grave than the inconvenience of abolishing traffic, let us

---

* Alcott and his English friends.

not pretend to have done with it, whilst we eat and drink and wear and breathe it.

Do not be too timid and squeamish about your actions. All life is an experiment. The more experiments you make the better. What if they are a little coarse, and you may get your coat soiled or torn? What if you do fail, and get fairly rolled in the dirt once or twice? Up again, you shall never be so afraid of a tumble.

Last night Henry Thoreau read me verses which pleased, if not by beauty of particular lines, yet by the honest truth, and by the length of flight and strength of wing; for most of our poets are only writers of lines or of epigrams. These of Henry's at least have rude strength, and we do not come to the bottom of the mine. Their fault is, that the gold does not yet flow pure, but is drossy and crude. The thyme and marjoram are not yet made into honey; the assimilation is imperfect. It seems as if the poetry was all written before time was.

I was a little chubby boy trundling a hoop in Chauncy Place, and spouting poetry from Scott and Campbell at the Latin School. But Time, the little grey man, has taken out of his vest-pocket a great, awkward house (in a corner of which I sit down and write of him), some acres of land, several full-grown and several very young persons, and seated them close beside me; then he has taken that chubbiness and that hoop quite away (to be sure he has left the declamation and the poetry), and here left a long, lean person threatening to be a little grey man, like himself.

I begged Alcott to paint out his project, and he proceeded to say that there should be found a farm of one hundred acres in excellent condition, with good buildings, a good orchard, and grounds which admitted of being laid out with great beauty; and this should be purchased and given to them, in the first place. I replied, You ask too much. This is not solving the problem; there are hundreds of innocent young persons, whom, if you will thus stablish and endow and protect, will find it no hard matter to keep their innocency. And to see their tranquil household, after all this has been done for them, will in no wise instruct or strengthen me. But he will instruct and strengthen me, who, there where he is, unaided, in the midst of poverty, toil, and traffic, extricates himself from the corruptions of the same and builds on his land a house of peace and benefit, good customs, and free thoughts. But, replied Alcott, how is this to be done? How can I do it who have a wife and family to maintain? I answered that he was not the person to do it, or he would not ask the question.

This fatal fault in the logic of our friends still appears: Their whole doctrine is spiritual, but they always end with saying, Give us much land and money.

Transcendentalism is the Saturnalia of faith. It is faith run mad.

Yesterday I read Dicken's *American Notes*. It answers its end very well, which plainly was to make a readable book, nothing more. Truth is not his object for a single instant, but merely to make good points in a lively sequence, and he proceeds very well. We can hear throughout every page the dialogue between the author and his publisher,—"Mr. Dickens, the book must be entertaining—that is the essential point. Truth? Damn truth! I tell you, it must be entertaining."

I think four walls one of the best of our institutions. A man comes to me, and oppresses me by his presence; he looks very large and unanswerable. I cannot dispose of him whilst he stays; he quits the room, and passes, not only out of the house, but, as it were, out of the horizon; he is a mere phantom or ghost. I think of him no more. I recover my sanity, the universe dawns on me again.

No man can be criticised but by a greater than he. Do not, then, read the reviews.

Conservatism stands on this, that a man cannot jump out of his skin; and well for him that he cannot, for his skin is the world; and the stars of heaven do hold him there: in the folly of men glitters the wisdom of God.

This old Bible, if you pitch it out of the window with a fork, it comes bounce back again.

A poet may eat bread for his breakfast, and bread and flesh for his dinner, but for his supper he must eat stars only.

I hear the whistle of the locomotive in the woods. Wherever that music comes it has its sequel. It is the voice of the civility of the Nineteenth Century saying, "Here I am." It is interrogative: it is prophetic: and this Cassandra is believed: "Whew! Whew! Whew! How is real estate here in the swamp and wilderness? Ho for Boston! Whew! Whew! Down with that forest on the side of the hill. I want ten thousand chestnut sleepers. I want cedar posts, and hundreds of thousands of feet of boards. Up! my masters of oak and pine! You have waited long enough—a good part of a century in the wind and stupid sky. Ho for axes and saws, and away with me to Boston! Whew! Whew!"

The world is the prey and dominion of thoughts. History is a foolish, pragmatic misstatement. As easily might you survey a cloud, which is now as big as your hat, and before you have measured its first angle, covers ten acres. Thoughts work and make what you call the world. Heroes are the lucky individuals who stand at the pole and are the largest and ripest.

The oak leaf is perfect, a kind of absolute realized, but every work of art is only relatively good;—the artist advances, and finds all his fine things naught.

The Yankee is one who if he once gets his teeth set on a thing, all creation can't make him let go; who, if he can get hold anywhere of a rope's end or a spar, will not let it go, but will make it carry him; if he can but find so much as a stump or a log, will hold on to it and whittle out of it a house and barn, a farm and stock, a mill-seat and a village, a railroad and a bank, and various other things equally useful and entertaining,—a seat in Congress or a foreign mission, for example. But these no doubt are inventions of the enemy.

Take away from me the feeling that I must depend on myself, give me the least hint that I have good friends and backers there in reserve who will gladly help me, and instantly I relax my diligence. I obey the first impulse of generosity that is to cost me nothing, and a certain slackness will creep over my conduct of my affairs. Here is a bank-note found of one hundred dollars. Let it fall into the hands of an easy man who never earned the estate he spends, and see how little difference it will make in his affairs. At the end of the year he is just as much behindhand as ever, and could not have done at all without that hundred. Let it fall into the hands of a poor and prudent woman, and every shilling and every cent of it tells, goes to reduce debt, or to add to instant and constant comfort, mends a window, buys a blanket or a pelisse, gets a stove instead of the old cavernous fireplace, all chimney.

Travelling is a very humiliating experience to me. I never go to any church like a railroad car for teaching me my deficiencies.

For any grandeur of circumstance length of time seems an indispensable element. Who can attach anything majestic to creatures so short-lived as we men? The time that is proper to spend in mere musing is too large a fraction of threescore years and ten to be indulged to that greatness of behavior. The brevity of human life gives a melancholy to the profession of the architect.

1843

Baltimore, Barnum's Hotel, January 7
Here to-day from Philadelphia. The railroad, which was but a toy coach the other day, is now a dowdy, lumbering country wagon. Yet it is not prosaic, as people say, but highly poetic, this strong shuttle which shoots across the forest, swamp, river, and arms of the sea, binding city to city. The Americans take to the little contrivance as if it were the cradle in which they were born.

Dreamlike travelling on the railroad. The towns through which I pass between Philadelphia and New York make no distinct impression. They are like pictures on a wall. The more, that you can read all the way in a car a French novel.

Nature asked, Whether troop and baggage be two things; whether the world is all troop or all baggage, or whether there be any troop that shall not one day be baggage? Easy, she thinks it, to show you the Universal Soul: we have all sucked that orange; but would you please to mention what is an Individual? She apologized for trifling with you in your nonage, and adding a little sugar to your milk that you might draw the teat, and a little glory afterward to important lessons, but declared she would never tell you another fib, if you had quite settled that Buddhism was better than hands and feet, and would keep that conviction in the presence of two persons. As for *far* and *too far*, she wondered what it meant. She admires people who read, and people who look at pictures, but if they read until they write, or look at pictures until they draw them, she curses them up and down. She has the oddest tastes and behavior. An onion, which is all coat, she dotes on; and among birds she admires the godwit; but when I hinted that a blue weed grew about my house called *Selfheal*, she said,—a coxcomb named it; but she teaches cobwebs to resist the tempest, and when a babe's cries drove away a lion, she almost devoured the darling with kisses. She says her office of Dragoman is vacant, though she has been much pestered with applications, and if you have a talent of asking questions, she will play with you all your life; but if you can answer questions, she will propose one, which, if you answer, she will die first. She hates authors, but likes Montaigne.

Webster is very dear to the Yankees because he is a person of very commanding understanding with every talent for its adequate expression. The American, foreigners say, always reasons, and he is the most American of the Americans. They have no abandonment, but dearly love logic, as all their churches have so long witnessed. His external advantages are very rare and admirable; his noble and majestic frame, his breadth and projection of brows, his coal-black hair, his great cinderous eyes, his perfect self-possession, and the rich and well-modulated thunder of his voice (to which I used to listen, sometimes, abstracting myself from his sense merely for the luxury of such noble explosions of sound) distinguish him above all other men. In a million you would single him out.

The faults that shade his character are not such as to hurt his popularity. He is very expensive, and always in debt; but this rather commends him, as he is known to be generous, and his countrymen make for him the apology of Themistocles, that to keep treasure undiminished is the virtue of a chest and not of a man. Then there is in him a large share of good nature and a sort of *bonhomie*. It is sometimes complained of him that he is a man of pleasure, and all his chosen friends are easy epicures and debauchees. But this is after Talleyrand's taste, who said of his foolish wife that he found nonsense very refreshing: so Webster, after he has been pumping his brains in the courts and the Senate, is, no doubt, heartily glad to get among cronies and gossips where he can stretch himself at his ease and drink his mulled wine. They also quote as his *three rules* of living: (1) Never to pay any debt that can by any possibility be avoided; (2) Never to do anything to-day that can be put off till to-morrow; (3) Never to do anything himself which he can get anybody else to do for him.

All is forgiven to a man of such surpassing intellect, and such prodigious powers of business which have so long been exerted. There is no malice in the man, but broad good humor and much enjoyment of the hour; so that Stetson said of him, "It is true that he sometimes commits crimes, but without any guilt."

He has misused the opportunity of making himself the darling of the American world in all coming time by abstaining from putting himself at the head of the Antislavery interest, by standing for New England and for man against the bullying and barbarism of the South.

I should say of him that he was not at all majestic, but the purest intellect that was ever applied to business. He is Intellect applied to affairs. He is the greatest of lawyers; but a very indifferent statesman for carrying his points. He carries points with the bench, but not with the caucus. No following has he, no troop of friends, but those whose intellect he fires. No sweaty mob will carry him on their shoulders. And yet all New England to the remotest farmhouse, or lumberers' camp in the woods of Maine, delights to tell and hear of anecdotes of his forensic eloquence.

As we go along the street, the eyes of all the passengers either ask, ask, continually of all they meet, or else assert, assert to all. Only rarely do we meet a face which has the balance of expression, neither asking leave to be, nor rudely egotistic, but equally receptive and affirmative.

It is very funny to go in to a family where the father and mother are devoted to the children. You flatter yourself for an instant that you have secured your friend's ear, for his countenance brightens; then you discover that he has just caught the eye of his babe over your shoulder, and is chirruping to him.

Mr. Adams chose wisely and according to his constitution, when, on leaving the Presidency, he went into Congress.

He is no literary old gentleman, but a bruiser, and loves the *mêlée*. When they talk about his age and venerableness and nearness to the grave, he knows better, he is like one of those old cardinals, who, as quick as he is chosen Pope, throws away his crutches and his crookedness, and is as straight as a boy. He is an old *roué* who cannot live on slops, but must have sulphuric acid in his tea.

I remembered what I have heard or dreamed, that the most terrific of hierarchs would be a mystic. Beware of Swedenborg *in power*. Swedenborg in minority, Swedenborg contemplative, is excellent company; but Swedenborg executive would be the Devil in crown and sceptre. Fagots!

Cheap literature makes new markets.

At the Five Points I heard a woman swearing very liberally as she talked with her companions; but when I looked at her face, I saw that she was no worse than other women; that she used the dialect of her class, as all others do, and are neither better nor worse for it.

When the rudder is invented for the balloon, railroads will be superseded.

Grief and Joy, Charity and Faith get derivative and referring. Dire Necessity is good and strong;—I love him, I hate him; I like, I dislike. Once there was a race that subsisted, but these seeming, spectral fellows that ask even when they curse and swear—or but affect to curse and swear! I wish there was no more good nature left in the world; tomahawks are better. I think the reason we value mystics so much is, as oaks indicate a strong soil, so a thick crop of mystics shows like redemption from our universal supplication of each other.

The Brook Farm Community is an expression in plain prose and actuality of the theory of impulse. It contains several bold and consistent philosophers, both men and women, who carry out the theory, odiously enough, inasmuch as this centripetence of theirs is balanced by no centrifugence; this wish to obey impulse is guarded by no old, old Intellect—or that which knows metes and bounds. The young people who have been faithful to this, their testimony, have lived a great deal in a short time, but have come forth with shattered constitutions. It is an intellectual Sansculottism.

The philosophers at Fruitlands have such an image of virtue before their eyes, that the poetry of man and nature they never see; the poetry that is in man's life, the poorest pastoral clownish life; the light that shines on a man's hat, in a child's spoon, the sparkle on every wave and on every mote of dust, they see not.

Two brave chanticleers* go up and down stripping the plumes from all the fine birds, showing that all are not in the best health. It makes much unhappiness on all sides; much crowing it occasions on the part of the two cockerels who so shrewdly discover and dismantle all the young beaux of the aviary. But alas, the two valiant cocks who strip are no better than those who are stripped, only they have sharper beak and talons. In plain prose, I grieved so much to hear the most intellectual youth I have met, Charles Newcomb, so disparaged, and our good and most deserving scholar, Theodore Parker, threatened as a morsel

* Alcott's two English friends.

to be swallowed when he shall come to-morrow, and all this by my brave friends, who are only brave, not helpful, not loving, not creative,—that I said, Cursed is preaching, —the better it is, the worse. A preacher is a bully: I who have preached so much,—by the help of God will never preach more.

Margaret [*Fuller*]. A pure and purifying mind, self-purifying also, full of faith in men, and inspiring it. She has great sincerity, force, and fluency as a writer, yet her powers of speech throw her writing into the shade. What method, what exquisite judgment, as well as energy, in the selection of her words; what character and wisdom they convey! You cannot predict her opinion. She sympathizes so fast with all forms of life, that she talks never narrowly or hostilely, nor betrays, like all the rest, under a thin garb of new words, the old droning cast-iron opinions or notions of many years' standing. What richness of experience, what newness of dress, and fast as Olympus to her principle. And a silver eloquence, which inmost Polymnia taught. Meantime, all this pathos of sentiment and riches of literature, and of invention, and this march of character threatening to arrive presently at the shores and plunge into the sea of Buddhism and mystic trances, consists with a boundless fun and drollery, with light satire, and the most entertaining conversation in America.

Persons are fine things, but they cost so much! for *thee* I must pay *me*.

The same persons should not constitute a Standing Committee on Reform. A man may say, I am the chief of sinners, but once. He is already damned, if having come once to the insight of that condition, he remains there to say it again.

It is a great joy to get away from persons, and live under the dominion of the Multiplication Table.

The world must be new as we know it, for see how lately it has bethought itself of so many articles of the simplest convenience; as, for example, wooden clothes-pins to pinch the clothes to the line, instead of metallic pins, were introduced since the Peace of 1783. My mother remembers when her sister, Mrs. Inman, returned from England at that time, and brought these articles with her furniture, then new in this country; then the india-rubber shoe; the railroad; the steamboat; and the air-tight stove; the friction match; and cut nails.

The difference between Talent and Genius is, that Talent says things which he has never heard but once, and Genius things which he has never heard. Genius is power; Talent is applicability.

Elizabeth Hoar says, "I love Henry, but do not like him." Young men, like Henry Thoreau, owe us a new world, and they have not acquitted the debt. For the most part, such die young, and so dodge the fulfilment. One of our girls said, that Henry never went through the kitchen without coloring.

In Roxbury, in 1825, I read Cotton's translation of Montaigne. It seemed to me as if I had written the book myself in some former life, so sincerely it spoke my thought and experience.

Tea and coffee are my wine, and I have finer and lighter wines than these. But some nectar an intellectual man will naturally use. For he will soon learn the secret that beside the energy of his conscious intellect, his intellect is capable of new energy by abandonment to the nature of things. All persons avail themselves of such means as they can to add this extraordinary power to their normal powers. One finds it in music, one in war, one in great pictures or sculpture; one in travelling; one in conversation; in politics, in mobs, in fires, in theatres, in love, in science; in animal intoxication. I take many stimulants and often make an art of my inebriation. I read Proclus for my opium; it excites my imagination to let sail before me the pleasing and grand figures of gods and dæmons and demoniacal men. I hear of rumors rife among the most ancient gods, of azonic gods who are itinerants, of dæmons with fulgid eyes, of the unenvying and exuberant will of the gods; the aquatic gods, the Plain of Truth, the meadow, the nutriment of the gods, the paternal port, and all the rest of the Platonic rhetoric quoted as household words. By all these and so many rare and brave words I am filled with hilarity and spring, my heart dances, my sight is quickened, I behold shining relations between all beings, and am impelled to write and almost to sing. I think one would grow handsome who read Proclus much and well.

Much poor talk concerning woman, which at least had the effect of revealing the true sex of several of the party who usually go disguised in the form of the other sex. Thus Mrs. B. is a man. The finest people marry the two sexes in their own person. Hermaphrodite is then the symbol of the finished Soul. It was agreed that in every act should appear the married pair: the two elements should mix in every act.

To me it sounded hoarsely, the attempt to prescribe didactically to woman her duties. Man can never tell woman

what her duties are: he will certainly end in describing a
man in female attire.

I can never think of women without gratitude for the bright
revelations of her best nature which have been made to
me, unworthy. The angel who walked with me in younger
days shamed my ambition and prudence by her generous
love in our first interview. I described my prospects. She
said, I do not wish to hear of your prospects.

April 10

The slowly retreating snow blocks the roads and wood
paths and shuts me in the house. But yesterday the warm
south wind drew me to the top of the hill, like the dove
from the ark, to see if these white waters were abated, and
there was place for the foot. The grass springs up already
between the holes in the snow, and I walked along the
knolls and edges of the hill wherever the winter bank was
melted, but I thrust my cane into the bank two feet perpendicular. I greeted the well-known pine grove which I
could not reach; the pine tops seemed to cast a friendly
gold-green smile of acquaintance toward me, for it was in
my heart that I had not yet quite got home from my late
journey, until I had revisited and rejoined these vegetable
dæmons. The air was kind and clear, the sky southward
was full of comets, so white and fan-shaped and ethereal
lay the clouds, as if the late visit of this foreign wonder
had set the fashion for the humbler meteors. And all
around me the new-come sparrows, robins, bluebirds, and
blackbirds were announcing their arrival with great spirit.

Daniel Webster is a great man with a small ambition. Nature has built him and holds him forth as a sample of the
heroic mould to this puny generation. He was virtual Presi-

dent of the United States from the hour of the Speech on
Foot's Resolutions in the United States Senate in 1832, be-
ing regarded as the Expounder of the Constitution and the
Defender of Law. But this did not suffice; he wished to be
an officer, also; wished to add a title to his name, and be a
President. That ruined him.

Travelling, forsooth! as if every traveller did not feel himself an impertinence when he came among the diligent in
their places. Do you suppose there is any country where
they do not scald the milkpans, and clout the infants,
and burn the brushwood?

How sincere and confidential we can be, saying all that lies
in the mind, and yet go away feeling that we have spun a
rope of sand, that all is yet unsaid, from the incapacity of
the parties to know each other, *although they use the same
words*. Could they but once understand that I loved to
know that they existed and heartily wished them God-
speed, yet out of my poverty of life and thought, had no
word or welcome for them when they came to see me,
and could well consent to their living in another town, from
any claim that I felt on them,—it would be great satisfaction. They did not like pictures, marbles, woodland, and
poetry; I liked all these, and Lane and Alcott too, as one
more figure in the various landscape.

And now, I said, will you not please to pound me a little
before I go, just by way of squaring the account, that I may
not remember that I alone was saucy? Alcott contented
himself with quarrelling with the injury done to greater
qualities in my company, by the tyranny of my Taste;—
which certainly was very soft pounding. And so I departed
from the divine lotus-eaters.

I went to Washington and spent four days. The two poles of an enormous political battery, galvanic coil on coil, self-increased by series on series of plates from Mexico to Canada and from the sea westward to the Rocky Mountains, here terminate and play and make the air electric and violent. Yet one feels how little, more than how much, Man is represented there. I think, in the higher societies of the universe, it will turn out that the angels are molecules, as the devils were always Titans, since the dulness of the world needs such mountainous demonstration, and the virtue is so modest and concentrating.

In every woman's conversation and total influence, mild or acid, lurks the *conventional devil*. They look at your carpet, they look at your cap, at your salt-cellar, at your cook and waiting-maid, conventionally,—to see how close they square with the customary cut in Boston and Salem and New Bedford.

Yesterday George Bradford walked and talked of the Community* and cleared up some of the mists which gossip had made: and expressed the conviction, shared by himself and his friends there, that plain dealing was the best defense of manners and morals between the sexes. I suppose that the danger arises whenever bodily familiarity grows up without spiritual intimacy. The reason why there is purity in marriage is, that the parties are universally near and helpful, and not only near bodily. If their wisdom come near and meet, there is no danger of passion. Therefore, the remedy of impurity is to come nearer.

Yesterday, English visitors, and I waited all day when they should go.

* Brook Farm.

If we could establish the rule that each man was a guest in his own house, and when we had shown our visitors the passages of the house, the way to fire, to bread, and water, and thus made them as much at home as the inhabitant, did then leave them to the accidents of intercourse, and went about our ordinary business, a guest would no longer be formidable.

Brook Farm Again! The freaks of the young philosophers show how much life they have, as jockeys, when a horse rolls on the ground, add a gold eagle to his price for every turn he makes. But nothing will take the place of fidelity.

Brook Farm will show a few noble victims, who act and suffer with temper and proportion, but the larger part will be slight adventurers and will shirk work.

My garden is an honest place. Every tree and every vine are incapable of concealment, and tell after two or three months exactly what sort of treatment they have had. The sower may mistake and sow his peas crookedly: the peas make no mistake, but come up and show his line.

Do not write modern antiques. They are paste jewels. You may well take an ancient subject where the form is incidental merely, like Shakspeare's plays, and the treatment and dialogue is simple, and most modern. But do not make much of the costume. For such things have no verity; no man will live or die by them: The way to write is to throw your body at the mark when your arrows are spent.

Walked with Ellery [Channing]. In the landscape felt the magic of color; the world is all opal, and these ethereal

tints the mountains wear have the finest effects of music
on us. Mountains are great poets, and one glance at this
fine cliff scene undoes a great deal of prose, and reinstates
us wronged men in our rights. All life, all society begins to
get illuminated and transparent, and we generalize boldly
and well. Space is felt as a great thing. There is some pinch
and narrowness to us, and we laugh and leap to see the
world, and what amplitudes it has of meadow, stream, up-
land, forest, and sea, which yet are but lanes and crevices
to the great Space in which the world swims like a cock-
boat in the sea. A little canoe with three figures put out
from a creek into the river and sailed downstream to the
Bridge, and we rejoiced in the Blessed Water inviolable,
magical, whose nature is Beauty, which instantly began to
play its sweet games, all circles and dimples and lovely
gleaming motions,—always Ganges, the Sacred River, and
which cannot be desecrated or made to forget itself. But
there below are these farms, yet are the farmers unpoetic.
The life of labor does not make men, but drudges.

The Farmer is an enchanted laborer, and after toiling his
brains out, sacrificing thought, religion, taste, love, hope,
courage at the shrine of toil, turns out a bankrupt as well as
the merchant. It is time to have the thing looked into, and
with a transpiercing criticism settled whether life is worth
having on such terms.

The stars I think the antidotes of pyrrhonism. In the fuss of
the sunlight and the rapid succession of moods, one might
doubt his identity; but these expressive points, always in
their place so immutable, are the tranquillizers of men.
No narcotic so sedative or sanative as this.

Man sheds grief as his skin sheds rain. A preoccupied mind
an immense protection. There is a great concession on all

hands to the ideal decorum in grief, as well as joy, but few hearts are broken.

I enjoy all the hours of life. Few persons have such susceptibility to pleasure: as a countryman will say, "I was at sea a month and never missed a meal," so I eat my dinner and sow my turnips, yet do I never, I think, fear death. It seems to me so often a relief, a rendering-up of responsibility, a quittance of so many vexatious trifles.

How poetic this wondrous web of property! J.P. sitting in his parlor talking of philanthropy has his pocket full of papers, representing dead labor done long ago, not by him, not by his ancestor, but by hands which his ancestor had skill to set at work and get the certificates of. And now these signs of the work of hands, long ago mouldered in the grave, are honored by all men, and for them J.P. can get what vast amounts of work done by new young hands,— canals, railways, houses, gardens, coaches, pastures, sheep, oxen, and corn.

One great wrong must soon disappear,—this right to burden the unborn with state loans.

I think we are not quite yet fit for Flying Machines, and therefore there will be none.

Carlyle must write thus or nohow, like a drunken man who can run, but cannot walk.

Fools and clowns and sots make the fringes of every one's tapestry of life, and give a certain reality to the picture. What could we do in Concord without Bigelow's and Wesson's bar-rooms and their dependencies? What without such fixtures as Uncle Sol, and old Moore who sleeps in

Doctor Hurd's barn, and the red charity-house over the brook? Tragedy and comedy always go hand in hand.

The sun and the evening sky do not look calmer than Alcott and his family at Fruitlands. They seemed to have arrived at the fact, to have got rid of the show, and so to be serene. Their manners and behavior in the house and in the field were those of superior men, of men at rest. What had they to conceal? What had they to exhibit? And it seemed so high an attainment that I thought, as often before, so now more because they had a fit home or the picture was fitly framed, that these men ought to be maintained in their place by the Country for its culture. Young men and young maidens, old men and women, should visit them and be inspired. I think there is as much merit in beautiful manners as in hard work.

I will not prejudge them successful. They look well in July. We will see them in December. I know they are better for themselves than as partners. One can easily see that they have yet to settle several things. Their saying that things are clear, and they sane, does not make them so.

Ellery Channing railed an hour in good set terms at the usurpation of the past, at the great hoaxes of the Homers and Shakespeares, hindering the books and men of today of their just meed. Oh certainly; I assure him that oaks and horse-chestnuts are entirely obsolete, that the Horticultural Society are about to recommend the introduction of cabbages as a shade tree, so much more convenient and every way comprehensible; all grown from the seed upward to its most generous crumpled extremity within one's own short memory; past contradiction the ornament of the world, and then so good to eat, as acorns and horse-chestnuts are not. Shade trees for breakfast!

Every person of worth, man or woman, whom I see, gives
me a pain as if I injured them, because of my incapacity to
do them justice in the intercourse that passes between us.
Two or more persons together deoxygenate the air, apa-
thize and paralyze me. I twist like the poor eel in the exhausted receiver, and my conviction of their sense and virtue only makes matters worse for me by accusing my
injustice. I am made for chronic relations, not for moments,
and am wretched with fine people who are only there for
an hour.

Mr. Webster loses nothing in comparison with brilliant
men in the legal profession: he is as much before them as
before the ordinary lawyer. At least I thought he appeared
among these best lawyers of the Suffolk Bar, like a schoolmaster among his boys.*

His wonderful organization, the perfection of his elocu-
tion, and all that thereto belongs,—voice, accent, intona-
tion, attitude, manner,—are such as one cannot hope to see
again in a century; then he is so thoroughly simple and wise
in his rhetoric. Understanding language and the use of the
positive degree, all his words tell, and his rhetoric is perfect, so homely, so fit, so strong. Then he manages his matter so well, he hugs his fact so close, and will not let it go,
and never indulges in a weak flourish, though he knows
perfectly well how to make such exordiums and episodes
and perorations as may give perspective to his harangue,
without in the least embarrassing his plan or confounding
his transitions. What is small, he shows as small, and makes
the great, great. In speech he sometimes roars, and his
words are like blows of an axe. His force of personal attack

---

* Emerson had visited the Court at Concord where a notable case of
misappropriation of bank funds was being tried.

is terrible, he lays out his strength so directly in honest blows, and all his powers of voice, arm, eye, and whole man are so heartily united and bestowed on the adversary that he cannot fail to be felt.

Rockwood Hoar said, nothing amused him more than to see Mr. Webster adjourn the Court every day, which he did by rising, and taking his hat and looking the Judge coolly in the face; who then bade the Crier adjourn the Court.

Rufus Choate is a favorite with the bar, and a nervous, fluent speaker, with a little too much fire for the occasion, yet with a certain temperance in his fury and a perfect self-command; but he uses the superlative degree, and speaks of affairs altogether too rhetorically. This property of $300,000, the property of a bank, he speaks of as "vast," and quite academically. And there was no perspective in his speech; the transitions were too slight and sudden. But the cast-iron tones of the man of men, the perfect machine that he is for arguing a case, dwarfed instantly Choate and all the rest of the learned counselors.

Webster behaves admirably well in society. These village parties must be dishwater to him, yet he shows himself just good-natured, just nonchalant *enough,* and has his own way without offending any one or losing any ground. He told us that he never read by candle-light.

Webster quite fills our little town, and I doubt if I shall get settled down to writing until he is well gone from the county. He is a natural Emperor of men; they remark in him the kingly talent of remembering persons accurately, and knowing at once to whom he has been introduced, and to whom not.

It seems to me the Quixotism of Criticism to quarrel with Webster because he has not this or that fine evangelical property. He is no saint, but the wild olive wood, ungrafted yet by grace, but according to his lights a very true and admirable man. His expensiveness seems to be necessary to him. Were he too prudent a Yankee it would be a sad deduction from his magnificence. I only wish he would never truckle; I do not care how much he spends.

That point of imperfection which we occupy—is it on the way *up* or *down?*

I wish to speak with all respect of persons, but sometimes I find it needs much heedfulness to preserve the due decorum, they melt so fast into each other.

In points of good breeding, what I most require and insist upon is deference. I like that every chair should be a throne and hold a king. And what I most dislike is a low sympathy of each with his neighbor's palate. I respect cats, they seem to have so much else in their heads besides their mess. I prefer a tendency to stateliness to an excess of fellowship. In all things I would have the island of a man inviolate. No degree of affection is to invade this religion.

The charge which a lady in much trust made to me against her companions was that people on whom beforehand all persons would put the utmost reliance were not responsible. They saw the necessity that the work must be done, and did it not; and it of course fell to be done by herself and the few principals.* I replied, that in my experience good people were as bad as rogues, that the conscience of the conscientious ran in veins, and the most punctilious in some particulars were latitudinarian in others.

* Probably refers to the Brook Farm Community.

Henry Thoreau sends me a paper with the old fault of un-limited contradiction. The trick of his rhetoric is soon learned: it consists in substituting for the obvious word and thought its diametrical antagonist. He praises wild moun-tains and winter forests for their domestic air; snow and ice for their warmth; villagers and wood-choppers for their ur-banity, and the wilderness for resembling Rome and Paris. With the constant inclination to dispraise cities and civili-zation, he yet can find no way to know woods and wood-men except by paralleling them with towns and townsmen. Channing declared the piece is excellent: but it makes me nervous and wretched to read it, with all its merits.

The thinker looks for God in the direction of the conscious-ness, the churchman out of it. If you ask the former for his definition of God, he would answer, "My possibility"; for his definition of Man, "My actuality."

Is life a thunderstorm that we can see now by a flash the whole horizon, and then cannot see our right hand?

Any form of government would content me in which the rulers were gentlemen, but it is in vain that I have tried to persuade myself that Mr. Calhoun or Mr. Clay or Mr. Webster were such; they are underlings, and take the law from the dirtiest fellows.

The capital defect of my nature for society (as it is of so many others) is the want of animal spirits. They seem to me a thing incredible, as if God should raise the dead.

God will have life to be real; we will be damned, but it shall be theatrical.

This morning Charles Lane left us after a two days' visit. He was dressed in linen altogether, with the exception of his shoes, which were lined with linen, and he wore no stockings. He was full of methods of an improved life; valued himself chiefly just now on getting rid of the animals; thinks there is no economy in using them on a farm.

When the poet spoke of the stars he should be innocent of what he said; for it seemed that the stars, as they rolled over him, mirrored themselves in his mind as in a deep well, and it was their image and not his thought that you saw.

Henry Ware,° with his benevolence and frigid manners, reminded men how often of a volcano covered with snow. This was a soldier that flung himself into all risks at all hours, not a solemn martyr kept to be burned once and make the flames proud. In calm hours and friendly company, his face expanded into broad simple sunshine; and I thought *le bon Henri* a pumpkin-sweeting.

Hard clouds, and hard expressions, and hard manners, I love.

The class of officers I recognize everywhere in town or country. These gallants come into the world to ruffle it, and by rough or smooth to find their way to the top. When I spoke to Nathaniel Hawthorne of the class who hold the keys of State Street and are yet excluded from the best Boston circles, he said, "Perhaps he has a heavy wife."

° Old friend of Emerson; his colleague at the Second Church; later professor at Harvard.

It is vain to attempt to get rid of the children by not mind-
ing them, ye parents dear; for the children measure their
own life by the reaction, and if purring and humming is
not noticed, they begin to squeal; if that is neglected, to
screech; then, if you chide and console them, they find
the experiment succeeds, and they begin again. The child
will sit in your arms if you do nothing, contented; but if you
read, it misses the reaction, and commences hostile opera-
tions.

My great-grandfather was Rev. Joseph Emerson of Malden,
son of Edward Emerson, Esq., of Newbury(port). I used
often to hear that when William, son of Joseph, was yet a
boy walking before his father to church, on a Sunday, his
father checked him: "William, you walk as if the earth
was not good enough for you." "I did not know it, Sir," he
replied, with the utmost humility. This is one of the household anecdotes in which I have found a relationship. 'T is
curious, but the same remark was made to me, by Mrs.
Lucy Brown, when I walked one day under her windows
here in Concord.

We come down with free thinking into the dear institutions, and at once make carnage amongst them. We are
innocent of any such fell purpose as the sequel seems to
impute to us. We were only smoking a cigar, but it turns
out to be a powder-mill we are promenading.

People came, it seems, to my lectures with expectation
that I was to realize the Republic I described, and ceased
to come when they found this reality no nearer. They mis-
took me. I am and always was a painter. I paint still with
might and main, and choose the best subjects I can. Many

have I seen come and go with false hopes and fears, and dubiously affected by my pictures. But I paint on. I count this distinct vocation which never leaves me in doubt what to do, but in all times, places, and fortunes gives me an open future, to be the great felicity of my lot.

Alcott came, the magnificent dreamer, brooding, as ever, on the renewal or reëdification of the social fabric after ideal law, heedless that he had been uniformly rejected by every class to whom he has addressed himself, and just as sanguine and vast as ever;—the most cogent example of the drop too much which Nature adds of each man's peculiarity. To himself he seems the only realist, and whilst I and other men wish to deck the dullness of the months with here and there a fine action or hope, he would weave the whole, a new texture of truth and beauty. . . . Very pathetic it is to see this wandering Emperor from year to year making his round of visits from house to house of such as do not exclude him, seeking a companion, tired of pupils.

We early men at least have a vast advantage: we are up at four o'clock in the morning and have the whole market,— we Enniuses and Venerable Bedes of the empty American Parnassus.

Alcott and Lane want feet; they are always feeling of their shoulders to find if their wings are sprouting; but next best to wings are cowhide boots, which society is always advising them to put on.

The moment we quote a man to prove our sanity, we give up all. No authority can establish it, and if I have lost confidence in myself I have the Universe against me.

Each man reserves to himself alone the right of being tedious.

At the performing of Handel's *Messiah* I heard some delicious strains and understood a very little of all that was told me. I walked in the bright paths of sound, and liked it best when the long continuance of a chorus had made the ear insensible to the music, made it as if there was none; then I was quite solitary and at ease in the melodious uproar. Once or twice in the solos, when well sung, I could play tricks, as I like to do, with my eyes,—darken the whole house and brighten and transfigure the central singer, and enjoy the enchantment.

The two parties in life are the believers and unbelievers, variously named. The believer is poet, saint, democrat, theocrat, free-trade, no church, no capital punishment, idealist.

The unbeliever supports the church, education, the fine arts, etc., as *amusements.*

But the unbelief is very profound: Who can escape it? I am nominally a believer: yet I hold on to property: I eat my bread with unbelief. I approve every wild action of the experimenters. I say what they say concerning celibacy, or money, or community of goods, and my only apology for not doing their work is preoccupation of mind. I have a work of my own which I know I can do with some success. It would leave that undone if I should undertake with them, and I do not see in myself any vigor equal to such an enterprise. My genius loudly calls me to stay where I am, even with the degradation of owning bank-stock and seeing poor men suffer, whilst the Universal Genius apprises me of this disgrace and beckons me to the martyrs and redeemer's office.

1844

Finish each day before you begin the next, and interpose a solid wall of sleep between two. This you cannot do without temperance.

I never seem well to do a particular work until another is done. I cannot write the poem, though you give me a week, but if I promise to read a lecture day after to-morrow, at once the poem comes into my head and now the rhymes will flow. And let the proofs of the *Dial* be crowding on me from the printer, and I am full of faculty how to make the lecture.

The astonishment of life is the absence of any appearances of reconciliation between the theory and practice of life.

Railroads make the country transparent.

Somebody said of me after the lecture at Amory Hall, within hearing of A.W., "The secret of his popularity is, that he has a *damn* for everybody."

It is curious that intellectual men should be most attractive to women. But women are magnetic; intellectual men are unmagnetic: therefore, as soon as they meet, communication is found difficult or impossible.

By acting rashly, we buy the power of talking wisely. People who know how to act are never preachers.

I have always found our American day short. The constitution of a Teutonic scholar with his twelve, thirteen, or fourteen hours a day, is fabulous to me. I become nervous and peaked with a few days editing the *Dial*, and watching the stage-coach to send proofs to printers. If I try to get many hours in a day, I shall not have any.

In America I grieve to miss the strong black blood of the English race: ours is a pale, diluted stream. What a company of brilliant young persons I have seen with so much expectation! the sort is very good, but none is good enough of his sort. Every one an imperfect specimen; respectable, not valid.

The Orientals behave well, but who cannot behave well who has nothing else to do? The poor Yankees who are doing the work are all wrinkled and vexed.

I am always environed by myself: what I am, all things reflect to me. The state of me makes Massachusetts and the United States out there.

Very sad, indeed, to see this half-god driven to the wall,* reproaching men, and hesitating whether he should not reproach the gods. The world was not, on trial, a possible element for him to live in. A lover of law had tried whether law could be kept in this world, and all things answered, No. He had entertained the thought of leaving it, and going where freedom and an element could be found. And if he should be found to-morrow at the roadside, it would be the act of the world. We pleaded guilty to perceiving the inconvenience and the inequality of property, and he said, "I will not be a convict." Very tedious and prosing and egotistical and narrow he is, but a profound insight, a

---

* Alcott, whose community at Fruitlands had proved a failure.

Power, a majestical man, looking easily along the centuries to explore *his contemporaries*, with a painful sense of being an orphan and a hermit here. I feel his statement to be partial and to have fatal omissions, but I think I shall never attempt to set him right any more. It is not for me to answer him: though I feel the limitations and exaggeration of his picture, and the wearisome personalities. His statement proves too much: it is a *reductio ad absurdum.* But I was quite ashamed to have just revised and printed last week the old paper denying the existence of tragedy, when this modern Prometheus was in the heat of his quarrel with the gods.

Alcott has been writing poetry, he says, all winter. I fear there is nothing for me in it. His overpowering personality destroys all poetic faculty.

It is strange that he has not the confidence of one woman. He would be greater if he were good-humoured, but such as he is, he "enlarges the known powers of man," as was said of Michael Angelo.

A man sends to me for money that he may pursue his studies in theology; he wants fifty or sixty dollars, and says he wants it the "last of this week or the fore part of next."

I wish to have rural strength and religion for my children, and I wish city facility and polish. I find with chagrin that I cannot have both.

Writers are so few that there are none; writing is an impossibility, until it is done. A man gives you his paper and hopes there is something in it, but does not know. There is nothing in it: do not open it. When a man makes what he calls an answer to a speculative question, he commonly changes the phrase of the question. But the only conversation we wish to hear is two affirmatives, and again two affirmatives, and so on.

Character brings to whatever it does a great superfluity of strength which plays a gay accompaniment; the air with variations. Hear Daniel Webster argue a jury case. He imports all the experience of the Senate, and the state, and the man of the world into the county court.

If I could freely and manly go to the mountains, or to the prairie, or to the sea, I would not hesitate for inconvenience: but to cart all my pots and kettles, kegs and clothespins, and all that belongs thereunto, over the mountains, seems not worth while. I should not be nearer to sun or star.

This morn [May 8] the air smells of vanilla and oranges.

Our people are slow to learn the wisdom of sending character instead of talent to Congress. Again and again they have sent a man of great acuteness, a fine scholar, a fine forensic orator, and some master of the brawls has crunched him up in his hand like a bit of paper. At last they sent a man with a back, and he defied the whole Southern delegation when they attempted to smother him, and has conquered them. Mr. Adams is a man of great powers, but chiefly he is a sincere man and not a man of the moment and of a single measure. And besides the success or failure of the measure, there remains to him the respect of all men for his earnestness. When Mr. Webster argues the case, there is the success, or the failure, and the admiration of the unerring talent and intellectual nature, but no respect for an affection to a principle. Could Mr. Webster have given himself to the cause of Abolition of Slavery in Congress, he would have been the darling of this continent of all the youth, all the genius, all the virtue in America. Had an angel whispered in his young ear, "Never mind the newspapers. Fling yourself on this principle of freedom. Show the legality of freedom; though they frown and bluster, they are already half-convinced and at last you shall have their votes,"—the tears of the love and joy and pride of the world would have been his.

God, the moral element, must ever be new, an electric spark; then it agitates and deifies us. The instant when it is fixed and made chronic, it is hollowness and cant. It is the difference between poets and preachers.

Ole Bull, a dignifying, civilizing influence. Yet he was there for exhibition, not for music; for the wonders of his execution, not as Saint Cecilia incarnated, who would be there to carry a point, and degrading all her instruments into meekest means. Yet he played as a man who found a violin in his hand, and so was bent to make much of that, but if he had found a chisel or a sword or a spyglass, or a troop of boys, would have made much of them. It was a beautiful spectacle. I have not seen an artist with manners so pleasing. What a sleep as of Egypt on his lips in the midst of his rapturous music!

For economy it is not sufficient that you make now and then a sharp reduction, or that you deny yourself and your family, to meanness, things within their system of expense; but it needs a constant eye to the whole. You yourself must be always present throughout your system. You must hold the reins in your own hands, and not trust to your horse.

The finest women have a feeling we cannot sympathize with in regard to marriage. They cannot spare the exaltation of love and the experiences of marriage from their history.

Henry Thoreau's conversation consisted of a continual coining of the present moment into a sentence and offering it to me. I compared it to a boy, who, from the universal snow lying on the earth, gathers up a little in his hand, rolls it into a ball, and flings it at me.

Henry said that the other world was all his art; that his pencils would draw no other; that his jackknife would cut nothing else. He does not use it as a means. Henry is a good substantial Childe, not encumbered with himself. He has no troublesome memory, no wake, but lives *ex tempore*, and brings to-day a new proposition as radical and revolutionary as that of yesterday, but different. The only man of leisure in the town. He is a good Abbot Samson: and carries counsel in his breast. If I cannot show his performance much more manifest than that of the other grand promisers, at least I can see that, with his practical faculty, he has declined all the kingdoms of this world. Satan has no bribe for him.

Woman. To-day, in our civilization, her position is often pathetic. What is she not expected to do and suffer for some invitation to strawberries and cream?

If two or three persons should come with a high spiritual aim and with great powers, the world would fall into their hands like a ripe peach.

The new races rise all pre-divided into parties, ready-armed and angry to fight for they know not what.

I think the best argument of the conservative is this bad one: that he is convinced that the angry democrat, who wishes him to divide his park and château with him, will, on entering into the possession, instantly become conservative, and hold the property and spend it as selfishly as himself. For a better man, I might dare to renounce my estate; for a worse man, or for as bad a man as I, why should I? All the history of man with unbroken sequence of examples establishes this inference. Yet it is very low and degrading ground to stand upon. We must never reason from history, but plant ourselves on the ideal.

A second visit to the Shakers. Their family worship was a painful spectacle; this shaking of their hands like the paws of dogs, before them as they shuffled in this dunce-dance seemed the last deliration. If there was anything of heart and life in this, it did not appear to me: and as Swedenborg said that the angels never look at the back of the head, so I felt that and saw nothing else. My fellow men could hardly appear to less advantage before me than in this senseless jumping. The music seemed to me dragged down nearly to the same bottom. And when you come to talk with them on their topic, which they are very ready to do, you find such exaggeration of the virtue of celibacy that you might think you had come into a hospital-ward of invalids afflicted with priapism. Yet the women were well dressed and appeared with dignity as honored persons. And I judge the whole society to be cleanly and industrious, but stupid people. And these poor countrymen with their nasty religion fancy themselves *the Church* of the world, and are as arrogant as the poor negroes on the Gambia River.

Novels make us skeptical by giving prominence to wealth and social position, but I think them to be fine occasional stimulants, and, though with some shame, I am brought into an intellectual state. But great is the poverty of their inventions. The perpetual motive and means of accelerating or retarding interest is the dull device of persuading a lover that his mistress is betrothed to another. Novels make us great gentlemen whilst we read them. How generous, how energetic should we be in the crisis described; but unhappy is the wife, or brother, or stranger who interrupts us whilst we read: nothing but frowns and tart replies from the reading gentleman for them. Our novel-reading is a passion for results; we admire parks and the love of beauties, and the homage of parliaments.

I can well hear a stranger converse on mysteries of love and romance of character; can easily become interested in his private love and fortunes; but as soon as I learn that he eats cucumbers, or hates parsnip, values his luncheon, and eats his dinner over again in his talk, I can never thenceforward hear that man talk of sentiment.

The lover transcends the person of the beloved; he is as sensible of her defects and weaknesses as another; he verily loves the tutelar and guiding Dæmon who is at each instant throwing itself into the eyes, the air and carriage of his mistress, and giving to them this unearthly and insurmountable charm.

A rose, a sunbeam, the human face, do not remind us of deacons.

Our mass meetings are a sad spectacle: they show great men put to a bad use, men consenting to be managed by committees, and worse, consenting to manage men. The retribution is instant diminution, bereavement of ideas and of power, of all loveliness and of all growth. It is in vain to bawl "constitution" and "patriotism"; those words repeated once too often have a most ironical hoarseness.

Ah! how different it is to render an account to ourselves of ourselves and to render account to the public of ourselves.

Let us, if we assume the dangerous pretension of being Abolitionists, and make that our calling in the world, let us do it symmetrically. The world asks, Do the Abolitionists eat sugar? Do they wear cotton? Do they smoke tobacco? Are they their own servants? Have they managed to put that dubious institution of servile labor on an agreeable and thoroughly intelligible and transparent foundation? The planter does not want slaves; give him money; give him a machine that will provide him with as much money as the slaves yield, and he will thankfully let them go; he does not love whips, or usurping overseers, or sulky, swarthy giants creeping round his house and barns by night with lucifer matches in their hands and knives in their pockets. No; only he wants his luxury, and he will pay even this price for it.

I understand very well in cities how the Southerner finds sympathy. The heat drives, every summer, the planter to the North. He comes from West and South and Southwest to the Astor and the Tremont Houses. The Boston merchant bargains for his cotton at his counting-house, then calls on him at the hotel, politely sympathizes with all his modes of thinking,—"He never sided with these violent men,"—poor Garrison, poor Phillips are on the coals.

Intense selfishness which we all share. Planter will not hesitate to eat his negro, because he can. We eat him in milder fashion by pelting the negro's friend. We cannot lash him with a whip, because we dare not. We lash him with our tongues. I like the Southerner the best; he deals roundly and does not cant.

I do not wonder at feeble men being strong advocates for slavery. They have no feeling or worthiness which assures them of their own safety. In a new state of things they are by no means sure it would go well with them. They live by certain privileges which the actual order of the community yields them. Take those and you take all. I do not wonder that such would fain raise a mob, for fear is very cruel.

A gentleman may have many innocent propensities, but if he chances to have the habit of slipping arsenic into the soup of whatever person sits next him at table, he must expect some inconvenience. He may call it his "peculiar institution," a mere way of his; he never puts it in his own soup, only in the soup of his neighbor, and even only in some of his neighbors'; for example, he is partial to light hair, and only spices the dish of such as have black hair, and he may persuade his chaplain to find him a text, and be very indignant and patriotic and quarrelsome and moral-religious on the subject, and swear to die in defence of this old and strong habit he has contracted.

Alcott does not do justice to the merits of labor. The whole human race spend their lives in hard work from simple and necessary motives, and feel the approbation of their conscience; and meet with this talker at their gate, who, as far as they see, does not labor himself, and takes up this grating tone of authority and accusation against them. His unpopularity is not at all wonderful. There must be not a few fine words, but very many hard strokes every day, to get what even an ascetic wants.

A loom which turns out huckabuck can never be talked into making damask.

PART V

1845-1848

During 1845 Emerson lectured in New England and New York on Napoleon, the first of what was later to grow into a course of lectures and, finally, into a book entitled *Representative Men*.

War with Mexico was declared in 1846. Thoreau, in protest, refused to pay his poll tax and was briefly jailed, as Alcott had been, for a similar scruple of conscience, three years before.

Emerson was lecturing as usual during the early months of 1847, including a course of six lectures delivered on the island of Nantucket for which he was paid ten dollars each, plus expenses. In October he sailed for England, having arranged that Thoreau should again live in his house during his absence. In England and Scotland, Emerson lectured with great success, and was widely entertained.

In May, 1848, Emerson crossed to France, then in political turmoil, and spent a busy month in Paris. Back in London, he gave more lectures, had a final fling at literary and fashionable society, and returned to America in July.

1845

In January arose the question again in our village Lyceum whether we should accept the offer of the ladies who proposed to contribute to the course a lecture on Slavery by Wendell Phillips.* I pressed the acceptance on the part of the curators of this proffer on two grounds; First, because the Lyceum was poor, and should add to the length and variety of their entertainment by all innocent means, especially when a discourse from one of the best speakers in the Commonwealth was volunteered; Second, because I thought, in the present state of this country, the particular

* Orator, reformer and leading abolitionist.

subject of Slavery had a commanding right to be heard in all places in New England, in season, and sometimes out of season; that, as in Europe the partition of Poland was an outrage so flagrant that all European men must be willing, once in every month or two, to be plagued with hearing over again the horrid story, so this iniquity of slavery in this country was a ghost that would not down at the bidding of Boston merchants, or the best democratic drill-officers, but the people must consent to be plagued with it from time to time until something was done, and we had appeased the negro blood so.

Nature seems a dissipated hussy. She seduces us from all work.

How gladly, after three months sliding on snow, our feet find the ground again!

What right have you scholars and thinkers to pretend to plans of philanthropy, who freeze and dispirit me by that selfish, murderous, hang-dog face?

We do not live an equal life, but one of contrasts and patchwork; now a little joy, then a sorrow, now a sin, then a generous or brave action. We must always be little whilst we have these alternations. Character is regular and homogeneous.

I talked yesterday with the Shaker Elders, Joseph Myrick and Grove Blanchard, and stated my chief objection to their community as a place of education, that there was too much interference. In heaven, a squadron of angels would be a squadron of gods, with profoundest mutual deference; so should men live.

The aim of writers is to tame the Holy Ghost, and produce it as a show to the city.

The Dæmons lurk and are dumb.

Let us, says Prudence, attempt something practicable. Why should we call meetings to vote against the law of gravitation, or organize a society to resist a revolution round the sun?

Henry Thoreau said that the Fourierists had a sense of duty which led them to devote themselves to their second best.

The State is our neighbors; our neighbors are the State. It is a folly to treat the State as if it were some individual, arbitrarily willing thus and so. It is the same company of poor devils we know so well, of William and Edward and John and Henry, doing as they are obliged to do, and trying hard to do conveniently what must and will be done. They do not impose a tax. God and the nature of things imposes the tax, requires that the land shall bear its burden, of road and of social order, and defence; and I confess I lose all respect for this tedious denouncing of the State by idlers who rot in indolence, selfishness, and envy in the chimney corner.

Common sense is the wick of the candle.

Men do blunder into victories. The compromise which prevails every day is the accepting of other people's aims for our own, through these treacherous sympathies, and so this expedient civilization subsists and gets on, which pleases nobody and torments the sincere. Yet it seems of little consequence at last whether we move on other people's tactics or on our own.

Experience is the only teacher, and we get his lesson indifferently in any school. I speak to A's state of mind; I write on a hint of B's learning; I enjoy myself in C's genius and tendency; E comes and says all this is wrong. Be it so, but I have always been thus facile, and here I am with prodigious enjoyments and hopes.

The worst thing I know of poverty is that if a man is dead, they call him *poor fellow*.

God's ways are parabolic projections that do not return into themselves.

Verses of true poets are hickory nuts, so fresh and sound.

The annexation of Texas looks like one of those events which retard or retrograde the civilization of ages. But the World Spirit is a good swimmer, and storms and waves cannot easily drown him. He snaps his finger at laws.

"As we grow old," said Alcott, "the beauty steals inward."

Men of talent create a certain artificial position, a camp in the wilderness somewhere, about which they contrive to keep much noise, firing of guns, and running to and fro of boys and idlers with what uproar they can. They have talents for contention, and they nourish a small difference into a loud quarrel, and persuade the surrounding population that it is the cause of the country and of man. But the world is wide; nobody will go there after to-morrow; the gun can defend nothing but itself; nor itself any longer than the man is by.

No, it is not the part of merit of a man to make his stove with his own hands, or cook and bake his own dinner: another can do it better and cheaper; but it is his essential virtue to carry out into action his own dearest ends, to dare to do what he believes and loves. If he thinks a sonnet the flower and result of the world, let him sacrifice all to the sonnet; if he loves the society of one or of several friends more than life, let him arrange his living and make everything yield to the procuring him that chief good. Now, we spend our money for that which is not bread, for paint and floor-cloths, for newspapers, and male and female servants that yield us the very smallest fraction of direct advantage. The friction of this social machine is grown enormous, and absorbs almost all the power applied.

We are bound hand and foot with our decorums and superstitions. England has achieved respectability at what a cost! America with a valet's eyes admires and copies in vain.

Conservatism has in the present society every advantage. All are on its side. Of those who pretend to ideas, all are really and in practice on the side of the State. They know that, if they should persist in actualizing their theories, it would be all convulsing and plunging. Their talk is the mere brag of liberalism. Yet, yet, they like to feel their wings.

Bonaparte represents the Business Men's Party against the Morgue. But the Morgue is only the Business Men's Party gone to seed. The lesson he teaches is that which vigor always teaches, that there is always room for it. He would not take "No" for an answer. He found impediments that would have stopped anybody else, but he saw what gibbering, quaking ghosts they were, and he put his hand through them: genius always sees room for one man more: he makes room for many.

A feeble man can only see the farms that are fenced and tilled; the houses that are built. At the end of the town, he is at the end of the world. The strong man sees not only the actual but the possible houses and farms. His eye makes estates and villages as fast as the sun breeds clouds.

I receive daily just so much vital energy as suffices to put on my clothes, to take a few turns in my garden and in my study with a book or a pen in my hand. If I attempt anything beyond this, if I so much as stretch out my hand to help my neighbour in his field, the stingy Genius leaves me faint and sprawling; I must pay for this vivacity by a prostration for two or three days following. These are costly experiments to try; I cannot afford two or three days when I count how many days it requires to finish one of my tasks; so I grow circumspect and disobliging beyond the example of all the misers.

What argument, what eloquence can avail against the power of that one word *niggers?* The man of the world annihilates the whole combined force of all the anti-slavery societies of the world by pronouncing it.

Alcott should be made effective by being tapped by a good suction-pump.

The solitude of the body is the populousness of the soul.

It is easy to hide for something,—to hide now, that we may draw the more admiration anon. Easy to sit in the shade, if we have a Plato's *Republic* teeming in the brain, which will presently be born for the joy and illumination of men; easy to withdraw and break somewhat morosely the *bien-séances* of society, visit not, and refuse visits, if we can make good to others and to ourselves a rare promise. But how if you have no security of such a result?—how if the fruit of your brain is abhortive?—if cramp and mildew, if dreams and the sons of dreams, if prose and crotchets and cold trifles, matter unreadable by other men and odious to your own eyes be the issue? How, if you must sit out the day in thoughtful attitude and experiment, and return to the necessities and conversation of the household without the support of any product, and they must believe and you may doubt that this waste cannot be justified. I call you to a confidence which surmounts this painful experience. You are to have a self-support which maintains you not only against all others, but against your own skepticism. Pain, indolence, sterility, endless ennui have also their lesson for you, if you are great.

The Saharas must be crossed as well as the Nile. It is easy to live for others; everybody does. I call on you to live for yourselves, so shall you find in this penury and absence of thought a purer splendor than ever clothed the exhibitions of wit.

You shall not know too much. There is a difference between a judge's and a deputy sheriff's knowledge of the world, and again between that of the last and a burglar's.

Put a woman into a small house, and after five years she comes out large and healthy, and her children are so. Put her into a large house, and after the same time she shall be haggard, sickly, with a sharp voice, and a wrinkled, carefull countenance, and her children suffer with her.

A whole volume of sermons might be made out of the chips of one sonnet.

Our virtue runs in a narrow rill: we have never a freshet. We ought to be subject to enthusiasms. One would like to see Boston and Massachusetts agitated like a wave with some generosity, mad for learning, for music, for philosophy, for association, for freedom, for art; but now it goes like a pedlar with its hand ever on its pocket, cautious, calculating.

How hard to find a man! It would take, as Taylor said, the lamp of Diogenes added to the splendor of the noonday sun. Otis talked too much. Webster has no *morale*. Choate wants weight. Alcott is unlimited, and unballasted. Bound, bound, let there be bound! But let there be not too strict bound. Alcott is a pail of which the bottom is taken out, and the Whig a pail from which you cannot get off the cover.

Among our social advantages what a signal convenience is fame! Do we read all authors, to grope our way to the best? No; but the world selects for us the best, and we select from the best, our best.

There is not the slightest probability that the college will foster an eminent talent in any youth. If he refuse prayers and recitations, they will torment and traduce and expel him, though he were Newton or Dante.

If an American should wake up some morning and discover that his existence was unnecessary, he would think himself excessively ill-used, and would declare himself instantly against the government of the Universe.

By atoms, by trifles, by sots, Heaven operates. The needles are nothing, the magnetism is all.

It was a pleasure, yesterday, to hear Father Taylor preach all day in our country church. He is mighty Nature's child. He rolls the world into a ball and tosses it from hand to hand. He says touching things, plain things, grand things, cogent things, which all men must perforce hear. He is incapable of thought, he cannot analyse or discriminate, he is a singing, dancing, drunkard of his wit—only he is sure of the sentiment. That is his mother's milk, that he feels in his bones, heaves in his lungs, throbs in his heart, walks in his feet, and gladly he yields himself to the sweet magnetism, and sheds it abroad on the people, rejoicing in his power. His whole genius is in minstrelsy; he calls it religion, Methodism, Christianity, and other names,—it is minstrelsy, he is a minstrel; all the rest is costume. For himself, it is easy to see that, though apparently of a moderate temperament, he would like the old cocks of the bar-room a thousand times better than their temperate monitors.

Men go through the world each musing on a great fable, dramatically pictured and rehearsed before him. If you speak to the man, he turns his eyes from his own scene, and slower or faster endeavors to comprehend what you say. When you have done speaking, he returns to his private music. Men generally attempt early in life to make their brothers first, afterwards their wives, acquainted with what is going forward in their private theatre, but they soon desist from the attempt, or finding that they also have some farce, or perhaps some ear and heart-rending tragedy for-

ward on their secret boards, on which they are intent, all
parties acquiesce at last in a private box with the whole play
performed before himself *solus*.

A cat falls on its feet; shall not a man? You think he has
character; have you kicked him? Talleyrand would not
change countenance; Edward Taylor, Henry Thoreau,
would put the assailant out of countenance.

The secret God will not impart himself to us for tea-table
talk; he frowns out moths and puppets, passes by us and
seeks out a solitary and religious heart.

The rogue or the statesman is not made to feel his insignificance among either divines or literary men; for, at a glance,
he sees that it is rogue again under the cassock, or with the
manuscripts, and they greet each other.

I am shamed on reflecting on the little new skill the years
bring me, at the power trifles have over me, at the importance of my dinner, and my dress, and my house, more than
at the slenderness of my acquisitions.

For we do acquire some patience, some temper, some
power of referring the particular to the general. We acquire
perspective so as to rank our experiences and know what
is eminent.

I was in the courthouse a little while to see the sad game.
But, as often happens, the judge and jury, the government
and the counsel for the prisoner, were on trial as much as
he.

Three or four stubborn necessary words are the pith and
fate of the business; all the rest is expatiating and qualify-

ing: three or four real choices, acts of will of somebody, the rest is circumstance, satellite, and flourish.

There was Webster, the great cannon loaded to the lips: he told Cheney that if he should close by addressing the jury, he should blow the roof off. As it was, he did nothing but pound. Choate put in the nail and drove it; Webster came after and pounded. The natural grandeur of his face and manners always satisfies; easily great; there is no strut in his voice or behavior, as in the others. Yet he is all wasted; he seems like a great actor who is not supported on the boards; and Webster, like the actor, ought to go to London. Ah! if God had given to this Demosthenes a heart to lead New England, what a life and death and glory for him. Now he is a fine symbol and mantel ornament— costly enough for those who must keep it: for the great head aches, and the great trunk must be curiously fed and comforted.

The apparatus of the Law is large and cumbrous and when one sees to how short an issue it leads it seems as if a judge would be as safe. All is for a vent to these two or three decisive phrases that come leaping out, no man knows when, at first or at last in the course of the trial. We go and sit out the tedious hearing for these moments.

We believe that if the angels should descend, we should associate with them easily, and never shame them by a breach of celestial propriety.

In the convention yesterday it was easy to see the drunkenness of eloquence. As I sat and listened, I seemed to be attending at a medical experiment. I have a bad time of it on these occasions, for I feel responsible for every one of the speakers, and shudder with cold at the thinness of the morning audience, and with fear lest all will fail at every bad speech. Mere ability and mellowness is then inestimable, Stephen C. Phillips was a great comfort to me, for he is a good house warmer, with his obvious honesty and good meaning, and his hurra-and-universal-scream sort of eloquence, which inundates the assembly with a flood of animal spirits, and makes all safe and secure, so that any and every sort of good speaking becomes at once practicable. His animal eloquence is as good as a stove in a cold house.

Genius consists in health, in plenipotence of that "top of condition" which allows of not only exercise but frolic of faculty. To coax and woo the strong Instinct to bestir itself and work its miracle is the end of all wise endeavor.

Gibbon built a pyramid and then enamelled it.

The eloquent man is he who is no beautiful speaker, but who is inwardly and desperately drunk with a certain belief.

In the water party, the skipper of the boat was the only interesting person; the rest made puns.

The Universe is like an infinite series of planes, each of which is a false bottom, and when we think our feet are planted now at last on the Adamant, the slide is drawn out from under us.

The scholar blunders along on his own path for a time, assured by the surprise and joy of those to whom he first communicates his results; then new solitudes, new marches; but after a time, on looking up he finds the sympathy gone or changed, he fancies himself accused by all the bystanders;

the faces of his friends are shaded by grief; and yet no tongue ever speaks of the cause. There is some indictment out against him, on which he is arraigned in many courts, and he cannot learn the charge. A prodigious power we have of begetting false expectations. These are the mistakes of others' subjectiveness. The true scholar will not heed them. Jump into another bush, and scratch your eyes in again. He passes on to acquit himself of their charges by developments as surprising as was his first word; by indirections and wonderful *alibis* which dissipate the whole crimination.

In this continent,—asylum of all nations,—the energy of Irish, Germans, Swedes, Poles, and Cossacks, and all the European tribes,—of the Africans, and of the Polynesians, —will construct a new race, a new religion, a new state, a new literature, which will be as vigorous as the new Europe which came out of the smelting-pot of the Dark Ages.

Every genius is defended from approval by great quantities of unavailableness, good only for himself. What property! says the hungry mind, as it sees it afar, and swims toward it as a fish to its food.

Jones Very is like the rain plentiful. He does not love individuals: he is annoyed by edge. I like sharp slats. Strength is wonderful.

The flame of the funeral pile is cool to the widow.

The absolutist is good and blessed, though he dies without sight of that paradise he journeys after; and he can forgive the earthworms who remain immersed in matter and know not the felicities he seeks. But not so well can he dispose of the middle man who receives and assents to his theories and yet, by habit and talent formed to live in the existing order, builds and prospers among the worldly men, extending his affection and countenance all the time to the absolutists. Ah, thou evil, two-faced half-and-half! how can I forgive thee? Evil, evil hast thou done. Thou it is that confoundest all distinctions. If thou didst not receive the truth at all, thou couldst do the cause of virtue no harm. But now the men of selfishness say to the absolutist, Behold this man, he has all thy truth, yet lo! he is with us and ours,—Ah, thou damnable Half-and-Half! choose, I pray you, between God and the Whig Party, and do not longer strew sugar on this bottled spider.

Yes; but Confucius. Confucius, glory of the nations, Confucius, sage of the Absolute East, was a middle man. He is the Washington of philosophy.

The good book grows whether the writer is awake or asleep.

Far the best part of every mind is not that which he knows, but that which hovers in gleams, suggestions, tantalizing, unpossessed, before him. His firm recorded knowledge soon loses all interest for him. But this dancing chorus of thoughts and hopes is the quarry of his future.

Shakspeare's fault that the world appears so empty. He has educated you with his painted world, and this real one seems a huckster's shop.

1846

A or B refuses the tax, or some tax, with solemnity, but eats and drinks and wears and perspires taxation all day. Let them not hew down the state with axe and gunpowder, but supersede it by irresistible genius; huddle it aside as ridiculous and obsolete by their quantity of being. Eloquence needs no constable.

The fault of Alcott's community is that it has only room for one.

If we cannot have a good rider, at least let us have a good horse: now, 't is a haggard rider of a haggard horse.

Give us the rare merits of impassivity, of marble texture, against which the mob of souls dashing is broken like crockery falling on stone: the endurance which can afford to fail in the popular sense, because it never fails in its own; it knows what it wants and advances to-day, and to-morrow, and every day, to that which belongs to it.

How much arrangement and combination and drudgery to bring about a pleasant hour, to hear an eloquent argument, or a fine poetic reading, or a little superior conversation; what rattle and jingle; how many miles must be ridden, how many woods and meadows, alder-borders and stone walls must be tediously passed!

I see not how a man can walk in a straight line, who has ever seen a looking-glass. He acts, and instantly his act is reflected to him by the opinion of men. He cannot keep his eyes off of these dancing images; and that is the death of glory, the death of duty in him.

I cannot hope to make any thorough lights into the caverns of the human consciousness. That were worth the ambition of angels! No! but only to make special, provincial, local lights? Yes; but we obey the impulse to affirm and affirm, and neither you nor I know the value of what we say.

Oh yes, he may escape from shackles and dungeons, but how shall he get away from his temperament?—how from his hereditary sins and infusions?—how from the yellow humors through which he must ever see the blue sky and the sun and stars? Sixty centuries have squatted and stitched and hemmed to shape and finish for him that strait jacket which he must wear.

What a discovery I made one day, that the more I spent the more I grew, that it was as easy to occupy a large place and do much work as an obscure place to do little; and that in the winter in which I communicated all my results to classes, I was full of new thoughts.

I like man, but not men. Instincts, tendencies,—they do no wrong: they are beautiful, and may be confided in and obeyed. Though they slay us, let us trust them. Why should eggs and tadpoles talk? All is mere sketch, symptomatic, possible, or probable, for us,—we dwellers in tents, we outlines in chalk, we jokes and buffooneries, why should we be talking? Let us have the grace to be abstemious. The etiquette of society should guard and consecrate a poet; he should not be visited, nor be shown at dinner-tables: too costly to be seen except on high holidays. He should be relieved of visits and trivial correspondence. His time is the time of his nation.

I do not wish to be amused, and the amusing persons are bores to me.

Is not the mystic like a rogue who comes to an honest man and says, "By your accumulated character you could deal an immense stroke at counterfeiting"?

The muse demands real sacrifices. You cannot be poet and a *paterfamilias* and a militia captain.

What pity that the mother and child cannot change states. The child is always awake, and the mother is always asleep.

Bring any club or company of intelligent men together again, after ten years, and if the presence of some penetrating and calming genius could dispose them all to recollection and frankness, what a confession of insanities would come up.

Anything that Goethe said, another might attain to say; but the profusion of sayings, every one of which is good and striking,—no man. Yet the "Autobiography" looks to-day like a storm of gold-headed canes.

Men quarrel with your rhetoric. Society chokes with a trope, like a child with the croup. They much prefer Mr. Prose, and Mr. Hoarse-as-Crows, to the dangerous conversation of Gabriel and the Archangel Michael, perverting all rules, and bounding continually from earth to heaven.

The boys kick and stamp for a noise when Abby Kelley and Stephen Foster* speak, not for any good reason, but because it is understood that people are to yell and throw eggs when the Fosters speak. 'T is a regular holiday for the boys through the land when these people go by; and if they do not make the noise, who will? You cannot allow too much for the levity of men. Inconceivable is the levity of men: everybody overrates their character. They have no

* Abolitionist orators.

meaning; they have heels, they wish to feel them, and it is the charm of noise *versus* the charm of eloquence.

When Alcott wrote from England that he was bringing home Wright and Lane, I wrote him a letter, which I required him to show them, saying, that they might safely trust his theories, but that they should put no trust whatever in his statement of facts. When they all arrived here,— he and his victims,—I asked them if he showed them that letter; they answered that he did: so I was clear.

The teamster, the farmer, are jocund and hearty, and stand on their legs: but the women are demure and subdued as Shaker women, and, if you see them out of doors, look, as Henry Thoreau said, "as if they were going for the Doctor." Has our Christianity saddled and bridled us?

The writer must live and die by his writing. Good for that, and good for nothing else.

Hawthorne invites his readers too much into his study, opens the process before them. As if the confectioner should say to his customers, "Now, let us make the cake."

The animals crawl on or fly over the rind of the planet, and the fishes and whales swim only at the surface of the water. You might skim the whole mammalia with a kitchen dipper. In the deep sea, and under the crust, all is still, nothing stirs. Human life and thought is not less external. Nobody is profoundly good or bad. Were they profound, they would satisfy.

New England is subservient. The President proclaims war, and those Senators who dissent are not those who know better, but those who can afford to, as Benton and Calhoun.

Democracy becomes a government of bullies tempered by editors. The editors standing in the privilege of being last devoured.

In the City of Makebelieve is a great ostentation bolstered up on a great many small ostentations. I think we escape something by living in the villages. In Concord here there is some milk of life, we are not so raving distracted with wind and dyspepsia. The mania takes a milder form. People go a-fishing, and know the taste of their meat. They cut their own whippletree in the woodlot, they know something practically of the sun and the east wind, of the underpinning and the roofing of the house, of the pan and the mixture of the soils.

In the City of Makebelieve all the marble edifices were veneered and all the columns were drums.

Boston or Brattle Street Christianity is the best Diagonal line that can be drawn between Jesus Christ and Abbott Lawrence.

Now I think of committees to read books, and on oath report of them. A scholar is crafty, and hides his reading; he is full of ends and reservations. I wish such report as a brother gives to a brother, or a husband to a wife. The committees must be as naked and liberal as gods in their agency.

Who cannot be famous, said Osman, since I am?

Things collect very fast of themselves, the difference between house and house is the wise omissions.

The Southerner is cool and insolent. "We drive you to the wall, and will again." Yes, gentlemen, but do you know why Massachusetts and New York are so tame?—it is because we own you, and are very tender of our mortgages which cover all your property.

A man is caught up and takes a breath or two of the Eternal, but instantly descends, and puts his eternity to commercial uses. A pretty kettle of fish we have here, men of this vast ambition, who wish an ethics commensurate with Nature, who sit expectant to be challenged to great performances, are left without any distinct aim. The only compliment society knows how to pay a man of genius is to wait on him and to ask him to deliver a Temperance Address.

The snails believe the geniuses are constitutionally skeptical. I lament that wit is a light mocker, that knowledge is the knowing that we cannot know, that genius is criticism. I lament to have life cheap; that a great understanding should play with the world as he tosses his walking-stick and catches it again. I wish the years and months to be long, the days centuries, loaded, fragrant: now we reckon them basely, as bank days, by some debt that we are to pay or that is to be paid us.

Society is a curiosity-shop full of odd excellences, a Brahmin, a Fakeer, a giraffe, an alligator, Colonel Bowie, Alvah Crocker, Bronson Alcott, Henry Thoreau; a world that cannot keep step, admirable melodies, but no chorus, for there is no accord.

The Yankee means to make moonlight work, if he can; and he himself, after he has spent all the business hours in Wall

Street, takes his dinner at a French boarding-house, that his soup and cutlet may not be quite unprofitable, but he shall learn the language between the mouthfuls.

Do they stand immovable there,—the sots,—and laugh at your so-called poetry? They may well laugh; it does not touch them yet. Try a deeper strain. There is no make-believe about these fellows; they are good tests for your skill; therefore, a louder yet, and yet a louder strain. There is not one of them but will spin fast enough when the music reaches him; but he is very deaf, try a sharper string. Angels in satinette and calico,—angels in hunting-knives and rifles,—swearing angels, roarers with liquor;—O poet, you have much to learn.

These—rabble—at Washington are really better than the snivelling opposition. They have a sort of genius of a bold and manly cast, though Satanic. They see, against the unanimous expression of the people, how much a little well-directed effrontery can achieve, how much crime the people will bear, and they proceed from step to step. Mr. Webster told them how much the war* cost, that was his protest, but voted the war, and sends his son to it. They calculated rightly on Mr. Webster. My friend Mr. Thoreau has gone to jail rather than pay his tax. On him they could not calculate. The Abolitionists denounce the war and give much time to it, but they pay the tax.

It seems now settled that the world is no longer a subject for reform: it is too old for that, and is to have custard and calves' jelly. We are no longer to apply drastic or alterative pills, nor attempt remedies at all, but if we have any new

* War with Mexico had just been declared.

game or some fireworks or ice cream,—if Jenny Lind come
hither, or Fanny Elssler return, it is all the case admits.

The State is a poor, good beast who means the best: it
means friendly. A poor cow who does well by you,—do not
grudge it its hay. It cannot eat bread, as you can; let it
have without grudge a little grass for its four stomachs. It
will not stint to yield you milk from its teat. You, who are a
man walking cleanly on two feet, will not pick a quarrel
with a poor cow. Take this handful of clover and welcome.
But if you go to hook me when I walk in the fields, then,
poor cow, I will cut your throat.

Don't run amuck against the world. Have a good case to
try the question on. It is the part of a fanatic to fight out a
revolution on the shape of a hat, or surplice, on paedo-
baptism, or altar rail, or fish on Friday. As long as the
state means you well, do not refuse your pistareen. You
have a tottering cause; ninety parts of the pistareen it
will spend for what you think also good: ten parts for mischief. You cannot fight heartily for a fraction. But wait
until you have a good difference to join issue upon.

Alcott thought he could find as good a ground for quarrel in the state tax as Socrates did in the edict of the
Judges. Then I say, Be consistent, and never more put an
apple or a kernel of corn into your mouth. Would you feed
the devil? Say boldly, "There is a sword sharp enough to
cut sheer between flesh and spirit, and I will use it, and
not any longer belong to this double-faced, equivocating,
mixed, Jesuitical universe."

The Abolitionists should resist, because they are literal-
ists; they know exactly what they object to, and there is a
government possible which will content them. Remove a
few specified grievances, and this present commonwealth
will suit them. They are the new Puritans, and as easily

satisfied. But you, nothing will content. No government short of a monarchy, consisting of one king and one subject, will appease you. Your objection, then, to the State of Massachusetts is deceptive. Your true quarrel is with the state of Man.

In the particular, it is worth considering that refusing payment of the state tax does not reach the evil so nearly as many other methods within your reach. The state tax does not pay the Mexican War. Your coat, your sugar, your Latin and French and German book, your watch does. Yet these you do not stick at buying.

But really a scholar has too humble an opinion of the population, of their possibilities, of their future, to be entitled to go to war with them, as with equals.

This prison is one step to suicide.

He knows that nothing they can do will ever please him. Why should he poorly pound on some one string of discord, when all is jangle?

1847

The chief good of life seems—this morning—to be born with a cheerful, happy temper, and well adjusted to the tone of the human race: for such a man feels himself in the harmony of things, and conscious of an infinite strength. He need not do anything. But if he is not well mixed and averaged, then he needs to achieve something, build a railroad, make a fortune, write an Iliad, as a compensation to himself for his abnormal position.

Here am I with so much all ready to be revealed to me, as to others, if only I could be set aglow. I have wished for a professorship. Much as I hate the church, I have wished the pulpit that I might have the stimulus of a stated task.

N. P. Rogers spoke more truly than he knew, perchance, when he recommended an Abolition Campaign to me. I doubt not, a course of mobs would do me much good. A snowflake will go through a pine board, if projected with force enough. I have almost come to depend on conversation for my most prolific hours. I who converse with so few and those of no adventure, connexion, or wide information.

I think I have material enough to serve my countrymen with thoughts and music, if only it was not scraps. But men do not want handfulls of gold-dust, but ingots.

The name of Washington City in the newspapers is every day of blacker shade. All the news from that quarter being of a sadder type, more malignant. It seems to be settled that no act of honour or benevolence or justice is to be expected from the American government, but only this, that they will be as wicked as they dare. No man now can have any sort of success in politics without a streak of infamy crossing his name.

Things have another order in these men's eyes. Heavy is hollow, and good is evil. A Western man in Congress the other day spoke of the opponents of the Texan and Mexican plunder as "every light character in the House," and our good friend in State Street speaks of "the solid portion of the community," meaning, of course, the sharpers. I feel, meantime, that those who succeed in life, in civilized society, are beasts of prey.

We live in Lilliput. Men are unfit to live, from their obvious inequality to their own necessities.

The question recurs whether we should descend into the ring. My own very small experience instructs me that the people are to be taken in very small doses. Vestry meetings and primary assemblies do not edify me.

Every man has his own courage, and is betrayed because he seeks in himself the courage of other persons.

My stories did not make them laugh, my facts did not quite fit the case, my arguments did not hit the white. Is it so? Then warm yourself, old fellow, with hot mince-pie and half a pint of port wine, and they will fit like a glove, and hit like a bullet.

Look at literary New England; one would think it was a national fast.

What a tool is money in a skilful hand. What a nuisance in a fool's.

Nation of Nantucket makes its own war and peace. Place of winds, bleak, shelterless, and, when it blows, a large part of the island is suspended in the air and comes into your face and eyes as if it was glad to see you.

Aunt Mary went out to ride horseback in her shroud.

Henry Truman Safford (born at Royalston, Vermont, January 6, 1836) in 1846 was examined for three hours by Rev. H. W. Adams, of Concord, New Hampshire, and Rev. C. N. Smith, of Randolph, Vermont, and at last was bidden, "Multiply in your head 365,365,365,365,365,365, by 365,365,-365,365,365,365,"—eighteen figures by eighteen. "He flew around the room like a top, pulled his pantaloons over the top of his boots, bit his hand, rolled his eyes in their sockets, sometimes smiling and talking, and then seeming to be

in agony, until in not more than one minute, he said, 133,-
491,850,208,566,925,016,658,299,941,583,225. The boy's father, Rev. C. N. Smith, and myself had each a pencil and
slate to take down the answer, and he gave it us in periods
of three figures each as fast as it was possible for us to
write them. And what was still more wonderful he began to
multiply at the left hand and to bring out the answer
from left to right giving first 133, 491, etc. Here, confounded
above measure, I gave up the examination. The boy looked
pale and said he was tired. He said it was the largest sum
he ever did."

The days come and go like muffled and veiled figures sent
from a distant friendly party, but they say nothing, and if
we do not use the gifts they bring, they carry them as silently away.

When I see my friend after a long time, my first question
is, Has anything become clear to you?

Unchastity with women is an acute disease, not a habit.

Life is a puzzle and a whirl, and the cards beat the best
players.

Criticism should not be querulous and wasting, all knife
and root-puller, but guiding, instructive, inspiring, a south
wind, not an east wind.

An Orientalist, who was a Hercules among the bugs and
curculios, recommended to me a Persian experiment of setting a lamp under the plum tree in a whitewashed tub with
a little water in it by night. But the curculio showed no

taste for so elegant a death. A few flies and harmless beetles perished and one genuine Yankee spider instantly wove his threads across the tub thinking that there was likely to be a crowd and he might as well set up his booth and win something for himself.

Railroads are to civilization what mathematics were to the mind. Their immense promise made the whole world nervous with hope and fear, and they leave society as they found it. The man gets out of the railroad car at the end of five hundred miles in every respect the same as he got in.

Thoreau sometimes appears only as a *gendarme,* good to knock down a cockney with, but without that power to cheer and establish which makes the value of a friend.

Bring the best wits together and they are so impatient of each other, so worldly, or so babyish, there is so much more than their wit, so many follies and gluttonies and partialities, so much age and sleep and care, that you have no academy.

But of what use to bring the men together, when they will torment and tyrannize over each other, and play the merchant and the statesman? Conversation in society is always on a platform so low as to exclude the Saint and the Poet after they have made a few trials.

Who does not remember the south wind days when he was a boy, when his own hand had a strawberry scent?

Of Alcott it is plain to see that he never loses sight of the order of things and thoughts before him. The thought he would record is something, but the place, the page, the book in which it is to be written are something also, not less than

the proposition. So that usually in the attention to the mar-
shalling, the thing marshalled dwindles and disappears. One
thing more. I used to tell him that he had no senses. And
it is true that they are with him merely vehicular, and do
not constitute a pleasure and a temptation of themselves.
We had a good proof of it this morning. He wanted to know
"Why the boys waded in the water after pond lilies?" Why,
because they will sell in town for a cent apiece and every
man and child likes to carry one to church for a cologne
bottle. "What!" said he, "have they a perfume? I did not
know it."

A public occasion, an expecting audience, or the pride of
printing a book, flagellate the drowsy muse.

The New Englander is attentive to trifles, values himself
on a sort of omniscience, knows when the cars start at every
depot; feels every waterpipe and furnace-flue in his house;
knows where the rafters are in the wall,—how can he be
absorbed in his thought? how can he be contemplative?
He must have a servant, he must call Tom to ask prices
and hours; what day of the month it is, and when the mail
closes? who is governor of the state, and where is the police office? But Tom does not come at a call. Nothing is so
rare in New England as Tom. Bad for the New Englander.
His skin is ocular. He is afflicted with the second thought.
Not for an instant can he be great and abandoned to a sentiment. Let the countrymen beware of cities. A city is the
paradise of trifles; and the current sets so strong that way
that the city seems a hotel and a shop, a gigantic clothes-
mart, toy-shop; and if one, perchance, meet in the street a
man of probity and wisdom, an accomplished and domestic
soul, we are taken by surprise, and he drives the owls and
bats, that had infested us, home to their holes again.

Life consists in what a man is thinking of all day.

If a man read a book because it interests him, and read in all directions for the same reason, his reading is pure, and interests me; but if he read with ulterior objects, if he reads that he may write, we do not impute it to him for righteousness. In the first case he is like one who takes up only so much land as he uses; in the second, he buys land to *speculate* with.

I have that faith in the necessity of all gifts that to implore writers to be a little more of this or that were like advising gunpowder to explode gently, or snow to temper its whiteness, or oak trees to be less profuse in leaves and acorns, or poplars to try the vinous habit and creep on walls. They do as they can, and they must instruct you equally by their failure as by their talent, that is, they must teach you that the world is farmed out to many contractors, and each arranges all things on his petty task, sacrifices all for that.

Polk and Webster must have power, and must truckle for it. With patrician airs, they can never be gentlemen. We understand very well what they mean when they say "patriotism," and unless we are very tired we do not laugh.

Thought is like the weather, or birth, or death: we must take it as it comes.

You may settle it in your hearts that when you get a great man, he will be hard to keep step with. Spoons and skimmers may well enough lie together; but vases and statues must have each its own pedestal.

In our best moments society seems not to claim equality, but requires to be treated like a child, to whom we administer camomile and magnesia, on our own judgment, without consultation. But when our own light flickers in the socket, suddenly the pupil seems riper, and more forward, and even assumes the mien of a patron whom we must court.

At Sea, October 14

The good ship darts through the water all night like a fish, quivering with speed, sliding through spaces, sliding from horizon to horizon.

Finding that I should not be wanted for a week in the lecture rooms, I came down to London, on Monday, and at ten at night the door was opened to me by Jane Carlyle, and the man himself was behind her with a lamp in the hall. They were very little changed from their old selves of fourteen years ago (in August) when I left them at Craigenputtock. "Well," said Carlyle, "here we are, shovelled together again!" The floodgates of his talk are quickly opened, and the river is a plentiful stream. We had a wide talk that night until nearly one o'clock, and at breakfast next morning again. At noon or later we walked forth to Hyde Park, and the palaces, about two miles from here, to the National Gallery, and to the Strand, Carlyle melting all Westminster and London into his talk and laughter, as he goes.

Here in his house, we breakfast about nine, and Carlyle is very prone, his wife says, to sleep till ten or eleven, if he has no company. An immense talker, and, altogether, as extraordinary in that as in his writing; I think even more so. You will never discover his real vigor and range, or how much more he might do than he has ever done, without seeing him. My few hours' discourse with him, long ago, in Scotland, gave me not enough knowledge of him; and I have now, at last, been taken by surprise by him.

He is not mainly a scholar, like the most of my acquaintances, but a very practical Scotchman, such as you would find in any saddler's or iron-dealers shop, and then only accidentally and by a surprising addition the admirable scholar and writer he is. He says over and over, for months, for years, the same thing. His sneers and scoffs are thrown in every direction. He breaks every sentence with a scoffing laugh—"windbag," "monkey," "donkey," "bladder," and let him describe whom he will, it is always "poor fellow." I said, "What a fine fellow are you to bespatter the whole world with this oil of vitriol!" "No man," he replied, "speaks truth to me." I said, "See what a crowd of friends listen to and admire you." He said, "Yes, they come to hear me, and they read what I write, but not one of them has the smallest intention of doing these things."

My little Edie cost me many a penny.*

Woman is cheap and vile in England.

The one rule to give to the traveller in England is, Do not sneak about diffidently, but make up your mind and carry your points.

The only girth or belt that can enable one to face these Patagonians of beef and beer is an absorbing work of your own. Otherwise, with their excessive life they hustle you out of their world.

---

* That is, when he saw some little begging girl, no bigger than his daughter, in the streets.

1848

At Edinburgh, I dined at Mrs. Crowe's with De Quincey, David Scott, and Dr. Brown. De Quincey is a small old man of seventy years, with a very handsome face,—a face marked by great refinement,—a very gentle old man, speaking with the utmost deliberation and softness, and so refined in speech and manners as to make quite indifferent his extremely plain and poor dress. For the old man, summoned by message on Saturday by Mrs. Crowe to this dinner, had walked on this rainy, muddy Sunday ten miles from his house at Lasswade and was not yet dry, and though Mrs. Crowe's hospitality is comprehensive and minute, yet she had no pantaloons in her house. He was so simply drest, that ten miles could not spoil him. It seemed, too, that he had lately *walked home*, at night, in the rain, from one of Mrs. Crowe's dinners. "But why did you not ride?" said Mrs. C.; "you were in time for the coach." Because, he could not find money to ride; he had met two street girls; one of them took his eight shillings out of his waistcoat pocket, and the other his umbrella. He told this sad story with the utmost simplicity, as if he had been a child of seven, instead of seventy. Here De Quincey is serene and happy, among just these friends with whom I found him; for he has suffered in all ways and lived the life of a wretch, for many years; and Samuel Brown, Mrs. C., and one or two more, have saved him from himself, and from the bailiff, and he is now cleaned, clothed, and in his right mind.

Dined at Lord Ashburton's, at Lady Harriet Baring's, attended Lady Palmerston's *soirée;* saw fine people at Lady Morgan's and at Lady Molesworth's, Lord Lovelace's, and other houses. But a very little is enough for me, and I find that all the old deoxygenation and asphyxia that have in town or in village existed for me in that word "a party," exist unchanged in London palaces. Of course the fault is wholly mine, but I shall at least know how to save a great deal of time and temper henceforward.

Grievous amount of dross about men of wit, they are so heavy, so dull, so oppressive with their bad jokes, and monstrous conceit, and stupefying individualism. Avoid the great man as one who is privileged to be an unprofitable companion. As a class the merchants are out of all comparison manlier and more sensible, and even the farmers are more real and agreeable. But this is babyish; I hate that a scholar should be an old goody.

If I stay here long, I shall lose all my patriotism and think that England has absorbed all excellences. I look at the immense wealth and the solid power concentrated, and am quite faint: then I look in the street at the little girls running barefoot through the rain, with broom in hand, to beg a halfpenny of the passenger at the crossing.

Only that mind draws me which I cannot read.

The objection, the loud denial, not less proves the reality and conquests of an idea than the friends and advocates it finds. Thus communism now is eagerly attacked, and all its weak points acutely pointed out by British writers and talkers; which is all so much homage to the Idea, whose first inadequate expressions interest them so deeply, and with which they feel their fate to be mingled.

One sees readily, in the embittered acuteness of the Oxonian reviewer in snuffing heresy from far, how hapless an unbeliever he is, and why he inveighs so angrily against that which he vainly resists in his own bosom.

People here expect a revolution. There will be no revolution, none that deserves to be called so. There may be a scramble for money. But as all the people we see want the things we now have, and not better things, it is very certain that they will, under whatever change of forms, keep the old system. When I see changed men, I shall look for a changed world. Whoever is skilful in heaping money now will be skilful in heaping money again.

Dined with John Forster, Esq., at Lincoln's Inn Fields, and found Carlyle and Dickens, and young Pringle. Forster, who has an obstreperous cordiality, received Carlyle with loud salutation, "My Prophet!" Forster called Carlyle's passion, "musket-worship." There were only gentlemen present and the conversation turned on the shameful lewdness of the London streets at night. "I hear it," he said, "I hear whoredom in the House of Commons. Disraeli betrays whoredom, and the whole House of Commons universal incontinence, in every word they say." I said that when I came to Liverpool, I inquired whether the prostitution was always as gross in that city as it then appeared, for to me it seemed to betoken a fatal rottenness in the state, and I saw not how any boy could grow up safe. But I had been told it was not worse nor better for years. Carlyle and Dickens replied that chastity in the male sex was as good as gone in our times; and in England was so rare that they could name all the exceptions. Carlyle evidently believed that the same things were true in America. He had heard this and that of New York, etc. I assured them that it was not so with us; that, for the most part, young men of good standing and good education, with us, go virgins to their nuptial bed, as truly as their brides. Dickens replied that incontinence is so much the rule in England that if his own son were particularly chaste, he should be alarmed on his account, as if he could not be in good health. "Leigh Hunt," he said, "thought it indifferent."

Carlyle is no idealist in opinions, but a protectionist in political economy, aristocrat in politics, epicure in diet, goes for murder, money, punishment by death, slavery, and all the pretty abominations, tempering them with epigrams.

I fancy, too, that he does not care to see anybody whom he cannot eat, and reproduce tomorrow, in his pamphlet or pillory. Alcott was meat that he could not eat, and Margaret Fuller likewise, and he rejected them, at once.

And 't is curious, the magnificence of his genius and the poverty of his aims. He draws his weapons from the skies, to fight for some wretched English property, or monopoly, or prejudice.

I heard Alboni sing last night in *Cenerentola,* and the *Times* today calls it the best of her triumphs. I found only the noble burst of voice beautiful, and the trills and gurgling and other feats not only not interesting, but, as in all other performers, painful; mere surgical, or rather, functional acts.

I saw Tennyson, first, at the house of Coventry Patmore, where we dined together. I was contented with him at once. He is tall, scholastic-looking, no dandy, but a great deal of plain strength about him, and though cultivated, quite unaffected; quiet, sluggish sense and strength, refined, as all English are, and good-humoured. There is in him an air of general superiority, that is very satisfactory. He has the air of one who is accustomed to be petted and indulged

by those he lives with. Take away Hawthorne's bashful-
ness, and let him talk easily and fast, and you would have a
pretty good Tennyson.

Carlyle describes him as staying in London through a
course of eight o'clock dinners every night for months until he is thoroughly fevered. Then, notice is given to one of
his friends, as lately to Aubrey de Vere, who has a fine estate in Ireland, to come and carry him off bodily. Tennyson
had capitulated, on three conditions: first, that he should
not hear anything about Irish distress; second, that he
should not come downstairs for breakfast; third, that he
might smoke in the house. So poor Tennyson, who had
been in the worst way, but had not force enough to choose
where to go, and so sat still, was now disposed of.

Tennyson was in plain black suit and wears glasses. He
has other brothers, and, I remember, Carlyle told me with
glee some story of one of them, who looked like Alfred, and
whom some friend, coming in, found lying on the sofa and
addressed him, "Ah, Alfred, I am glad to see you," and he
said, "I am not Alfred, I am Septimus; I am the most morbid of all the Tennysons." I suppose he is self-indulgent and
a little spoiled and selfish by the warm and universal favor
he has found. Lady Duff Gordon told me that the first day
she saw him he lay his whole length on the carpet, and
rolled himself to her feet and said, "Will you please to put
your feet on me for a stool." Coventry Patmore described
him as very capricious and as once spending the evening
with a dozen friends, "not, to be sure, his equals, but as
nearly his equals as any that could be collected." Yet Tennyson would not say a word, but sat with his pipe, silent, and
at last said, "I am going to Cheltenham; I have had a glut
of men." When he himself proposed, one day, to read Tennyson a poem which he had just finished, that Tennyson
might tell him of anything which his taste would exclude,

Tennyson replied, "Mr. Patmore, you have no idea how many applications of this sort are made to me."

The one thing odious to me now is joking. What can the brave and strong genius of C. himself avail? What can his praise, what can his blame avail me, when I know that if I fall or if I rise, there still awaits me the inevitable joke? The day's Englishman must have his joke, as duly as his bread.

I suppose you could never prove to the mind of the most ingenious mollusk that such a creature as a whale was possible.

What games sleep plays with us! We wake indignant that we have been so played upon, and should have lent ourselves to such mountains of nonsense. All night I was scarifying with my wrath some conjuring miscreant, but unhappily I had an old age in my toothless gums, I was as old as Priam, could not articulate, and the edge of all my taunts and sarcasms, it is to be feared, was quite lost. Yet, spite of my dumb palsy, I defied and roared after him, and rattled in my throat, until wife waked me up. Then I bit my lips. So one day we shall wake up from this longer confusion, and be not less mortified that we had lent ourselves to such rigmarole.

In approaching Paris, it seemed a nation of soldiers. The climate seemed altered, and 't is incredible that this Syrian capital—all the people poured into the street—should be so near to London.

I find the French all soldiers, all speakers. The *aplomb* which these need, every Frenchman has; every *gamin* a certain trimness or trigness and a certain fancy cut like a dandy boat at a regatta. A certain ingenuity and verbal clearness of statement they require, and that satisfies them that they have a new and lucid and coherent statement, though it is artificial, and not an idea.

Torchlight processions have a seek-and-slay look, dripping burning oil-drops, and the bearers now and then smiting the torch on the ground, and then lifting it into the air.

The question of history is, what each generation has done with its surplus produce? One bought crusades, one churches, one villas, one horses, and one railroads.

I have been exaggerating the English merits all winter and disparaging the French. Now I am correcting my judgment of both, and the French have risen very fast.

I have seen Rachel in *Phèdre*, in *Mithridate*, and now last night in *Lucréce*. The best part of her performance is the terror and energy she can throw into passages of defiance or denunciation. Her manners and carriage are throughout pleasing by their highly intellectual cast. And her expression of the character is not lost by your losing some word or look, but is continuous and is sure to be conveyed. She is extremely youthful and innocent in her appearance, and when she appeared after the curtain fell to acknowledge the acclamations of the house and the heaps of flowers that were flung to her, her smile had a perfect good nature and a kind of universal intelligence.

Paris has great merits as a city. Its river is made the greatest pleasure to the eye by the quays and bridges; its fountains are noble and copious; its gardens or parks far more available to the pleasure of the people than those of London. What a convenience to the senses of men is the *Palais Royal;* the swarming Boulevards, what an animating promenade; the furnished lodgings have a seductive independence; the living is cheap and good; then what a luxury it is to have a cheap wine for the national beverage as uniformly supplied as beer in England. The manners of the people are full of entertainment, so spirited, chatty, and coquettish, as lively as monkeys. And now the whole nation is bearded and in military uniform. I have no doubt also that extremes of vice are found here, and that there is a liberty and means of animal indulgence hardly known by name, or even by rumor, in other towns.

The cafés are not to be forgotten, filled with newspapers, blazing with light, sauntering places, *oubliettes* or remember-nothings. One in Paris who would keep himself up with events must read every day about twelve newspapers of the two hundred that are printed there. Then in the street the *affiches* on every spot of dead wall attract all eyes and make the text of all talk for the gazing group. The Government reserve to their own the exclusive use of white paper. All others are in colours.

After twenty-five days spent in Paris, I took the railroad for Boulogne, stopped at Amiens half an hour and saw the cathedral, which has nothing equal to it in Paris. At Boulogne (where six thousand English reside for cheapness) I took the night steamboat for Folkestone.

The world is always childish, and with each new gewgaw of a revolution or new constitution that it finds, thinks it shall never cry any more.

In England every man you meet is some man's son; in America, he may be some man's father.

People eat the same dinner at every house in England. 1, soup; 2, fish; 3, beef, mutton, or hare; 4, birds; 5, pudding and pastry and jellies; 6, cheese; 7, grapes, nuts, and wine. During dinner, hock and champagne are offered you by the servant, and sherry stands at the corners of the table. Healths are not much drunk in fashionable houses. After the cloth is removed, three bottles, namely, port, sherry, and claret, invariably circulate. What rivers of wine are drunk in all England daily! One would say, every guest drinks six glasses.

I stayed in London till I had become acquainted with all the styles of face in the street, and till I had found the suburbs and then straggling houses on each end of the city. Then I took a cab, left my farewell cards, and came home.

In the English landscape the combed fields have the softest look, and seem touched with a pencil and not with a plough.

I was accustomed to characterize Alcott, in England, by saying he was the one man I had met who could read Plato without surprise.

Dragged day and night continually through the water by this steam engine, at the rate of near twelve knots, or fourteen statute miles, the hour; in the nearing America my inviting port, England loses its recent overweight, America resumes its commanding claims.

One long disgust is the sea. No personal bribe would hire one who loves the present moment. Who am I to be treated in this ignominious manner, tipped up, shoved against the side of the house, rolled over, suffocated with bilge mephitis and stewing-oil? These lack-lustre days go whistling over us and are those intercalaries I have often asked for, and am cursed now with,—the worthless granting of my prayer.

The gods deal very strictly with us, make out quarter-bills, and exact specie payment, allow no partnerships, no stock companies, no arrangements, but hold us personally liable to the last cent. Ah, say I, I cannot do this and that, my cranberry field, my burned woodlot, the rubbish lumber about the summer house, my grass, my crop, my trees; —can I not have some partner; can't we organize our new Society of poets and lovers, and have somebody with talent for business to look after these things, some deacons of trees and grass and cranberries, and leave me to letters and philosophy?

But the nettled gods say, No, go to the devil with your arrangements. You, you, you personally, you alone, are to answer body and soul for your things. Leases and covenants are to be punctually signed and sealed. Arithmetic and the practical study of cause and effect in the laws of Indian corn and rye meal is as useful as betting is in England to teach accuracy of statement, or duelling in France or Ireland to make men speak the truth.

Henry Thoreau is like the wood-god who solicits the wandering poet and draws him into antres vast and desarts idle, and bereaves him of his memory, and leaves him naked, plaiting vines and with twigs in his hand.

I spoke of friendship but my friends and I are fishes in our habit. As for taking Thoreau's arm, I should as soon take the arm of an elm tree.

Ellery Channing remarks in Alcott the obstruction of his egoism. Cultivated men always must be had; everybody sends for them as for peaches. But what to do with this man, when you have first to kick away the man in order to get at what he knows.

Henry Thoreau, working with Alcott on the summer house, said, he was nowhere, doing nothing.

There are always two things to be done by the novelist; first, the aspirations of the mind are to be revered, that is, Faith; and, secondly, the way things actually fall out, that is, Fate. Fate and Faith, these two; and it seems as if justice were done, if the Faith is vindicated in the sentiments of the heroes of the tale, and Fate in the course and issue of the events.

I observe that all the bookish men have a tendency to believe that they are unpopular. Parker gravely informs me by word and by letter that he is precisely the most unpopular of all men in New England. Alcott believes the same thing of himself, and I, no doubt, if they had not anticipated me in claiming this distinction, should have claimed it for myself.

George Sand is a great genius, and yet owes to her birth in France her entire freedom from the cant and snuffle of our dead Christianity.

The Railroads is the only sure topic for conversation in
these days. That is the only one which interests farmers,
merchants, boys, women, saints, philosophers, and fools.

And now we have one more rival topic, California gold.

The Railroad is that work of art which agitates and
drives mad the whole people; as music, sculpture, and picture have done on their great days respectively.

I know what I shall find if Alcott brings me manuscripts. I
shall have a Salisbury Plain full of bases of pyramids, to
each of which I am to build an apex.

[Last days of September]
I go twice a week over Concord with Ellery [Channing],
and, as we sit on the steep park at Conantum, we still have
the same regret as oft before. Is all this beauty to perish?
Shall none remake this sun and wind, the sky-blue river, the
river-blue sky; the yellow meadow spotted with sacks and
sheets of cranberry-pickers; the red bushes; the iron-gray
house with just the color of the granite rock; the paths of
the thicket, in which the only engineers are the cattle graz-
ing on yonder hill; the wide, straggling wild orchard in
which Nature has deposited every possible flavor in the
apples of different trees? Whole zones and climates she
has concentrated into apples. We think of the old benefactors who have conquered these fields; of the old man
Moore, who is just dying in these days, who has absorbed
such volumes of sunshine like a huge melon or pumpkin
in the sun,—who has owned in every part of Concord a
woodlot, until he could not find the boundaries of these,
and never saw their interiors. But we say, where is he who
is to save the present moment, and cause that this beauty
be not lost?

Ellery declares that the Railroad has proved too strong

for all our farmers and has corrupted them like a war, or the incursion of another race;—has made them all amateurs, given the young men an air their fathers never had; they look as if they might be railroad agents any day. We shall never see Cyrus Hubbard, or Ephraim Wheeler, or Grass-and-Oats, or Oats-and-Grass, or Barrett or Hosmer, in the next generation. These old Saxons have the look of pine trees and apple trees, and might be the sons got between the two; conscientious laborers with a science born with them from out the sap vessels of these savage sires.

I still feel a little uneasiness about these novels. Why should these sorceries have a monopoly of our delicious emotions? —The novel still weakly uses the cheap resources of property married away instead of earned, and that is the chief conjuring-stick it has; for the instincts of man always attach to property, as he knows what accumulations of spiritual force go to the creation of that, and sobs and heart-beats and sudden self-sacrifice very easily result from the dealing with it. But the novel will find the way to our interiors, one day, and will not always be novel of costume merely. These stories are to stories of real life what the figures which represent the fashions of the month on the front page of the magazine are to portraits and inspired pictures.

I value men as they can complete their creation. One man can hurl from him a sentence which is spheral, and at once and forever disengaged from the author. Another can say excellent things, if the sayer and the circumstances are known and considered; but the sentences need a running commentary, and are not yet independent individuals that can go alone.

On Kicking up our heels. We have a ridiculous wisdom, like that which a man has of his corns, or of his gouty foot, and has become by experience cunning in setting it down so as not to hurt him, so we of our limitations. We have learned not to strut or talk of our wings, or affect angelic moods, but to keep the known ways, knowing that at the end of these fine struts is the Lunatic Asylum.

The Spirit of Knowledge is serious, honest, and trustworthy.

We say nothing against astronomy and vegetation, because we are roaring here in our bed with rheumatism. We doubt not there are bounding fawns, and lilies with graceful, springing stem; so neither do we doubt or fail to love the eternal law of which we are such shabby practicers. A cripple was our father and an Ethiop was our mother, and we worship the Liberty which we shall not see with our eyes, nor help but with our prayer.

Our philosophy is to *wait.* We have retreated on Patience, transferring our oft-shattered hope now to larger and eternal good. We meant well, but our uncle was crazy and must be restrained from waking the house. The roof leaked, we were out of wood, our sisters were unmarried and must be maintained; there were taxes to pay, and notes, and, alas, a tomb to build: we were obliged continually to postpone our best action, and that which was life to do could only be smuggled in to odd moments of the month and year. Then we say, Dear God, but the life of man is not by man, it is consentaneous and far-related, it came with the sun and Nature, it is crescive and vegetative, and it is with it as with the sun and the grass. I obey the beautiful Necessity. The powers that I want will be supplied as *I* am supplied, and the philosophy of waiting is sustained by all the oracles of the Universe.

God never made such a bungler as I am at any practical work, therefore I keep clear of the garden and the phalanstery.

Henry Thoreau sports the doctrines of activity: but I say, What do *we*? We want a sally into the regions of wisdom, and do we go out and lay stone wall or dig a well or turnips? No, we leave the children, sit down by a fire, compose our bodies to corpses, shut our hands, shut our eyes, that we may be entranced and see truly.

Alcott is a certain fluid in which men of a certain spirit can easily expand themselves and swim at large, they who elsewhere found themselves confined. He gives them nothing but themselves. Of course, he seems to them the only wise and great man. But when they meet people of another sort, critics and practical, and are asked concerning Alcott's wisdom, they have no books to open, no doctrines to impart, no sentences or sayings to repeat, and they find it quite impossible to communicate to these their good opinion.

Me he has served now these twelve years in that way; he was the reasonable creature to speak to that I wanted.

There is in California a gold ore in great abundance in which the gold is in combination with such elements that no chemistry has yet been able to separate it without great loss. Alcott is a man of unquestionable genius, yet no doctrine or sentence or word or action of his which is excellent can be detached and quoted.

He is like Channing, who possesses a painter's eye, an appreciation of form and especially of color, that is admirable, but who, when he bought pigments and brushes and painted a landscape on a barrel head could not draw a tree so that his wife could know it was a tree. So Alcott the philosopher has not an opinion or an apothegm to produce.

I shall write on his tomb, *Here lies Plato's reader*. Read he can with joy and *naïveté* inimitable, and the more the style rises, the more natural and current is seems to him. And yet his appetite is so various that the last book always seems to him the best. *Here lies the Amateur*.

I notice that people who wash much have a high mind about it, and talk down to those who wash little. Carlyle washes, and he has come to believe that the only religion left us is ablution, and that Chadwick, the man who is to bring water for the million, is the Priest of these times. So at home I find the morning bathers are proud and haughty scorners, and I begin to believe that the composition of water must be one part hydrogen and three parts conceit.

When Nature removes a great man, people explore the horizon for a successor.

I am afraid books do stand in our way; for the best heads are writers, and when they meet and fall into profound conversation, they never quite lose all respects of their own economy and pour out the divinest wine, but each is a little wary, a little checked, by the thought of the rare helps this hour might afford him to some page which he has written. Each is apt to become abstracted and lose the remark of the other through too much attention to his own. Yet I have no book and no pleasure in life comparable to this.

Here I come down to the shore of the Sea and dip my hands in its miraculous waves. Here I am assured of the eternity, and can spare all omens, all prophecies, all religions, for I see and know that which they obscurely announce. I seem rich with earth and air and heaven; but the next morning I have lost my keys.

To escape this economy of writers, women would be better friends; but they have the drawback of the perplexities of sex.

Another walk this Saturday afternoon with Ellery through the woods to the shore of Flint's Pond. The witch-hazel was in full bloom and from the highland we saw one of the best pictures of the New Hampshire Mountains. But Ellery said that when you come among them they are low, and nothing but cow pastures. I say, let us value the woods; they are full of solicitation. My wood lot has no price. I could not think of selling it for the money I gave for it. It is full of unknown mysterious values. What forms, what colours, what powers, null, it is true, to our ignorance, but opening inestimably to human wit. The crows filled the landscape with a savage sound; the ground was covered with new fallen leaves which rustled so loud as we trampled through them that we could hear nothing else.

Love is necessary to the righting the estate of woman in this world. Otherwise nature itself seems to be in conspiracy against her dignity and welfare; for the cultivated, high-thoughted, beauty-loving, saintly woman finds herself unconsciously desired for her sex, and even enhancing the appetite of her savage pursuers by these fine ornaments she has piously laid on herself. She finds with indignation that she is herself a snare, and was made such. I do not wonder at her occasional protest, violent protest against nature, in fleeing to nunneries, and taking black veils. Love rights all this deep wrong.

I find out in an instant if my companion does not want me; I cannot comprehend how my visitor does not perceive that I do not want him. It is his business to find out that I, of course, must be civil. It is for him to offer to go. I certainly shall not long resist.

Yesterday, another walk with Ellery well worth commemoration, if that were possible; but no pen could write what we saw: it needs the pencils of all the painters that ever existed to aid the description. We went to White Pond; a pretty little Indian basin, lovely now as Walden once was; we could almost see the sachem in his canoe in a shadowy cove. But making the circuit of the lake on the shore, we came at last to see some marvellous reflections of the colored woods in the water, which held us fast to the effect, almost to the going down of the sun. The water was very slightly rippled, which took the proper character from the pines, and the birches, and a few oaks, which composed the grove; and the submarine wood seemed all made of Lombardy poplar, with such delicious green, stained by gleams of mahogany from the oaks, and streaks of white from the birches, every moment growing more excellent. It was the world seen through a prism.

In walking with Ellery you shall always see what was never before shown to the eye of man. And yet for how many ages of lonely days has that pretty wilderness of White Pond received the sun and clouds into its transparency, and woven each day new webs of birch and pine, shooting into wilder angles and more fantastic crossing of these coarse threads, which, in the water, have such momentary elegance.

Only write a dozen lines, and rest on your oars forever, you are dear and necessary to the human race and worth all the old trumpery Plutarchs and Platos and Bacons of the world.

Every loafer knows the way to the rum shop, but every angel does not know the way to his nectar.

A good deal of thought and reading is no better than smoking, yet we give ourselves airs thereon, and not on our cigars.

It is a finer thing to hold a man by his ears than by his eyes, as the Beauty does; by his belly, as the rich man does; by his fears, as the State does.

What is indispensable to inspiration? Sleep. There are two things, both indispensable: sound sleep; and the provocation of a good book or a companion.

How Nature, to keep her balance true, invented a Cat. What phantasmagoria in these animals! Why is the snake so frightful, which is the line of beauty, and every resemblance to it pleases? See what disgust and horror of a rat, loathsome in its food, loathsome in its form, and a tail which is villanous, formidable by its ferocity; yet interposed between this horror and the gentler kinds is the cat, a beautiful horror, or a form of many bad qualities, but tempered and thus strangely inserted as an offset, check, and temperament, to that ugly horror. See then the squirrel strangely adorned with his tail, which is his saving grace in human eyes.

In the hotels the air is buttered and the whole air is a volatilized beefsteak.

X and Y and so many honest *bourgeois* in our population

vote on the expectation and assurance of a specific reward. It is as honest and natural in them to expect the *place*, as in an ox to expect his hay and stalks; and they are as legitimately angry and implacable, if they are baulked of it.

I see no security in laws, but only in the nature of men; and in that reactive force which develops all kinds of energy at the same time; energy of good with energy of evil; the ecstasies of devotion with the exasperations of debauchery. The sons of Democrats will be Whigs, and the fury of republicanism in the father is only the immense effort of Nature to engender an intolerable tyrant in the next age.

A blockhead makes a blockhead of me.

Henry [Thoreau] says, "Alcott is the best natured man I ever met. The rats and mice make their nests in him."

Yesterday afternoon cold, fine ride with Ellery to Sudbury Inn, and mounted the side of Nobscot. Finest picture through wintry air of the russet Massachusetts. The landscape is democratic, not gathered into one city or baronial castle, but equally scattered into these white steeples, round which a town clusters in every place where six roads meet, or where a river branches or falls, or where the pan of soil is a little deeper. The horizon line marched by hills tossing like waves in a storm: firm indigo line. 'T is a pretty revolution which is effected in the landscape by simply turning your head upside down, or, looking through your legs: an infinite softness and loveliness is added to the picture. It changes the landscape from November to June, or, as Ellery declared, makes *Campagna* of it at once; so, he said, Massachusetts is Italy upside down.

PART VI

1849-1855

Emerson lectured in New England during 1849. Alcott moved to Boston, and did not return to Concord for nine years. In the following year, *Representative Men* was published and Margaret Fuller was drowned with her Italian husband and her child when the boat on which she was returning from Europe was wrecked on Fire Island. Emerson lectured in New York and Philadelphia and toured the "New West," sailing down the Ohio and up the Mississippi to Galena, crossing Illinois by stagecoach, Michigan by the new railroad, Lakes Erie and Ontario by boat, and home by train.

Outrage at the Fugitive Slave Law and at Webster's part in its passage dominated the entries for 1851. In March, Emerson gave a course of lectures in Pittsburgh, traveling to that city partly by canal boat, where he slept on the floor "in a wreath of legs."

During the next three years Emerson lectured widely, traveling north to Canada and west as far as Wisconsin. In 1854 Emerson's mother died. During this period the pressure of successful lecturing and the writing of *English Traits* (published in 1856) curtailed the journal entries.

1849

If a man is going to California, he announces it with some hesitation; because it is a confession that he has failed at home.

The timeliness of this invention of the locomotive must be conceded. To us Americans it seems to have fallen as a political aid. We could not else have held the vast North

America together which now we engage to do. It was strange, too, that when it was time to build a road across to the Pacific, a railroad, a shiproad, a telegraph, and, in short, a perfect communication in every manner for all nations,—'t was strange to see how it is secured. The good World-soul understands us well. How simple the means. Suddenly the Californian soil is spangled with a little gold-dust here and there in a mill-race in a mountain cleft: an Indian picks up a little, a farmer, and a hunter, and a soldier, each a little; the news flies here and there, to New York, to Maine, to London, and an army of a hundred thousand picked volunteers, the ablest and keenest and boldest that could be collected, instantly organize and embark for this desert, bringing tools, instruments, books, and framed houses, with them. Such a well-appointed colony as never was planted before arrive with the speed of sail and steam on these remote shores, bringing with them the necessity that the government shall instantly proceed to make the road which they themselves are all intimately engaged to assist.

At Alcott's last Tuesday (March 20) we had a meeting of thirty men, and discussed the expediency of a Club and Clubroom. Alcott was festal and Olympian, as always, when friends come; his heart is then too great; his voice falters and chokes in his throat. Every newcomer seems large, sacred, and crowned to him. It was proposed that the club should rent the room in which we sat (Alcott's), and that he should be declared perpetual secretary.

It is much wanted by the country scholars, a *café* or reading-room in the city, where, for a moderate subscription, they can find a place to sit in and find their friends, when in town, and to write a letter in, or read a paper. Better still, if you can add certain days of meeting when important questions can be debated, communications read, etc., etc.

Enthusiasm is a fine thing, my son, so it be guided by prudence, says the grocer; which is like Ellery Channing's saying of C——, "Yes, he would draw very well, if he had any talent for it."

It is chemical mixture, and not mechanical, which makes the writer. The others have not intelligence enough to know they are not writers.

Who buys Channing's house buys a sunset. It should be sold in a fair day; then the purchaser gets rivers, mountains, villages, in the bargain. I would not, if I owned that place, sell it. I would hold onto it as long as I could see.

I meet in the street people full of life. I am, of course, at ebb tide; they at flood; they seem to have come from the South, or from the West, or from Europe. I see them pass with envy at this gift which includes all gifts.

From a better man than myself (I used to say) I can easily expect a finer thought: from a worse, I am incredulous. But that *Better* we so slowly believe.

'T is pity our dismasted, rudderless hulks drifting about on the sea of life should not be taken into port. When the school and college drop them, let Plato take them up, and life would no longer be forlorn, and they left to the stock quotations by day, and cards at night.

Immortality. I notice that as soon as writers broach this question they begin to quote. I hate quotations. Tell me what you know.

I pay the schoolmaster, but 't is the schoolboys that educate my son.

Socrates and Franklin may well go hungry and in plain clothes, if they like; but there are people who cannot afford this, but whose poverty of nature needs wealth of food and clothes to make them decent.

I think, if I were professor of Rhetoric,—teacher of the art of writing well to young men,—I should use Dante for my text-book. Come hither, youth, and learn how the brook that flows at the bottom of your garden, or the farmer who ploughs the adjacent field, your father and mother, your debts and credits, and your web of habits are the very basis of poetry, and the material which you must work up. Dante knew how to throw the weight of his body into each act, and is, like Byron, Burke, and Carlyle, the Rhetorician. I find him full of the *nobil volgare eloquenza;* that he knows "God damn," and can be rowdy if he please, and he does please. Yet is Dante not reason or illumination and that essence we were looking for, but only a new exhibition of the possibilities of genius? Here is an imagination that rivals in closeness and precision the senses. But we must prize him as we do a rainbow, we can appropriate nothing of him.

When I was born, private and family prayer was in the use of all well-bred people, and now it is not known.

Mr. Harrison Gray Otis said, "that it was of no use to tie up a woman's property; by kissing or kicking, her husband would get it away from her."

The French change their Constitution as often as their shirt.

It could not be said of Buna,* that she lived entirely for her dinner,—though she was tenderly, patiently absorbed in that capital event of the day;—no; for she was not less dedicated to her supper, nor less to her breakfast. He had studied her character imperfectly who thought she lived in these. No; she wished to keep her feet warm, and she was addicted to a soft seat, and expended a skill and generalship on securing the red chair and a corner *out* of the draught and *in* the air, worthy of a higher seat in heaven. Neither on these was she exhausted.

In a frivolous age, Buna was earnest. She screamed, she groaned, she watched at night, she waited by day for her omelet and her lamp with smooth handle, and when she went out of the house it was a perfect *row* for half an hour. Buna had catarrh, pleurisy, rush of blood to the head, apoplexy, diabetes, diarrhœa, sunstroke, atrophy, worms, palsy, erysipelas, consumption, and dropsy.

It is no matter how fine is your rhetoric, or how strong is your understanding, no book is good which is not written by the Instincts.

The Indian squaw with a decisive hat has saved herself a world of vexation. The tragedy of our women begins with the bonnet; only think of the whole Caucasian race damning the women to cover themselves with this frippery of rye straw and tags, that they may be at the mercy of every shower of rain. A meeting-house full of women and a shower coming up,—it is as if we had dressed them all in

---

* Emerson's name for one of his more obnoxious visitors.

paper. Put on the squaw's man's hat, and you amputate so much misery.

Yesterday a ride and walk with Thoreau to Acton. We climbed to the top of Nagog Hill, and afterward of Nashobah, the old domain of Tahatawan and his praying Indians. The houses in Acton seemed to be filled with fat old people who looked like old tomatoes; their faces crumpled into red collops, fatting and rotting at their ease.

How difficult to deal erect with the Days! Each of these events which they bring,—this Concord thieving, the muster, the ripening of plums, the shingling of the barn, all throw dust in your eyes, and distract your attention.

Aunt Mary never liked to throw away any medicine; but, if she found a drop of laudanum here, and a pill or two there, a little quinine and a little antimony, mixed them up and swallowed them. So when she came to the tea-table —"Oh, no, she never took tea";—"Can you get a little shells?" The cocoa came, and Aunty took cocoa, because it was soothing, and put a little tea in it to make her lively, and if there was a little coffee, that was good for getting rid of the taste.

Love is the bright foreigner, the foreign self.

To-day, carpets; yesterday, the aunts; the day before, the funeral of poor S.; and every day, the remembrance in the library of the rope of work which I must spin;—in this way life is dragged down and confuted. We try to listen to the hymn of gods, and must needs hear this perpetual *cock-a-doodle-doo*, and *ke-tar-kut* right under the library windows. They, the gods, ought to respect a life, you say, whose ob-

jects are their own. But steadily they throw mud and
eggs at us, roll us in the dirt, and jump on us.

Solitary Imprisonment is written on his coat and hat, on
the lines of his face, and the limbs of his body, on his brow
and on the leaves of laurel on his brow. He wrestles hard
with the judge, and does not believe he is in earnest. "Solitary Imprisonment," replied the Judge. Yet with some miti-
gation. Three times a day his keeper comes to the window,
and puts bread and water on the shelf. The keeper's dog he
may play with, if he will. Bow-wow-wow, says the dog. People may come from Asia to see him, if they like. He only is
permitted to become his friend.

For good reading there must be, of course, a yielding,
sometimes entire, but always some yielding to the book.
Then the reader is refreshed with a new atmosphere and
foreign habits. But many minds are incapable of any surrender.

For the conduct of life, let us not parade our rags, let us
not, moved by vanity, confess and tear our hair at the corners of the streets, or in the sitting-room; but, as age and in-
firmity steal on us, contentedly resign the front seat and
the games to these bright children, our better representa-
tives, nor expect compliments or inquiries—much less, gifts
or love—any longer (which to expect is ridiculous), and,
not at all wondering why our friends do not come to us,
—much more wondering when they do,—decently withdraw ourselves into modest and solitary resignation and
rest.

Some of the sweetest hours of life, on retrospect, will be
found to have been spent with books. Yes; but the sweetness was your own. Had you walked, or hoed, or swum,

or sailed, or kept school, in the same hours, it would have endeared those employments and conditions.

Macaulay's History is full of low merits: it is like English manufactures of all kinds, neat, convenient, portable, saleable, made on purpose for the Harpers to print a hundred thousand copies of. So far can Birmingham go.

Michael Angelo paints with more will; Raffaello, with the obedience of water and flame. Everybody would paint like Raffaello, if the power of painting were added to everybody.

What I want to know is, the meaning of what I do; believing that any of my current Mondays or Tuesdays is Fatebook for me; and believing that hints and telegraphic signals are arriving to me every moment out of the interior eternity. I am tormented with impatience to make them out. We meet people who seem to overlook our game, and read us with a smile, but they do not tell us what they read.

The universe is only in transit, or, we behold it shooting the gulf from the past to the future.

Alcott is like a slate pencil which has a sponge tied to the other end, and, as the point of the pencil draws lines, the sponge follows as fast, and erases them. He talks high and wide, and expresses himself very happily, and forgets all he has said. If a skilful operator could introduce a lancet and sever the sponge, Alcott would be the prince of writers.

Every day shows a new thing to veteran walkers. Yesterday reflections of trees in the ice: snowflakes, perfect rowels,

on the ice; beautiful groups of icicles all along the eastern
shore of Flint's Pond, in which, especially where encrusting
the bough of a tree, you have the union of the most flowing
with the most fixed. Ellery all the way squandering his
jewels as if they were icicles, sometimes not comprehended
by me, sometimes not heard. How many days can Methusalem go abroad and see somewhat new? When will he
have counted the changes of the kaleidoscope?

Why a writer should be vain, and a farmer not, though the
writer admires the farmer, and the farmer doesn't admire
the writer, does not appear.

Like the New England soil, my talent is good only whilst
I work it. If I cease to task myself, I have no thoughts. This
is a poor sterile Yankeeism. What I admire and love is
the generous and spontaneous soil which flowers and fruits
at all seasons.

People like exaggerated events, and activity,—like to run to
a house on fire, to a murder, an execution;—like to tell of a
bankruptcy, of a death, of a crime, or of an engagement.
They like a rattling town, where a great deal of business is
done. The student shuns all this. They like to be in a state
of exaggeration. Of course, manly greatness consists in being so much that the mere wash of the sea, the observed
passage of the stars, or the *almost heard* current of time, is
event enough and the full soul cries, Let not the noise of
what you call events disturb me!

Duties are as much impediments to greatness as cares. If
a man sets out to be rich, he cannot follow his genius; neither can he any more, if he wishes to be an estimable son,
brother, husband, nephew, and cousin.

1850

I affirm the divinity of man; but as I know well how much is my debt to bread and coffee and flannel and heated room, I shun to be Tartuffe, and do affirm also with emphasis the value of these fomentations. But I cannot reconcile that absolute with this conditional.

Love is temporary and ends with marriage. Marriage is the perfection which love aimed at, ignorant of what it sought. Marriage is a good known only to the parties,—a relation of perfect understanding, aid, contentment, possession of themselves and of the world,—which dwarfs love to green fruit.

The English journals snub my new book; as, indeed, they have all its foregoers. Only now they say that this has less vigor and originality than the others. Where, then, was the degree of merit that entitled my books to their notice? They have never admitted the claims of either of them. The fate of my books is like the impression of my face. My acquaintances, as long back as I can remember, have always said, "Seems to me you look a little thinner than when I saw you last."

At Alcott's conversation on "The Times" each person who opened his lips seemed in snuffing the air to snuff nitrous oxide, and away he went,—a spinning dervish,—pleasing himself, annoying the rest. A talent is a nuisance. Each rode his nag with devotion round the walls of the universe; I found no benefit in this jar and jangle. There was much ability and good meaning in the room, but some persons present who should not have been there, and these, like an east wind, checked every growth.

Byron's life suggests that a partnership of authors would have the same immense advantage for literature that concert has in war, in music, and in trade: Byron's, because in his case, as in so many (in mine, for example, who am hardly a writer), his talent is conspicuously partial, and needs a complement. But if one with solid knowledge—a man of massive mind, or a man of ideas, powerful generalizations, or both—had united with Byron, with his unmatched expressiveness, his heat, his firm ductile thread of gold, a battery had been built, against which nothing could stand. But in his isolation Byron is starved for material, has no thoughts; and his fiery affections are only so many women, though rigged out in men's clothes, garnished, too, with beards and mutachios. They vapor.

It is well worth thinking on. Thus, if Thoreau, Ellery, and I could (which is perhaps impossible) combine works heartily (being fired by such a desire to carry one point as to fuse all our repulsions and incompatibilities), I doubt not we could engender something superior for quality and for effect to any of the thin, cold-blood creatures we have hitherto flung into the light.

There is a curious shame in our faces. The age is convict, confessing, sits on the anxious benches. We say there is no religion, no poetry, no heroism, no rage; death is unperfumed; age of debility, correctness, levity, of the looking-glass. Not to be bruised by the bruisers, not to despond in cities, is a mark of merit.

The riddle of the age has always a private solution.

The talent sucks the substance of the man. How often we repeat the disappointment of inferring general ability from conspicuous particular ability.

It is not the least characteristic sign of the Times that Alcott should have been able to collect such a good company of the best heads for two Monday evenings, for the expressed purpose of discussing the Times. What was never done by human beings in another age was done now; there they met to discuss their own breath, to speculate on their own navels, with eyeglass and solar microscope, and no man wondered at them. But these very men came in the cars, by steam-ferry and locomotive to the meeting, and sympathized with engineers and Californians. Mad contradictions flavor all our dishes.

Alcott can never finish a sentence, but revolves in spirals until he is lost in air.

Abuse is a pledge that you are felt. If they praise you, you will work no revolution.

A good book is a Damascus blade made by the welding of old nails and horse-shoes. Everything has seen service, and been proved by wear and tear in the world for centuries, and yet now the article is brand-new.

Society disgusts and the poet resolves to go into retirement and indulge this great heart and feed his thoughts henceforward with botany and astronomy;—behold on the instant his appetites are exasperated, he wants dinners and concerts, scholars and fine women, theatre and club. And life consists in managing adroitly these antagonisms to intensate each other. Life must have continence and abandonment.

Garrison is venerable in his place, like the tart Luther; but he cannot understand anything you say, and neighs like a horse when you suggest a new consideration, as when I told him that the *fate*-element in the negro question he had never considered.

How many centres we have fondly found which proved soon to be circumferential points! How many conversations or books seemed epochs at the moment, which we have now actually forgotten!

Shakspeare was like a looking-glass carried through the street.

I am a bad traveller, and the hotels are mortifications to all sense of well-being in me. The people who fill them oppress me with their excessive virility, and would soon become intolerable if it were not for a few friends, who, like women, tempered the acrid mass.

The badness of the times is making death attractive.

On Friday, July 19, Margaret [Fuller] dies on rocks of Fire Island Beach within sight of and within sixty rods of the shore. To the last her country proves inhospitable to her; brave, eloquent, subtle, accomplished, devoted, constant soul! If Nature availed in America to give birth to many such as she, freedom and honour and letters and art too were safe in this New World.

Her life was romantic and exceptional: so let her death be; it sets the seal on her marriage, avoids all questions of society, all of employment, poverty, and old age, and besides was undoubtedly predetermined when the world was created.

She had great tenderness and sympathy, as Aunt Mary has none. If Aunt Mary finds out anything is dear and sacred to you, she instantly flings broken crockery at that.

If I should be honest, I should say my exploring of life presents little or nothing of respectable event or action, or, in myself, of a personality. Too composite to offer a positive unity, but it is a recipiency, a percipiency. And I, and far weaker persons, if it were possible, than I, who pass for nothing but imbeciles, do yet affirm by their percipiency the presence and perfection of Law as much as all the martyrs.

Every glance at society—pale, withered people with gold-filled teeth, ghastly, and with minds in the same dilapidated condition, drugged with books for want of wisdom—suggests at once the German thought of the progressive god, who has got thus far with his experiment, but will get out yet a triumphant and faultless race.

Men as naturally make a state as caterpillars a web.

Yesterday took that secluded Marlboro' road with Channing in a wagon. Every rock was painted "Marlboro'," and we proposed to take the longest day in the year and ride to Marlboro',—that flying Italy. We went to Willis's Pond in Sudbury and paddled across it, and took a swim in its water, coloured like sugar-baker's molasses. Nature, Ellery thought, is less interesting. Yesterday Thoreau told me it was more so, and persons less. I think it must always combine with man. Life is ecstatical, and we radiate joy and honour and gloom on the days and landscapes we converse with.

But I must remember a real or imagined period in my youth when they who spoke to me of Nature were religious, and made it so, and made it deep: now it is to the young sentimentalists frippery, and a milliner's shop has as much reason and worth.

I confine my ambition to true reporting, though I only get one new fact in a year.

It is curious that we so peremptorily require beauty, and if it do not exist in any one, we feel at liberty to insult over that subject, without end. Thus the poor Donkey is not handsome, and so is the gibe of all mankind in all ages, notwithstanding his eminent usefulness; whilst those handsome cats, the lion, leopard, tiger are allowed to tear and devour because handsome mischiefs, and are the badges of kings.

Rambling talk with Henry Thoreau last night, in accordance with my proposal to hold a session, the first for a long time, with malice prepense, and take the bull by the horns. We disposed pretty fast of America and England, I maintaining that our people did not get ripened, but, like the peaches and grapes of this season, wanted a fortnight's more sun and remained green, whilst in England, because of the density, perhaps, of cultivated population, more caloric was generated and more completeness obtained.

I like the English better than our people, just as I like merchants better than scholars; for, though on a lower platform, yet there is no cant, there is great directness, comprehension, health, and success. So with English.

In the face of the facts which appear as soon as a couple

of meditative men converse, I demand another sort of biography than any of which we have experience, bold, experimental, varied, availing itself of these unspeakable, incomputable advantages which this meditative conversation at once discloses as within reach.

I complain that grandeurs do not ultimate themselves in grandeurs, but in paltriness. The idea of God ends in a paltry Methodist meeting-house.

And you think another day another scream of the eternal wail?

Yesterday I read Margaret's letters to C.S., full of probity, full of talent and wit, full of friendship, ardent affections, full of noble aspiration. They are tainted with a female mysticism which to me appears so merely an affair of constitution that it claims no more respect or reliance than the charity or patriotism of a man who has just dined well and *feels good*. When I talked with G.H., I remember the eggs and butter seemed to have got into his eyes. In our noble Margaret her personal feeling colours all her judgments of persons, of books, of pictures, and of the laws of the world. This is easily felt in common women, and a large deduction is civilly made on the spot by whosoever replies to their remark. But when the speaker has such brilliant talent and literature as Margaret, she gives so many fine names to these merely sensuous and subjective objects that the hearer is long imposed upon, and thinks so precise and glittering nomenclature cannot be of mere *muscæ volitantes*, but must be of some real ornithology hitherto unknown to him.

It is curious that Margaret made a most disagreeable impression on her friends at first,—created a strong prejudice which she had then to conquer.

Creep-mouse manners.

When we find that our habitual aridity, incapacity, and egotism can be overpowered by a generous cause, all impediment brushed away, and our long unused faculties arouse in perfect array, and at last obedient to the will, so that we nobodies are suddenly great and eloquent,—we can forgive the long hybernation, and impute our past insignificance to the triviality of the game.

I recall the man who so amused the stage-coach once from Middleborough with his contrivances for defending his own coffin in his grave from body-snatchers. He had contrived a pistol to go off—*pop!* from this end, and a pistol—*pop!* from that end of the coffin, and he was plainly spending his life in the sweets of the revenge he was going to take hereafter on the young doctors that should creep to his graveyard.

We are wasted with our versatility; with the eagerness to grasp on every possible side, we all run to nothing. I cannot open an agricultural paper without finding objects enough for Methusalem. I jilt twenty books whenever I fix on one. I stay away from Boston, only because I cannot begin there to see those whom I should wish, the men and the things. I wish to know France. I wish to study art. I wish to read laws.

Napoleon III acquired such skill in the art of lying that "the journals complained you could not depend on the exact contrary of that which he stated."

1851

Tennyson's *In Memoriam* is the common-places of condolence among good Unitarians in the first week of mourning. The consummate skill of the versification is the sole merit.

I found when I had finished my new lecture that it was a very good house, only the architect had unfortunately omitted the stairs.

Women carry sail, and men rudders. Women look very grave sometimes, and affect to steer, but their pretended rudder is only a masked sail. The rudder of the rudder is not there.

Nothing can be more foolish than this reproach, which goes from nation to nation, of the love of dollars. It is like oxen taxing each other with eating grass, or a society of borers in an oak tree accusing one another of eating wood; or, in a great society of cheese-mites, if one should begin making insinuations that the other was eating cheese.

We wake up with painful auguring, and, after exploring a little to know the cause, find it is the odious news in each day's paper, the infamy that has fallen on Massachusetts, that clouds the daylight and takes away the comfort out of every hour. We shall never feel well again until that detestable law is nullified in Massachusetts and until the Government is assured that once for all it cannot and shall not be executed here. All I have and all I can do shall be given and done in opposition to the execution of the law.*

* The Fugitive Slave Law.

Since Webster's speech in last March, all the interim has really been a period of calamity to New England. That was a steep step downward. I had praised the tone and attitude of the country. My friends had mistrusted it. They say now, It is no worse than it was before; only it is manifest and acted out. Well I think *that* worse. It shows the access of so much courage in the bad, so much check of virtue, terror of virtue, withdrawn. The tameness is shocking.

I am sorry to say it, but New Hampshire has always been distinguished for the servility of its eminent men. Mr. Webster had resisted for a long time the habit of his *compatriots*,—I mean no irony,—and by adopting the spirited tone of Boston had recommended himself as much as by his great talents to the people of Massachusetts; but blood is thicker than water, the deep servility of New Hampshire politics which has marked all prominent statesmen from that district, with the great exception of Mr. Hale, has appeared late in life with all the more strength that it had been resisted so long, and he has renounced,—what must have cost him some perplexity,—all the great passages of his past career on which his fame is built. His great speeches are,—his discourse at Plymouth denouncing slavery; his speech against Hayne and Southern aggression; his eulogy on Adams and Jefferson, a speech which he is known by and in which he stands by the Fathers of the Revolution for the very resistance which he now denounces; and lastly, his speeches and recent writings on Hungarian liberty. At this very moment his attitude, assumed as Foreign Secretary, is printed in all newspapers before the people in the most awkward contradiction to his own domestic position, precisely like *Hail Columbia,* when sung at a slave auction.

I opened a paper today in which he pounds on the old

strings in a letter to the Washington Birthday feasters at New York. "Liberty! liberty!" Pho! Let Mr. Webster, for decency's sake, shut his lips once and forever on this word. The word *liberty* in the mouth of Mr. Webster sounds like the word *love* in the mouth of a courtezan.

The little fact comes out more plainly that you cannot rely on any man for the defence of truth who is not constitutionally of that side. Wolf, however long his nails have been pared, however neatly he has been shaved and tailored and taught and tuned to say "virtue" and "religion," cannot be relied on when it comes to a pinch; he will forget his morality, and say morality means sucking blood.

Mr. Choate, whose talent consists in a fine choice of words which he can hang indiscriminately on any offender, has pushed the privilege of his profession so far as to ask, "What would the Puritans of 1620 say to the trashy sentimentalism of modern reformers?" And thus the stern old fathers of Massachusetts who, Mr. Choate knows, would have died at the stake before soiling themselves with this damnation, are made to repudiate the "trashy sentimentalism" of the Ten Commandments. The joke is too impudent.

Mr. Webster has deliberately taken out his name from all the files of honour in which he had enrolled it,—from all association with liberal, virtuous, and philanthropic men, and read his recantation on his knees at Richmond and Charleston. He has gone over in an hour to the party of force. He has undone all that he has spent his years in doing,—he has discredited himself. He may bluster. It is his tactics. We shall make no more mistakes. He has taught us the ghastly meaning of liberty, in his mouth. It is kidnapping and hunting to death men and women, it is making treason a matter of fine and imprisonment and armed intervention of the resistance of an immoral law.

The very question of property, the house and land we

occupy, have lost all their sunlight, and a man looks gloom-
ily on his children, and thinks, What have I done that you
should begin life in dishonour?

Nothing seems to me more bitterly futile than this bluster about the Union. A year ago we were all lovers and
prizers of it. Before the passage of that law which Mr.
Webster made his own, we indulged in all the dreams
which foreign nations still cherish of American destiny. But
in the new attitude in which we find ourselves, the degradation and personal dishonour which now rest like miasma
on every house in Massachusetts, the sentiment is entirely
changed. No man can look his neighbor in the face. We
sneak about with the infamy of crime in the streets and
cowardice in ourselves, and frankly, once for all, the Union
is sunk, the flag is hateful, and will be hissed.

The Union! Oh, yes, I prized that, other things being
equal; but what is the Union to a man self-condemned,
with all sense of self-respect and chance of fair fame cut
off,—with the names of conscience and religion become
bitter ironies, and liberty the ghastly nothing which Mr.
Webster means by that word? The worst mischiefs that
could follow from Secession and new combination of the
smallest fragments of the wreck were slight and medica-
ble to the calamity your Union has brought us. Another
year, and a standing army, officered by Southern gentlemen
to protect the Commissioners and to hunt the fugitives,
will be illustrating the new sweets of Union in Boston,
Worcester, and Springfield. It did not appear and it was
incredible that the passage of the Law would make the
Union odious; but from the day it was attempted to be
executed in Massachusetts, this result has appeared, that
the Union is no longer desirable. Whose deed is that?

One more consideration occurs,—the mischief of a legal
crime; the demoralization of the community. Each of these

persons who touches it is contaminated. There has not been in our lifetime another moment when public men were personally lowered by their political action. But here are gentlemen whose names stood as high as any, whose believed probity was the confidence and fortification of all, who, by fear of public opinion, or by that dangerous ascendency of Southern manners, have been drawn into the support of this nefarious business, and have, of course, changed their relations to men. We poor men in the country, who might have thought it an honour to shake hands with them, would now shrink from their touch; nor could they enter our humblest doors.

And as for Andover and Boston preachers who deduce kidnapping from their Bible,—tell the poor, dear doctor, if this be Christianity, it is a religion of dead dogs, let it never pollute the ears and hearts of noble children again.

Oh, bring back then the age when valor was virtue, since what is called morality means nothing but pudding!—pardon the spleen of a professed hermit.

Mr. Webster cannot choose but regret his loss. Tell him that those who make fame accuse him with one voice. Tell him that he who was their pride in the woods and mountains of New England is now their mortification, they never name him, they have taken his book of speeches from the shelf and put it in the stove; and all the fribble of the *Daily Advertiser,* and of its model, the *New York Journal of Commerce,* will not quite compensate him. I have no fear that any roars of New York mobs will be able to drown this voice in Mr. Webster's ear. It can outwhisper all the salvos of their cannon.

It will be his distinction to have changed in one day, by the most detestable law that was ever enacted by a civilized state, the fairest and most triumphant national escutcheon the sun ever shone upon, the free, the expanding, the hospitable, the irresistible America, home of the homeless, and pregnant with the blessings of the world, into a jail or barracoon for the slaves of a few thousand Southern planters, and all the citizens of this hemisphere into kidnappers and drivers for the same. Is that a name will feed his hungry ambition?

Webster and Choate think to discredit the higher law by personalities; they insinuate much about transcendentalists and abstractionists and people of no weight. It is the cheap cant of lawyers and of merchants in a failing condition and of rogues. These classes usually defend an immorality by the practice of men of the world, and talk of dreamers and enthusiasts. Every woman that has been debauched has been so by being made to believe that it is the mode, it is custom, and none but the priest and a few devout visionaries ever think otherwise.

Mr. Webster is fond of fame; his taste is likely to be gratified. For there is not a man of thought or ingenuity but at every dinner table, in every private letter, in every newspaper I take up, is forced to say something biting of this enemy of the honour of Massachusetts. He has the curse of all this country which he has afflicted.

One way certainly the Nemesis is seen. Here is a measure of pacification and union. What is its effect?—that it has made one subject, one only subject for conversation and painful thought throughout the Union, Slavery. We eat it, we drink it, we breathe it, we trade, we study, we wear it. We are all poisoned with it, and after the fortnight the symptoms appear, purulent, making frenzy in the head and rabidness.

The present crisis is not analogous to the Revolution. No liberty of the controlling classes is now threatened. If the South, or if the Federal Government threatened the liberty of any class, I doubt not there would be as violent reaction as was then. This is merely a case of conscience, not of anger, a call for compassion, a call for mercy.

That is one thing; now it is not less imperative that this nation should say, This Slavery shall not be, it poisons and depraves everything it touches.

There can never be peace whilst this devilish seed of war is in our soil. Root it out, burn it up, pay for the damage, and let us have done with it. It costs a hundred millions. Twice so much were cheap for it.

Union is a delectable thing, and so is wealth, and so is life, but they may all cost too much, if they cost honour.

All the drops of his [Webster's] blood have eyes that look downward.

This filthy enactment [the Fugitive Slave Law] was made in the nineteenth century, by people who could read and write. I will not obey it, by God.

In feeble individuals, the sex and the digestion are all.

The world is babyish, and the use of wealth is: it is made a toy. Men of sense esteem wealth to be the assimilation of Nature to themselves, the converting the sap and juices of the planet to the nutriment and incarnation of their design. Power is what they want, not candy, and they will pay any prices. Power for what? Power to execute their idea,— which, in any well-constituted man, of course, appears the end to which the universe exists and all its resources might be well applied.

Thoreau wants a little ambition in his mixture. Fault of this, instead of being the head of American engineers, he is captain of huckleberry party.

He is the richest man who pays the largest debt to his shoemaker.

It will hereafter be noted that the events of culture in the Nineteenth Century were, the new importance of the genius of Dante, Michel Angelo, and Raffaello to Americans; the reading of Shakespeare; and, above all, the reading of Goethe. Goethe was the cow from which all their milk was drawn.

They all took the "European Complaint" and went to Italy. Then there was an uprise of Natural History, and if you would see the fashionable and literary celebrities, you must go to the soirées of the Marquis of Northampton, President of the Royal Society, or to the Geological Club at Somerset House.

It seems, however, as if all the young gentlemen and gentlewomen of America spent several years in lying on the grass and watching "the grand movements of the clouds in the summer sky" during this century.

Goethe is the pivotal man of the old and new times with us. He shuts up the old, he opens the new. No matter that you were born since Goethe died,—if you have not read Goethe, or the Goetheans, you are an old fogy, and belong with the antediluvians.

It is indeed a perilous adventure, this serious act of venturing into mortality, swimming in a sea strewn with wrecks, where none indeed go undamaged. It is as bad as going to Congress; none comes back innocent.

The Judgment Day is in reality the past. We have all been judged, and we have judged all. We would gladly think highly of Nature and Life, but what a country-muster, what a Vanity-Fair full of noise, squibs and egg-pop it is! Pass your last week in review, and what figures move on the swelling scene! 'T is a one-cent farce;—am I deceived;

—or is the low and absurd a little predominant in the piece?

The attention of mankind is now fixed on ruddering the balloon, and probably the next war—the war of principles —is to be fought in the air.

Alcott thinks the American mind a little superior to English, German, Greek, or any other. Shall I say it has the confirmation of having been held of his own country by every son of Adam?

Half measures fail. Don't be leaky.

Miss Peabody* ransacks her memory for anecdotes of Margaret's youth, her self-devotion, her disappointments, which she tells with fervency, but I find myself always putting the previous question. These things have no value unless they lead somewhere. If a Burns, if a De Staël, if an artist is the result, our attention is pre-engaged; but quantities of rectitude, mountains of merit, chaos of ruins are of no account without result;—'t is all mere nightmare; false instincts; wasted lives.

Now, unhappily, Margaret's writing does not justify any such research. All that can be said is that she represents an interesting hour and group in American cultivation; then that she was herself a fine, generous, inspiring, vinous, eloquent talker, who did not outlive her influence; and a kind of justice requires of us a monument, because crowds of vulgar people taunt her with want of position.

Once upon the sense of beauty, and vulgar manners, tricks, bad eating, loud speaking, yelps, and all the miscreation of

* Elizabeth Peabody, Alcott's assistant in his school and sister-in-law of Nathaniel Hawthorne. Margaret is, of course, Margaret Fuller.

ugliness become intolerable, and we are reconciled to the intense selfishness and narrowness of "good society," thinking that, bad as it is, the better alternative as long as health lasts.

We are intent on Meteorology, to find the law of the variable winds, to the end that we may not get our hay wet. I also wish a Farmer's Almanac of the mental moods, that I may farm my mind. There are undulations of power and imbecility and I lose days sitting at my table, which I should gain to my body and mind if I knew beforehand that no thought would come that day.

To-day is holden at Worcester the "Woman's Convention." I think that as long as they have not equal rights of property and right of voting they are not on the right footing.

For the rest, I do not think a woman's convention, called in the spirit of this at Worcester, can much avail. It is an attempt to manufacture public opinion, and of course repels all persons who love the simple and direct method. I find the evils real and great. If I go from Hanover Street to Atkinson Street,—as I did yesterday,—what hundreds of extremely ordinary, paltry, hopeless women I see, whose plight, inscribed on their forms, "Leave all hope behind," is piteous to think of. If it were possible to repair the rottenness of human nature, to provide a rejuvenescence, all were well, and no specific reform, no legislation would be needed. For as soon as you have a sound and beautiful woman, a figure in the style of the antique Juno, Diana, Pallas, Venus, and the Graces, all falls into place, the men are magnetized, heaven opens, and no lawyer need be called in to prepare a clause, for woman moulds the lawgiver. I should therefore advise that the Woman's Convention should be holden in the Sculpture Gallery, that this high remedy might be suggested.

Beware of engagements. Learn to say No, and drop resolutely all false claims.

Live for the year, not for the day.

It would be hard to recall the rambles of last night's talk with Henry Thoreau. But we stated over again, to sadness almost, the eternal loneliness. How insular and pathetically solitary are all the people we know.

1852

'T is said, a man can't be aught in politics without some cordial support in his own district; nor can a man dupe others long, who has not duped himself first.

Eternity is very long; opportunity is a very little portion of it, but worth the whole of it. If God gave me my choice of the whole planet, or my little farm, I should certainly take my farm.

Tom Appleton said at the dinner the other day, "Canvasback ducks eat the wild celery, and the common black duck, if it eats the wild celery, is just as good—only, damn them, they won't eat it."

If a young man come home from college, and find his father coming in every day to dinner in his shirt-sleeves, from the field,—he is forced himself to adopt, at once, some lucrative employment. But if he finds his father at ease in the parlour,—he will never go to work himself.

Few know how to read. Women read to find a hero whom they can love; men, for amusement; editors, for something to crib; authors, for something that supports their view: and hardly one reads comprehensively and widely.

Little things are often filled with great beauty. The cigar makes visible the respiration of the body, an universal fact, of which the ebb and flow of the sea-tide is only one example.

The illustrations in modern books mark the decline of art. 'T is the dram-drinking of the eye, and candy for food; as whales and horses and elephants, produced on the stage, show decline of drama.

A man is a torpedo to a man. I see him with wonder; he looks open and radiant, a god in the world; he understands astronomy, love, and heroism. But I touch him, and am frozen by him. Wonderful power to benumb possesses this Brother. Beware of a pair of eyes! What a puzzle! He is little enough, and nobody; as he comes down the hill, the sun shining in his eyes, the east wind blowing, he is only sensible, like an ox, of petty inconveniences. But he takes a book, or hears a fact or sentiment, he dilates; he knows nature, and the unspoken, unpenetrated universe. In this exaltation all bars sink, he is open as the element,—one man is suddenly tantamount to the race. These powers, so great, yet so haphazard discovered,—how easily he might have missed them! Well, now he has them, and the magnificent dreams begin. All history, nay, all fable, Alexander, Haroun Al-raschid, Hari himself, could do no more than this unaided person will. We hear and believe. But, from month to month, from year to year, he delays, and does not. He has passed out of the exaltation, and his hands are not equal to his thought, nor are the hands of his mind equal to the eyes of his mind.

The belief of some of our friends in their duration suggests one of those musty householders who keep every broomstick and old grate, put in a box every old tooth that falls out of their heads, preserve the ancient frippery of their juvenile wardrobe, and they think God saves all the old souls which he has used up. What does he save them for?

Nature's best feat is enamouring the man of these children, like kissing the knife that is to cut his throat,—they sucking, fretting, mortifying, ruining him, and upsetting him at last, because they want his chair, and he, dear old donkey, well pleased to the end.

There is such an obvious accumulation of dexterity in the use of tools in the old scholar and thinker that it is not to be believed Nature will be such a spendthrift as to sponge all this out, like figures from a slate.

Men achieve a certain greatness, to their own surprise, whilst they were striving to achieve quite another conventional one.

Poetry seems to begin in the slightest change of name, or, detecting identity under variety of surface. Boys please themselves with crying to the coachman, "Put on the string," instead of *lash*. With calling a fire-engine a *tub;* and the engine men *Tigers*. A boy's game of balls is called *Four Old Cats*. Poetry calls a snake a *worm*. In a shipwreck, the sea novel finds "*cordilleras* of water." I can never lose the ludicrous effect of using the word *tin* for *money*.

Miss B——, a mantuamaker in Concord, became a "Medium," and gave up her old trade for this new one; and is to charge a pistareen a spasm, and nine dollars for a fit. This is the Rat-revelation, the gospel that comes by taps in the wall, and thumps in the table-drawer.

The spirits make themselves of no reputation. They are rats and mice of society. And one of the demure disciples of the rat-tat-too, the other day, remarked that "this, like every other communication from the spiritual world, began very low."

The head of Washington hangs in my dining-room for a few days past, and I cannot keep my eyes off of it. It has a certain Appalachian strength, as if it were truly the first-fruits of America, and expressed the Country. The heavy, leaden eyes turn on you, as the eyes of an ox in a pasture. And the mouth has a gravity and depth of quiet, as if this MAN had absorbed all the serenity of America, and left none for his restless, rickety, hysterical countrymen.

Henry Thoreau rightly said, the other evening, talking of lightning-rods, that the only rod of safety was in the vertebrae of his own spine.

A man avails much to us, like a point of departure to the seaman, or his stake and stones to the surveyor. I am my own man more than most men, yet the loss of a few persons would be most impoverishing;—a few persons who give flesh to what were, else, mere thoughts, and which now I am not at liberty to slight, or in any manner treat as fictions. It were too much to say that the Platonic world I might have learned to treat as cloud-land, had I not known Alcott, who is a native of that country, yet I will say that he makes it as solid as Massachusetts to me; and Thoreau gives me, in flesh and blood and pertinacious Saxon belief, my own ethics. He is far more real, and daily practically obeying them, than I; and fortifies my memory at all times with an affirmative experience which refuses to be set aside.

I live a good while and acquire as much skill in literature as an old carpenter does in wood. It occurs, then, what pity! that now, when you know something, have at least learned so much good omission, your organs should fail you; your eyes, health, fire, and zeal of work, should decay daily. Then I remember that it is the mind of the world which is the good carpenter, the good scholar, sailor, or blacksmith, thousand-handed, versatile, all-applicable, in all these indifferent channels entering with wild vigor, excited by novelty in that untried channel confined by dikes of pedantry. In you, this rich soul has peeped, despite your horny, muddy eyes, at books and poetry. Well, it took you up, and showed you something to the purpose; that there was something there. Look, look, old mole! there, straight up before you, is the magnificent Sun.

Whiggery has found for itself a new formula in Boston, this, namely, that, when we go to drive, the breeching is as indispensable as the traces. Its claim is that it blocks the wheels; that the Democratic party goes with a rush for Cuban Invasion, Mexico, Canada, and all: that the Whig party resists these; assuming, however, that the total population is bad, and means badly. But all this despair comes of incapacity; their eyes being only on money, they do not conceive hope or faith. They are the shop-till party.

Statesmen are the superficiality of surface. For, if slavery is a good, then is lying, theft, arson, incest, homicide, each and all goods, and to be maintained by Union Societies.

> Why did all manly gifts in Webster fail?
> He wrote on nature's grandest brow, *For Sale*.

How delicate, difficult, unattainable the golden mean which Nature yet knows how to attain of temperament and culture in a young girl's carriage and manners. Here are girls beautiful without beauty, and ugly with it. Birth has much to do with it and condition much, and society very much; and wealth, and beauty, and tradition, and connection, are all elements; but no rules can be given, and the hazards are so great that the *status* and *métier* of a young girl, from fourteen to twenty-five, are beforehand pathetically perilous.

I waked at night, and bemoaned myself, because I had not thrown myself into this deplorable question of Slavery, which seems to want nothing so much as a few assured voices. But then, in hours of sanity, I recover myself, and say, "God must govern his own world, and knows his way out of this pit, without my desertion of my post, which has none to guard it but me. I have quite other slaves to free than those negroes, to wit, imprisoned spirits, imprisoned thoughts, far back in the brain of man,—far retired in the heaven of invention, and which, important to the republic of Man, have no watchman, or lover, or defender, but I."

When a man sits under the dentist, he fancies his teeth have some acres of extent.

If I have a message to send, I prefer the telegraph to the wheelbarrow.

The church is there for check of trade. But on examination all the deacons, ministers, and saints of this church are

steering with all their sermons and prayers in the direction
of the Trade. If the city says, "Freedom and no tax," they
say so, and hunt up plenty of texts. But if the city says,
"Freedom is a humbug. We prefer a strong government,"
the pulpit says the same, and finds a new set of applicable
texts. But presently Trade says, "Slavery too has been misunderstood: it is not so bad; nay, it is good; on the whole,
it is the best possible thing." The dear pulpit and deacons
must turn over a new leaf, and find a new string of texts,
which they are forward to do.

Last Sunday I was at Plymouth on the beach, and looked
across the hazy water—whose spray was blowing on to the
hills and orchards—to Marshfield. I supposed Webster must
have passed, as indeed he had died at three in the morning. The sea, the rocks, the woods, gave no sign that America and the world had lost the completest man. Nature had
not in our days, or not since Napoleon, cut out such a masterpiece. He brought the strength of a savage into the height
of culture. He was a man *in equilibrio;* a man within and
without, the strong and perfect body of the first ages, with
the civility and thought of the last. "*Os, oculosque Jovi
par.*" And what he brought, he kept. Cities had not hurt
him; he held undiminished the power and terror of his
strength, the majesty of his demeanour.

He had a counsel in his breast. He was a statesman, and
not the semblance of one. Most of our statesmen are in their
places by luck and vulpine skill, not by any fitness. Webster was there for cause: the reality; the final person, who
had to answer the questions of all the *fainéants,* and who
had an answer.

But alas! he was the victim of his ambition; to please the
South betrayed the North, and was thrown out by both.

We entreat you not to believe that anything is yet attained. All is in the gristle and preparation. Your commerce is but a costly comfort,—ease of life,—no more; it belts the world for raisins, and oranges, and oil and wine, and gums, and drugs, and hides, and silk; but what for thought? and what for humanity?

Is science and the heart always to be merely endured, and tolerated and never to walk to the quarterdeck and take the command?

The people don't want liberty,—they want bread; and, though republicanism would give them more bread after a year or two, it would not until then, and they want bread every day.

It is the distinction of *Uncle Tom's Cabin* that it is read equally in the parlour and the kitchen and the nursery of every house. What the lady read in the drawing-room in a few hours is retailed to her in the kitchen by the cook and the chambermaid, week by week; they master one scene and character after another.

Dr. Kirkland and Professor Brazer* mutually resolved one day to break off smoking for six months. Soon after they met at a dinner party at Colonel P.'s, where all the appointments were excellent. Cigars were offered, and Brazer declined them. Dr. Kirkland lighted one, and after smoking with much content for a time, he said to nobody in particular, as he puffed away the smoke,—"It is doubtful whether we show more want of self-control in breaking good resolutions, or self-conceit in keeping them."

* The President of Harvard College, and the Latin Professor.

Mr. William Wistar met a youth at a dinner party, who took a cigar. "How old are you?" said Mr. W. "Sixteen years." "You are at school, are you not?" "I am at the university." "You are just about as old as my boy;—do you know him?" "Yes," answered the youth, "and I am damned glad to find the breed has improved."

"The classes and the races too weak to master the new conditions of life must give way." —KARL MARX.

1853

It is a bitter satire on our social order, just at present, . . . for example the plight of Mr. Alcott, the most refined and the most advanced soul we have had in New England, who makes all other souls appear slow and cheap and mechanical; a man of such a courtesy and greatness, that (in conversation) all others, even the intellectual, seem sharp and fighting for victory, and angry;—he has the unalterable sweetness of a muse,—yet because he cannot earn money by his pen or his talk, or by school-keeping or bookkeeping or editing or any kind of meanness,—nay, for this very cause, that he is ahead of his contemporaries,—is higher than they,—and keeps himself out of the shop-condescensions and smug arts which they stoop to, or, unhappily, need not stoop to, but find themselves, as it were, born to,—therefore, it is the unanimous opinion of New England judges that this man must die,—we shall all hear of his death with pleasure, and feel relieved that his board and clothes are saved! We do not adjudge him to hemlock, or to garroting,—we are much too hypocritical for that,—but we not the less surely doom him, by refusing to protest against this doom, or combine to save him, and to set him

on employments fit for him and salutary to the State, or to
the Senate of fine Souls, which is the heart of the state.

In Boston is no company for a fine wit. There is a certain *poor-smell* in all the streets, in Beacon Street and
Park and Mt. Vernon, as well as in the lawyers' offices,
and the wharves, the same meanness and sterility, and
leave-all-hope-behind, as one finds in a boot manufacturer's
premises, or a bonnet-factory; vamps, pasteboard, lillinette,
and an eye to profit. The want of elevation, the absence of
ideas, the sovereignty of the abdomen, reduces all to the
same poorness.

If a girl is mad to marry, let her take a ride of ten miles,
and see meadows and mountains she never saw before;
two villages, and an old mansion house; and the odds are,
it will change all her resolutions. World is full of fools who
get a-going and never stop: set them off on another tack,
and they are half cured.

Henry [Thoreau] is military. He seemed stubborn and implacable; always manly and wise, but rarely sweet. One
would say that, as Webster could never speak without an
antagonist, so Henry does not feel himself except in opposition. He wants a fallacy to expose, a blunder to pillory, requires a little sense of victory, a roll of the drums, to call
his powers into full exercise.

Sylvan could go wherever woods and waters were, and no
man was asked for leave—once or twice the farmer with-
stood, but it was to no purpose,—he could as easily prevent
the sparrows or tortoises. It was their land before it was his,
and their title was precedent. Sylvan knew what was on
their land, and they did not; and he sometimes brought
them ostentatious gifts of flowers or fruits or shrubs which

they would gladly have paid great prices for, and did not tell them that he took them from their own woods.

Moreover the very time at which he used their land and water (for his boat glided like a trout everywhere unseen), was in hours when they were sound asleep. Long before they were awake he went up and down to survey like a sovereign his possessions, and he passed onward, and left them before the farmer came out of doors. Indeed, it was the common opinion of the day that Mr. Thoreau made Concord.

I admire answers to which no answer can be made.

The insufferable folly of keeping the weal of millions at risk, and every interest of science, of charity, of morals, and of humanity, at a halt, on so despicable a chance as the will of a single Russian gentleman,* will not long impose on the common sense of mankind. Some third way will be thought of between anarchy and this puerile makeshift of an irresponsible rogue.

'T is curious that Christianity, which is idealism, is sturdily defended by the brokers, and steadily attacked by the idealists.

We cannot afford to live long, or Nature, which lives by illusions, will have disenchanted us too far for happiness.

In the stories of the Round Table, the horses show rather more good sense and conduct than their riders.

If a divine physician could come and say, "Ah, you are hurt,—you are bleeding to death,—not out of your body, but, far worse, out of your mind. You that are reckoned

*Czar Nicholas I, whose act of occupying the city of Constantinople brought on the Crimean War.

the pink of amiable and discreet men,—you are in a raging typhoid, already comatose, blind, and deaf. All the worse that you do not know it. Men run away from the smallpox. But see the smallpox of small society,—the vermin, the tapeworm of politics, and of trifling city life, is eating your vitals.—Save yourself."

If a man knows a hundred men, he treats each according to each's nature, and renders dust to dust, and miracle to miracle.

Solitude and the country, books, and openness, will feed you; but go into the city—I am afraid there is no morning in Chestnut Street, it is full of rememberers, they shun each other's eyes, they are all wrinkled with memory of the tricks they have played, or mean to play, each other.

Alcott was here, a baker who bakes a half a dozen worlds as easily as the cook so many loaves: the most obstinate unitarian that ever existed. He believes in cause and effect and comes out of such vast caverns up to the surface of conversation that he has to rub his eyes and look about him not to break the proprieties of this trifling world.

Women. How difficult to deal with them. You must interfere continually to steer their talk or they will be sure, if they meet a button or a thimble, to run against it and forget all in the too powerful associations of the work-table and the pantry. Can't keep it impersonal. Can't keep it afloat in the stream.

Unless we had Boswell, we should hardly know how to account for Johnson's fame, his wit is so muffled and choked in his scholastic style.

It is characteristic of the Teutonic mind to prefer the idea to the phenomenon, and of the Celtic, to prefer the phenomenon to the idea.

Alas for the majority! that old inevitable dupe and victim. What a dreary Iliad of woes it goes wailing and mad withal. Some dog of a Cleon or Robespierre or Douglas or Butler is always riding it to ruin.

1854

Knowledge runs steadily down from class to class down to the lowest people, from the highest, as water does.

Henry Thoreau charged Blake,* if he could not do hard tasks, to take the soft ones, and when he liked anything, if it was only a picture or a tune, to stay by it, find out what he liked, and draw that sense or meaning out of it, and do *that:* harden it, somehow, and make it his own. Blake thought and thought on this, and wrote afterwards to Henry, that he had got his first glimpse of heaven. Henry was a good physician.

We can see well into the past; we can guess shrewdly into the future; but that which is rolled up and muffled in impenetrable folds is To-day.

Those who stay away from the election think that one vote will do no good: 't is but one step more to think one vote will do no harm.

What a notable green-grocer was spoiled to make Macaulay!

* Harrison G. O. Blake, a friend of Thoreau.

Now and then a man exquisitely made can and must live alone; but coop up most men, and you undo them.

If Minerva offered me a gift and an option, I would say give me continuity. I am tired of scraps. I do not wish to be a literary or intellectual chiffonier. Away with this Jew's ragbag of ends and tufts of brocade, velvet, and cloth-of-gold; let me spin some yards or miles of helpful twine, a clew to lead to one kingly truth, a cord to bind wholesome and belonging facts.

We affirm and affirm, but neither you nor I know the value of what we say.

The history of humanity is no hopping squib, but all its discoveries in science, religion, and art are consecutive and correlated,—every discovery leading to a new discovery.

It does seem as if a vow of silence coupled with systematic lessons might teach women the outline and new direction of the philosopher, but they give themselves no leisure to hear; they are impatient to talk.

The world is always as bad as it dares to be, and if the majority are evil it is because the minority are not good. If the heathen rage, it is because the Christians doubt.

We only use different names; he calls it attar of rose, and I call it bilgewater.

Our boys get caught in their own nets, marry the means, and defeat the ends.

The wars of other people and of history growl at a distance, but your war comes near, looks into your eyes, in politics, in professional pursuit, in choices in the street, in daily habit, in all the questions of the times, in the keeping or surrendering the control of your day, and your horse, and your opinion; in the terrors of the night; in the frauds and skepticism of the day.

A man can only write one book. That is the reason why everybody begs readings and extracts of the young poet until thirty-five. When he is fifty, they still think they value him, and they tell him so; but they scatter like partridges, if he offer to read his paper. They think it is because they have some job to do. But they never allowed a job to stand in the way when he was twenty-five.

I suppose, every one has favorite topics, which make a sort of museum or privileged closet of whimsies in his mind, and which he thinks is a kind of aristocracy to know about. Thus, I like to know about lions, diamonds, wine, and Beauty; and Martial, and Hafiz.

I put the duty of being read, invariably on the author. If he is not read, whose fault is it? If he is very learned and yet heavy, it is a double-shot which fells both himself and his readers.

All the thoughts of a turtle are turtle. Underwitted persons who live in a perpetual sense of inferiority, if also they have the misfortune to have a bad temper, seek to avenge themselves by contriving little insults, which have the effect of making others momentarily inferior.

Universities are, of course, hostile to geniuses.

Last night, talking with Ellery Channing, it appeared still more clear,—the two nations in England,—one in all time fierce only for mince pie,—the old, granniest, beef-eating solemn trifler, a Cheapside 'prentice, and growing to be a Cheapside lord;—the other a fine, thoughtful, religious, poetical believer,—fit for hero, fit for martyr, deriving in his flights only the solidity, and square elbows, and method, from his Cheapside brother, and rewarding him with puritanism, with drama, with letters and liberty.

The art of conversation, or the qualification for a good companion, is a certain self-control, which now holds the subject, now lets it go, with a respect to the emergencies of the moment.

James Furness said, "There was only one person in the world he envied, and that was his wife."

The English believe that by mountains of fact they can climb into the heaven of thought and truth: so the builders of Babel believed.

1855

I do not know that I am ready, like my Dervish* in his more total devotion, to throw my babes into the Stream. No, I am householder, and father, and citizen, far too much for that. But what blazing evidence his vices (so esteemed) afford to the pure beauty that intoxicates him!

How far better his outward shiftlessness and insensibility to what are reckoned the primary claims, than the Bulwer

* Alcott.

view of intellect, as a sort of bill of exchange easily convertible into fine chambers, wines, and cigars.

People fatigue us because they are apes and drilled.

Governor Reynolds, of Illinois, said, "The people were always right." One said, "But they crucified Our Saviour; were they right then?" The Governor looked about him and then replied, "Yes, they were right then, for if they had not crucified him, he could not have been our Saviour."

Men ride on a thought, as if each bestrode an invisible horse, which, if it became visible, all their seemingly mad plunging motions would be explained.

As boys write verses from delight in the music or rhyme, before they learn to delight in the sense, so, when grown older, they write from love of the rhetoric, sooner than for the argument, and, in most instances, a sprightly genius chooses the topic and treatment that gives him room to say fine things, before the sad heroic truth.

I trust a good deal to common fame, as we all must. If a man has good corn, or wood, or boards, or pigs, to sell, or can make better chairs or knives, crucibles or church organs, than anybody else, you will find a broad hard-beaten road to his house, though it be in the woods.* And if a man knows the law, people find it out, though he live in a pine shanty, and resort to him. And if a man can pipe or sing, so as to wrap the prisoned soul in an elysium; or can paint landscape, and convey into oils and ochres all the

* The popular quotation, erroneously attributed to Emerson,—"If a man make a better mouse-trap" etc.,—appears to have been adapted from this entry.

enchantments of Spring or Autumn; or can liberate or intoxicate all people who hear him with delicious songs and verses; 't is certain that the secret cannot be kept: the first witness tells it to a second, and men go by fives and tens and fifties to his door. What a signal convenience is fame.

It is becoming in the scholar to insist on central soundness, rather than on superficial applications. I am to give a wise and just ballot, though no man else in the republic doth. I am not to compromise or mix or accommodate. I am to demand the absolute right, affirm that, and do that; but not push Boston into a false, showy, and theatrical attitude, endeavoring to persuade her she is more virtuous than she is. Thereby I am robbing myself, more than I am enriching the public. After twenty, fifty, a hundred years, it will be quite easy to discriminate who stood for the right, and who for the expedient.

The vulgar, comprising ranks on ranks of fine gentlemen, clergymen, college presidents and professors, and great Democratic statesmen bellowing for Liberty, will of course go for safe degrees of liberty,—that is, will side with property against the Spirit, subtle and absolute, which keeps no terms.

The lover delights in the surprise of face and form yet so dearly related to him. The more foreign, the better. The lady's eye seemed always looking at distant lands and distant people: she could never be domesticated. It was like a young deer or a young leopard, or a forest bird, newly caught and brought into your yard. Still descend to him, prefer him, but, for Heaven's sake, do not lose this exotic charm, which fills his imagination.

Jones Very, who thought it an honour to wash his own face, seems to me less insane than men who hold themselves cheap.

We know the austere law of liberty,—that it must be re-conquered day by day, that it subsists in a state of war, that it is always slipping away from those who boast it, to those who fight for it.

Hurrying America makes out of little vanities its great men, as, now, the three leading men in America are of a small sort, who never saw a grander arch than their own eyebrow.

A man is not to aim at innocence, any more than he is to aim at hair; but he is to keep it.

A scholar is a man with this inconvenience, that, when you ask him his opinion of any matter, he must go home and look up his manuscripts to know.

If the women demand votes, offices, and political equality, refuse it not. 'T is very cheap wit that finds it so funny.

Our fear of death is like our fear that summer will be short, but when we have had our swing of pleasure, our fill of fruit, and our swelter of heat, we say we have had our day.

I want a horse that will run all day like a wolf.

I dread autobiography which usurps the largest part, some-times the whole of the discourse of very worthy persons whom I know.

Le Claire House, Davenport, Iowa, December 31
Rules of the house. "No gentlemen permitted to sit at the table without his coat." "No gambling permitted in the house."

I have crossed the Mississippi on foot three times.

PART VII

1856-1873

In January, 1856, Emerson lectured through Illinois, Wisconsin, Michigan and Ohio in extreme cold and with great discomfort which he accepted, as always, uncomplainingly. In the autumn, his English experiences of eight years before were published, after long testing and sifting on the lecture platform, under the title *English Traits*.

The next winter found Emerson again on a western lecture tour. This year John Brown visited Concord, and the *Atlantic Monthly* was founded.

Hard times constricted the lecture tours in 1858. For reasons unknown there were few journal entries during the year. In the following year came the John Brown raid. Emerson's deepest feelings had been stirred by the slavery question, and on the day of Brown's execution he delivered an address at a commemorative meeting at Concord.

In the year of Lincoln's election, Emerson lectured, as usual, in the Middle West; also in Canada. The preparation of *Conduct of Life* curtailed the journal entries for this year.

Except for his visit to Washington and meetings with Lincoln and other Union leaders in 1862, the stirring events of the Civil War were reflected but dimly in the pages of the journals. This, also, was the year of Thoreau's death.

To celebrate the Emancipation Proclamation, a Musical Festival of Rejoicing was held at Boston in 1863, at which Emerson read his famous "Boston Hymn." Also in that year he served as member of the Board of Visitors at West Point.

After the close of the Civil War the first traces of a slow decline in Emerson's intellectual vitality became evident. Belated honors came to him: from Harvard, an LL.D. and election as an Overseer; also an appointment as lecturer on philosophy. In 1871 he made a trip to California and in the following year, after his house was partially destroyed by fire, visited Europe and sailed up the Nile.

During the seventies, Emerson's memory gradually failed and there are few journal entries. Death—from pneumonia—came on April 27, 1882.

1856

Beloit, January 9

I fancied in this fierce cold weather—mercury varying from 20° to 30° below zero for the last week—that Illinois lands would be at a discount, and the agent, who at Dixon was selling great tracts, would be better advised to keep them for milder days, since a hundred miles of prairie in such days as these are not worth the poorest shed or cellar in the towns. But my easy landlord assured me "we had no cold weather in Illinois, only now and then Indian summer and cool nights." He looked merrily at his window panes, opaque with a stratum of frost, and said that his was a fashionable first-class hotel, with window lights of ground glass.

This climate and people are a new test for the wares of a man of letters. All his thin, watery matter freezes; 't is only the smallest portion of alcohol that remains good. At the lyceum, the stout Illinoian, after a short trial, walks out of the hall. The Committee tell you that the people want a hearty laugh. Well, I think the people are always right (in a sense), and that the man of letters is to say, These are the new conditions to which I must conform. Shakespeare or Franklin or Aesop, coming to Illinois, would say, I must give my wisdom a comic form, and well I know to do it, and he is no master who cannot vary his forms, and carry his own end triumphantly through the most difficult.

Mr. Sweet, a telegraph agent on the Chicago and Rock River line, said, he can tell the name of the operator, by the accent of his dispatch, by the ear, just as readily as he knows the handwriting of his friends. Every operator has his own manner of accent. Boys make the best operators, and, in six months, a boy of sixteen was worth $45.00 a month in an office at Chicago.

The hard times of Illinois were from 1837 to 1845 and onward; when pork was worth twelve shillings a hundred, and men journeyed with loads of wheat and pork a hundred miles or more to Chicago, and sold their wheat for twenty-six cents a bushel, and were obliged to sell their team to get home again. Mr. Jenks, a stage agent and livery-stable keeper, told us of his experiences, and when he left Chicago to go eastward, he would not have given $3.00 for a warranty deed of the State of Illinois.

People here are alive to a benefaction derived from railroads which is inexpressibly great, and vastly exceeding any intentional philanthropy.

My banker here at Adrian is of opinion that, to run on a bank for gold is a criminal offence, and ought to be punished by the state's prison! He delights, he frankly told me, to make such people pay three or four per cent a month for money.

Hospitality consists in a little fire, a little food, but enough, and an immense quiet.

Truth is always new and wild as the wild air, and is alive.

If I knew only Thoreau, I should think coöperation of good men impossible. Must we always talk for victory, and never once for truth, for comfort, and joy? Centrality he has, and penetration, strong understanding, and the higher gifts,—the insight of the real, or from the real, and the moral rectitude that belongs to it; but all this and all his resources of wit and invention are lost to me, in every experiment, year after year, that I make, to hold intercourse with his mind. Always some weary captious paradox to fight you with, and the time and temper wasted.

The most important effect of Copernicus was not on astronomy, but on Calvinism,—tapping the conceit of man; and geology introduces new measures of antiquity.

Now and then leaps a word or a fact to light which is no man's invention, but the common instinct. Thus, "all men are born free and equal"—though denied by all politics, is the key-word of our modern civilization.

Woman should find in man her guardian. Silently she looks for that, and when she finds, as she instantly does, that he is not, she betakes her to her own defences, and does the best she can. But when he is her guardian, all goes well for both.

The property proves too much for the man, and now all the men of science, art, intellect, are pretty sure to degenerate into selfish housekeepers dependent on wine, coffee, furnace, gaslight, and furniture. *Then* things swing the other way, and we suddenly find that civilization crowed too soon; that what we bragged as triumphs were treacheries; that we have opened the wrong door, and let the enemy into the castle; that civilization was a mistake; that nothing is so vulgar as a great warehouse of rooms full of furniture and trumpery; that, in the circumstances, the best wisdom were an auction, or a fire; since the foxes and birds have the right of it, with a warm hole to fend the weather, and no more.

Elizabeth Hoar said of Aunt Mary,—"She thinks much more of her bonnet and of other people's bonnets than they do"; and she sends Elizabeth from Dan to Beersheba to find a bonnet that does not conform; while Mrs. Hoar, whom she severely taxes with conforming, is satisfied with anything she finds in the shops. She tramples on the common humanities all day, and they rise as ghosts and torment her at night.

Whipple* said of the author of "Leaves of Grass," that he had every leaf but the fig leaf.

The audience that assembled to hear my lectures in these six weeks was called "the *effete* of Boston."

It is curious that Thoreau goes to a house to say with little preface what he has just read or observed, delivers it in lump, is quite inattentive to any comment or thought which any of the company offer on the matter, nay, is merely interrupted by it, and when he has finished his report departs with precipitation.

The comfort of Alcott's mind is, the connexion in which he sees whatever he sees. He is never dazzled by a spot of colour, or a gleam of light, to value that thing by itself; but forever and ever is prepossessed by the undivided one behind it and all. I do not know where to find in men or books a mind so valuable to faith.

I shall go far, and see many, before I find such an extraordinary insight as Alcott's. In his fine talk, last evening, he

* Edwin Percy Whipple, American critic and essayist.

ran up and down the scale of powers, with as much ease and precision as a squirrel the wires of his cage, and is never dazzled by his means, or by any particular, and a fine heroic action or a poetic passage would make no impression on him, because he expects heroism and poetry in all. Ideal Purity, the poet, the artist, the man, must have. I have never seen any person who so fortifies the believer, so confutes the skeptic. And the almost uniform rejection of this man by men of parts, Carlyle and Browning inclusive, and by women of piety, might make one despair of society. If they could find him in a book a thousand years old, with a legend of miracles appended, there would be churches of disciples: but now they wish to know if his coat is out at the elbow.

Education. Don't let them eat their seed-corn; don't let them anticipate, ante-date, and be young men, before they have finished their boyhood. Let them have the fields and woods, and learn their secret and the base- and foot-ball, and wrestling, and brickbats, and suck all the strength and courage that lies for them in these games; let them ride bare-back, and catch their horse in his pasture, let them hook and spear their fish, and shin a post and a tall tree, and shoot their partridge and trap the woodchuck, before they begin to dress like collegians, and sing in serenades, and make polite calls.

It must be admitted, that civilization is onerous and expensive; hideous expense to keep it up;—let it go, and be Indians again; but why Indians?—that is costly, too; the mud-turtle and trout life is easier and cheaper, and oyster, cheaper still.

Play out the game, act well your part, and if the gods have blundered, we will not.

Yesterday to the Sawmill Brook with Henry [Thoreau]. He
was in search of yellow violets which he waded into the water for; and which he concluded, on examination, had been
out five days. Having found his flowers, he drew out of his
breast pocket his diary and read the names of all the plants
which should bloom on this day, May 20; whereof he
keeps account as a banker when his notes fall due. But
his attention was drawn to the redstart which flew about
with its *cheap, cheap chevet,* and presently to two fine
grosbeaks, rose-breasted, whose brilliant scarlet "bids the
rash gazer wipe his eye," and which he brought nearer with
his spyglass, and whose fine, clear note he compares to that
of a "tanager who has got rid of his hoarseness." Then he
heard a note which he calls that of the night-warbler, a
bird he has never identified, has been in search of for
twelve years, which, always, when he sees it, is in the act
of diving down into a tree or bush, and which 't is vain to
seek; the only bird that sings indifferently by night and by
day. I told him, he must beware of finding and booking
him, lest life should have nothing more to show him. He
said, "What you seek in vain for half your life, one day
you come full upon—all the family at dinner. You seek
him like a dream, and as soon as you find him, you become
his prey." He thinks he could tell by the flowers what day
of the month it is, within two days.

Water is the first gardener: he always plants grasses and
flowers about his dwelling. There came Henry with music-
book under his arm, to press flowers in; with telescope in
his pocket, to see the birds, and microscope to count sta-
mens; with a diary, jack-knife, and twine; in stout shoes,
and strong grey trousers, ready to brave the shrub-oaks and
smilax, and to climb the tree for a hawk's nest. His strong

legs, when he wades, were no insignificant part of his armour.

I am impressed at the indignation meeting* last night, as ever, on like occasions, with the sweet nitrous oxide gas which the speakers seem to breathe. Once they taste it, they cling like mad to the bladder, and will not let it go. And it is so plain to me that eloquence, like swimming, is an art which all men might learn, though so few do.

I go for those who have received a retaining fee to this party of Freedom, before they came into the world. I would trust Garrison, I would trust Henry Thoreau, that they would make no compromises. I would trust Horace Greeley, I would trust my venerable friend Mr. Hoar, that they would be staunch for freedom to the death; but both of these would have a benevolent credulity in the honesty of the other party, that I think unsafe.

South Carolina is in earnest. I see the courtesy of the Carolinians, but I know meanwhile that the only reason why they do not plant a cannon before Faneuil Hall, and blow Bunker Hill Monument to fragments, as a nuisance, is because they have not the power. They are fast acquiring the power, and if they get it, they will do it.

There are men who as soon as they are born take a beeline to the axe of the inquisitor.

Professor Poikilus had one advantage over the rest of the University, that when the class gaped or began to dimin-

---

* To denounce the attack on Senator Charles Sumner by Preston Brooks of South Carolina.

ish, he would with great celerity throw his heels into the
air, and stand upon his head, and continue his lecture in
that posture, a turn which seemed to invigorate his audience, who would listen with marked cheerfulness as long
as he would speak to them in that attitude.

How the landscape mocks the weakness of man! it is vast,
beautiful, complete, and alive; and we can only dibble and
step about, and dot it a little.

1857

Chicago, Tremont House

'T is very droll to hear the comic stories of the rising values
here, which, ludicrous though they seem, are justified by
facts presently. Mr. Corwin's story of land offered for $50,-
000, and an hour given to consider of it. The buyer made
up his mind to take it, but he could not have it; it was five
minutes past the hour, and it was now worth $60,000.
After dinner, he resolved to give the price, but he had over-
stayed the time again, and it was already $70,000; and it
became $80,000, before night,—when he bought it. I be-
lieve it was Mr. Corwin's joke, but the solemn citizens
who stood by, heard it approvingly, and said, "Yes, that is
about the fair growth of Chicago *per hour.*" However, a
quite parallel case to this, I am told, actually occurred in
the sale of the "American House" lot, which rose in a day
from perhaps $40,000 to 50, 60, 70, 80, or 90,000, at which
price it was sold. Mr. Foster, of Evansville, when I asked
about the once rival towns which competed with Chicago,
said, "Yes, at New City they once thought there was to be
a great centre, and built sixty houses." "Was there not a
river and harbor there?" "Oh yes, there was a guzzle out of
a sandbank, but now there are still the sixty houses, and

when I passed by the last time, there was one owl which was the only inhabitant."

Mr. W. B. Ogden told me that he came here from New York twenty-one years ago. In New York he had, in association with some others, made a large purchase here to the amount of $100,000. He had never been here, but wished to have a reason for coming beyond merely seeing the country; had never then been beyond Buffalo westward.

He arrived here one morning, June 11, 1836. He learned that one of the parties of whom he had purchased was in the house, on his arrival at the tavern or fort, and this person sent for him to come up and see him. This Mr. Bronson had heard some rumor that his brother had sold the land to a company in New York, but hoped it was not so. Mr. Ogden showed him his deed. Bronson said it was all right, but it was injudicious in his brother. Ogden said he was glad to hear that, for he had feared he had made a foolish bargain. While he was in Bronson's room, somebody tapped at the door, and wished to know if the man who represented *Block No. 1* was here? Mr. Ogden knew nothing of it; but Bronson told the man, Yes, Ogden represented that purchase. "Well, will you sell Block No. 1?" Ogden replied he knew nothing of it, but after breakfast he would go and see the land. After breakfast, they crossed in a little boat, and looked about in the swamp and woods, and came to a stake. "Here," said Bronson, "is Block No. 1." Well, they were followed by several persons, and, among others, the one he had seen. These came up, and the man said, "What will you take for this property?" Ogden said he knew nothing of its value, but if they would make him an offer, he would inform himself, and answer. The man said, "We will give you $35,000 for eight blocks from No. 1 to No. 8." Ogden said, "I never altered a muscle of my face, but I looked him in the face, to see if he were joking, and expected they would all laugh; but they all looked solemn, and the speaker no more crazy than the rest. So I took Bronson's arm, and walked apart, and said, 'Is this a joke, or are they crazy, or is this the value of the land?' 'Yes, this is the supposed value.' 'Is it worth more?' 'Perhaps, but you must wait.' So I went back, and said, as gravely as I could, that I would take it; but I expected them to laugh, but that would not harm me. But the man said, 'Well we will pay 10 per cent down, and we will pay it now.' But I said, 'We will go back to the tavern.' But the man was uneasy, and wished to pay now. I said, 'I shall not vary from what I have said.' But the man inclined to pay now. So he took out of his pocket ten $1000 notes of the U. S. Bank, and I put them in my waistcoat pocket."

And from that time Mr. Ogden proceeded to sell piece after piece of the land (about 150 acres) till in one year he had nearly sold the whole for $1,000,000.

Captain John Brown of Kansas gave a good account of himself in the Town Hall, last night, to a meeting of citizens. One of his good points was, the folly of the peace party in Kansas, who believed that their strength lay in the greatness of their wrongs, and so discountenanced resistance. He wished to know if their wrong was greater than the negro's, and what kind of strength that gave to the negro?

He believes on his own experience that one good, believing, strong-minded man is worth a hundred, nay, twenty thousand men without character, for a settler in a new country; and that the right men will give a permanent direction to the fortunes of a state. For one of these bullying, drinking rowdies,—he seemed to think cholera, smallpox, and consumption were as valuable recruits.

The first man who went into Kansas from Missouri to

interfere in the elections, he thought, "had a perfect right to be shot."

When a man says to me, "I have the intensest love of nature," at once I know that he has none.

I once knew of a man who drew a poor girl into his chamber. The girl quickly came to her penitence, and said she was bitterly ashamed. "Ashamed," said the man; "what is there to be ashamed of?" The speeches of our statesmen at Washington are much in the same clear key of correct sentiment.

The hater of property and of government takes care to have his warranty-deed recorded, and the book written against Fame and learning has the author's name on the title-page.

A man signing himself George R—— (of Madison, Wis.) and who seems to be drunk, writes me, that "the secret of drunkenness is, that it insulates us in thought, whilst it unites us in feeling."

Longfellow avoids greedy smokers. A cigar lasts one hour: but is not allowed to lose fire. "Give me the luxuries, the necessities may take their chance."

To teach us the first lesson of humility, God set down man in these two vastitudes of Space and Time, yet is he such an incorrigible peacock that he thinks them only a perch to show his dirty feathers on.

This morning I had the remains of my mother and of my son Waldo removed from the tomb of Mrs. Ripley to my lot in "Sleepy Hollow." The sun shone brightly on the coffins, of which Waldo's was well preserved—now fifteen years. I ventured to look into the coffin. I gave a few white-oak leaves to each coffin, after they were put in the new vault, and the vault was then covered with two slabs of granite.

July 28

Yesterday, the best day of the year, we spent in the afternoon on the river. A sky of Calcutta; light, air, clouds, water, banks, birds, grass, pads, lilies, were in perfection, and it was delicious to live. Ellery and I went up the South Branch, and took a bath from the bank behind Cyrus Hubbard's, where the river makes a bend. Blackbirds in hundreds; swallows in tens sitting on the telegraph lines; and one heron (*ardea minor*) assisted. In these perfect pictures, one thinks what weary nonsense is all this painful collection of rubbish,—pictures of rubbish masters,—in the total neglect of this and every lovely river valley, where the multitudinous life and beauty make these pictures ridiculous, cold chalk and ochre.

I can count on my fingers all the sane men that ever came to me. Were I to insist on silence until I was fully met, and all my faculty called out and tasked by my companion, I should have a solitary time of it. Those who visit me are young men, imperfect persons, people with some partial thought, or local culture.

Thoughts. Will he coax and stroke these deities? I do. I can no more manage these thoughts that come into my head than thunderbolts. But once get them written down, I come and look at them every day, and get wonted to their faces, and by and by, am so far used to them that I see their family likeness, and can pair them and range them better, and if I once see where they belong and join them in that order, they will stay so.

Yesterday with Ellery at Flint's Pond. The pond was in its summer glory, the chestnuts in flower, two fishermen in a boat, thundertops in the sky, and the whole picture a study of all the secrets of landscape.

The great afternoon spends like fireworks, or festival of the gods, with a tranquil exultation, as of a boy that has launched his first boat, or his little balloon, and the experiment succeeds.

The woodchopper, by using the force of gravity, lets the planet chop his stick.

Good writing sips the foam of the cup. There are infinite degrees of delicacy in the use of the hands; and good workmen are so distinguished from laborers; and good horsemen, from rude riders; and people of elegant manners, from the vulgar. In writing, it is always at the surface, and can chip off a scale, where a coarser hand and eye find only solid wall.

If a man is set on collecting diamonds, or Arabian horses, or an arboretum, or a particular piece of land, or a telescope, his heat makes the value.

The abolitionists are not better men for their zeal. They have neither abolished slavery in Carolina, nor in me. If they cannot break one fetter of mine, I cannot hope they will of any negro. They are bitter, sterile people whom I flee from, to the unpretentious whom they disparage.

Gauss, I believe it is, who writes books that nobody can understand but himself, and himself only in his best hours.

Henry [Thoreau] avoids commonplace, and talks birch bark to all comers, reduces them all to the same insignificance.

The Atlantic Monthly. A journal is an assuming to guide the age—very proper and necessary to be done, and good news that it shall be so. But this journal, is this it? Has Apollo spoken?

The best the Editor can do is, to see that nothing goes into the book but important pieces; every chapter must record of real experiences. It suffices that it be weighty. It matters not whether 't is upon Religion, or Balloons, or Kneebuckles, so only that there is nothing fantastic or factitious in the subject and writing. Great scope and illumination ought to be in the Editor, to draw from the best in the land, and to defy the public, if he is only sure himself that the piece has worth, and is right. Publics are very placable, and will soon find out when they have a master. The value of money-capital is to be able to hold out for a few months, and go on printing, until the discerning minority of the public have found out that the book is right, and must be humbly and thankfully accepted.

What an obstinate illusion is that which in youth gives respect to the old!

I owe real knowledge and even alarming hints to dreams, and wonder to see people extracting emptiness from mahogany tables, when there is vaticination in their dreams. For the soul in dreams has a subtle synthetic power which it will not exert under the sharp eyes of day. It does not like to be watched or looked upon, and flies to real twilights, as the rappers do in their wretched mummeries. If in dreams you see loose and luxurious pictures, an inevitable tie drags in the sequel of cruelty and malignity. If you swallow the devil's bait, you will have a horizon full of dragons shortly.

When I higgled for my dime and half-dime in the dream, and lost,—the parrots on the chimney tops, and church pinacles scoffed at me, Ho! ho!

Is there no check to this class of privileged thieves that infest our politics? We mark and lock up the petty thief, or we raise the hue and cry in the street, and do not hesitate to draw our revolvers out of the box, when one is in the house. But here are certain well-dressed, well-bred fellows, infinitely more mischievous, who get into the government and rob without stint, and without disgrace. They do it with a high hand, and by the device of having a party to whitewash them, to abet the act, and lie, and vote for them. And often each of the larger rogues has his newspaper, called "his organ," to say that it was not stealing, this which he did; that if there was stealing, it was you who stole, and not he.

I took such pains not to keep my money in the house, but to put it out of the reach of burglars by buying stock, and had no guess that I was putting it into the hands of these very burglars now grown wiser and standing dressed as Railway Directors.

Wisdom has its root in goodness, and not goodness its root in wisdom. A thought is embosomed in a sentiment, which broadens indefinitely around it, and the attempt to detach and blazon the thought by itself is like a show of cut flowers.

When the microscope is improved, we shall have the cells analysed, and all will be electricity, or somewhat else.

You must draw your rule from the genius of that which you do, and not from by-ends. Don't make a novel to establish a principle of political economy. You will spoil both. Don't set out to teach Theism from your Natural History, like Paley and Agassiz. You spoil both.

Paper money is a wonderful convenience, which builds up cities and nations, but it has this danger in it, like a camphene lamp, or a steam boiler, it will sometimes explode. So excellent a tool we cannot spare, but must take it with its risks. We know the dangers of the railroad, but we prefer it with its dangers to the old coach, and we must not forego the high civility of paper and credit, though once in twenty years it breaks the banks, and puts all exchange and traffic at a stand.

1858

When a dog barks on the stage of a theatre, the audience are interested. What acting can take their attention from the dog? But if in the real action which their scene represents, a dog had barked, it would not have been heard.

Taking to pieces is the trade of those who cannot construct.

It is impossible to be a gentleman, and not be an abolitionist.

The populace drag down the gods to their own level.

What unreckoned elements the orator carries with him, for example, silence. He performs as much or more with judicious pauses, as by his best stroke.

Wealth consists in having at every moment a commanding position as regards your ends. A man in debt has not. Every hour is bringing certain opportunities to do somewhat desirable. But we are not free to use to-day, or to promise to-morrow, because we are already mortgaged to yesterday, having eaten our cake before we had earned it.

1859

To be isolated, is to be sick, and so far dead. That is, the life of the *All* must stream through us, to make the man and the moment great.

I am a natural reader, and only a writer in the absence of natural writers. In a true time, I should never have written.

I have now for more than a year, I believe, ceased to write in my Journal, in which I formerly wrote almost daily. I see few intellectual persons, and even those to no purpose, and sometimes believe that I have no new thoughts, and that my life is quite at an end. But the magnet that lies in my drawer, for years, may believe it has no magnetism, and, on touching it with steel, it knows the old virtue; and, this morning, came by a man with knowledge and interests like mine, in his head, and suddenly I had thoughts again.

The world is reckoned by dull men a dead subject, whilst it is quick and blazing. The house and farm are thought fixed and lasting, whilst they are rushing to ruin every moment. The difference between skilful and unskilful men is

—that the one class are timed to this movement, and move with it, can load as they go, can read as they run, can write in a cab; whilst the heavy men wait for the eagle to alight, for the swallow to roost like a barn fowl, for the river to run by, for the pause in the conversation, which never comes till the guests take their hats.

Events are not as the brute circumstance that falls, but as the life which they fall upon. Out of the same carbon and ammonia, the rose will make a rose, and the nettle a nettle. The same air in the trachea of an ass will bray, in the trachea of a nightingale will sing.

I have been writing and speaking what were once called novelties, for twenty-five or thirty years, and have not now one disciple. Why? Not that what I said was not true; not that it has not found intelligent receivers; but because it did not go from any wish in me to bring men to me, but to themselves. I delight in driving them from me. What could I do, if they came to me?—they would interrupt and encumber me. This is my boast that I have no school follower. I should account it a measure of the impurity of insight, if it did not create independence.

Here came the sub-soil plougher, H.J.*

Henry James said of woman, "That the flesh said, It is for me, and the spirit said, It is for me."

Egotism is a kind of buckram that gives momentary strength and concentration to human beings.

* Henry James, Senior, father of the novelist.

A great man is always a contradiction to his age and to fore-going history.

People live like these boys who watch for a sleigh-ride and mount on the first that passes, and when they meet another that they know, swing themselves on to that, and ride in another direction, until a third passes, and they change again; 't is no matter where they go, as long as there is snow and company.

There is no strong performance without a little fanaticism in the performer.

You need not write the History of the World, nor the Fall of Man, nor King Arthur, nor Iliad, nor Christianity; but write of hay, or of cattle shows, or trade sales, or of a ship, or of Ellen, or Alcott, or of a couple of schoolboys, if only you can be the fanatic of your subject, and find a fibre reaching from it to the core of your heart, so that all your affection and all your thought can freely play.

Nature wishes that woman should attract man, but she has cunningly made them with a little sarcasm in expression, which seems to say, "Yes, I am willing to attract, but to attract a little better kind of man than any I yet see."

In reading prose, I am sensible as soon as a sentence drags, but in reading poetry, as soon as one word drags.

Am I not, one of these days, to write consecutively of the beatitude of the intellect? It is too great for feeble souls, and they are over-excited. The wineglass shakes, and the wine is spilled. What then? The joy which will not let me sit in my chair, which brings me bolt upright to my feet, and sends me striding around my room, like a tiger in his cage, and I cannot have composure and concentration enough even to set down in English words the thought which thrills me—is not that joy a certificate of the elevation? What if I never write a book or a line? for a moment, the eyes of my eyes were opened.

'T is a great misfortune of certain temperaments that they are by their own force, or too much determination, thrown out of all sympathy, and are therefore inconvertible. They cannot be made to see when they are in the wrong, and when they are rushing to ruin, taking the bits in their teeth, they are then triumphantly assured of their innocency, and mere Phocions, scorning the universe of objectors. Argument, appeal to bystanders, to a world of bystanders, masses of opposing fact, all is wasted; 't is only oil to flame, only mountains of confirmation to their insanity. In these tragic cases, their own talent, acuteness, cannot help them, even genius, as in Aunt Mary, only widens the hopeless chasm.

We like a person of will and of thought because there is nobody behind his chair. It is the year one, and the Emperor is here.

On Wachusett, I sprained my foot. It was slow to heal, and I went to the doctors. Dr. Henry Bigelow said, "Splint and absolute rest." Dr. Russell said, "Rest, yes; but a splint, no." Dr. Bartlett said, "Neither splint nor rest, but go and walk." Dr. Russell said, "Pour water on the foot, but it must be warm." Dr. Jackson said, "Stand in a trout brook all day."

When I sprained my foot I soon found it was all one as if I had sprained my head, if I must sit in my chair. Then I

thought Nature had sprained her foot; and that King Lear
had never sprained his, or he would have thought there
were worse evils than unkind daughters. When I see a man
unhappy, I ask, has a sprained foot brought him to this pass?

Dread the collectors, whether of books, of shells, of coins,
of eggs, of newspapers; they become alike trustless. Their
hunger over-rides their honesty. A *forte* always makes a
foible.

Remember Norton's story of the gentleman who passed
the antique coin which he believed to be unique around
his dinner-table, and lost it. One guest alone refused to be
searched, and, after it was found on the floor, excused his
refusal by announcing he had a duplicate of the coin at
that moment in his pocket.

From a Speech at the Dinner to Dr. Holmes, August 29
MR. PRESIDENT,—

When I read the *Atlantic*, I have had much to think of the
beneficence of wit, its vast utility; the extreme rarity, out of
this presence, of the pure article. Science has never measured the immense profundity of the Dunce-Power. The
globe of the world—the diameter of the solar system, is
nothing to it. Everywhere, a thousand fathoms of sandstone
to a teaspoonful of wit. And yet people speak with apprehension of the dangers of wit, as if there were, or could
be, an excess.

We all remember, in 1849, it was thought California
would make gold so cheap that perhaps it would drive lead
and zinc out of use for covering roofs and sink-spouts, but
here we have had a Mississippi River of gold pouring in
from California, Australia, and Oregon for ten years, and all
has not yet displaced one pewter basin from our kitchens,
and I begin to believe that if Heaven had sent us a dozen

men as electrical as Voltaire or Sidney Smith, the old Dulness would hold its ground, and die hard.

Why, look at the fact, Whilst, once, wit was extremely rare and sparse-sown,—rare as cobalt, rare as platina,—here comes the Doctor and flings it about like sea-sand, threatens to make it common as newspapers; is actually the man to contract to furnish a chapter of Rabelais or Sidney Smith once a month—bucketsful of Greek fire against tons of paunch and acres of bottom. Of course, the danger was that he would throw out of employment all the dunces, the imposters, the slow men, the stock writers; in short, all the respectabilities and professional learning of the time. No wonder the world was alarmed.

And yet the old House of Unreason stands firm at this day, when he is fifty years old, and he is bound to live a hundred in order to spend the half of his treasure.

The beggars arrive every day, some on foot, the Sardinians and Sicilians, who cannot argue the question of labor and mendicity with you, since they do not speak a word of English; then the Monumentals, who come in landaus or barouches, and wish your large aid to Mount Vernon, Plymouth, Ball's Webster, or President Quincy in marble; then the chipping lady from the Cape, who has three blind sisters, and I know not how many dumb ones, and she had been advised to put them in the Poor House. No, not she. As long as she had health, she would go about and sell these books for them, which I am to buy, and she tosses her head, and expects my praise and tears for her heroic resolution; though I had a puzzled feeling that, if there was sacrifice anywhere, it was in me, if I should buy them; and I am sure I was very little inclined to toss my head on the occasion.

I think wealth has lost much of its value, if it have not wine. I abstain from wine only on account of the expense.

'T is surprising how often I am reminded of my Aunt Mary Emerson in reading Boswell lately. Johnson impresses his company as she does, not only by the point of the remark, but also when the point fails, because he makes it. Like hers, his obvious religion or superstition, his deep wish that they should think so or so, weighs with them, so rare is depth of feeling, or a constitutional value for a thought or opinion, among the light-minded men and women who make up society. And this, though in both cases their companions know that there is a degree of shortcoming, and of insincerity, and of talking for victory.

The imagination enters into all the details and ennobles life. Even the shopboy smoking his cigar assumes the attitude and air of rich gentlemen, and is raised in his own eyes.

There are men whose opinion of a book is final. If Ellery Channing tells me, "Here is a good book," I know I have a day longer to live. But there are plenty of able men whose report in that kind is not to be trusted.

The believing we do something when we do nothing is the first illusion of tobacco.

1860

The engineer was goading his boilers with pitch-pine knots.

The traveller looked out of the car window; the fences passed languidly by; he would scan curiously every post. But very soon the jerk of every pulse of the engine was felt; the whistle of the engineer moaned short moans, as it swept across any highway. He gazed out over the fields; the fences were tormented; every rail and rider writhed and twisted past the window; the snowbanks swam past like fishes; and the speed seemed to increase every moment. The near trees and bushes wove themselves into coloured ribbons. The rocks, walls, the fields themselves streaming like a mill-race. The train tore on with jumps and jerks that tested the strength of oak and iron. The passengers seemed to suffer their speed. Meantime, the wind cried like a child, complained like a sawmill, whistled like a fife, mowed like an idiot, roared like the sea, and yelled like a demon.

When an Eastern man is cheated by a Hoosier, he is said to be *Wabashed*.

When our friends die, we not only lose them, but we lose a great deal of life which in the survivors was related to them.

Election. The news of last Wednesday morning (7th) was sublime, the pronunciation of the masses of America against Slavery.

1861

We have no guess what we are doing, even then when we do our best; perhaps it will not appear for an age or two yet; then the dim outline of the reef and new continent we madrepores were making, will sketch itself to the eyes of the dullest sailor.

The furious slaveholder does not see that the one thing he is doing, by night and by day, is to destroy slavery. They who help and they who hinder are all equally diligent in hastening its downfall. Blessed be the inevitabilities.

I watched the fair boy and girl—one as fair and sweet as the other; both surprised with a new consciousness, which made every hour delicious; each laying little traps for the attention of the other, and each jumping joyfully into the traps.

Because I have no ear for music, at the Concert of the Quintette Club it looked to me as if the performers were crazy, and all the audience were making-believe crazy, in order to soothe the lunatics, and keep them amused.

I often say to young writers and speakers that their best masters are their fault-finding brothers and sisters at home, who will not spare them, but be sure to pick and cavil, and tell the odious truth. It is smooth mediocrity, weary elegance, surface finish of our voluminous stock-writers, or respectable artists, which easy times and a dull public call out, without any salient genius, with an indigence of all grand design, of all direct power. A hundred statesmen, historians, painters, and small poets are thus made: but Burns, and Carlyle, and Bettine, and Michel Angelo, and Thoreau were pupils in a rougher school.

It is very hard to go beyond your public. If they are satisfied with your poor performance, you will not easily make better. But if they know what is good and delight in it, you will aspire, and burn, and toil, till you achieve it.

The chamber of flame in which the martyr passes is more magnificent than the royal apartment from which majesty looks out on his sufferings.

Do thy duty of the day. Just now, the supreme public duty of all thinking men is to assert freedom. Go where it is threatened, and say, "I am for it, and do not wish to live in the world a moment longer than it exists." Phillips has the supreme merit in this time, that he and he alone stands in the gap and breach against the assailants. Hold up his hands. He did me the honour to ask me to come to the meeting at Tremont Temple, and, esteeming such invitation a command, though sorely against my inclination and habit, I went, and, though I had nothing to say, showed myself. If I were dumb, yet I would have gone and mowed and muttered or made signs. The mob roared whenever I attempted to speak, and after several beginnings, I withdrew.

I read many friendly and many hostile paragraphs in the journals about my new book, but seldom or never a just criticism. As long as I do not wince, it cannot be that the fault is touched. When the critics hit you, I suppose you will know it. I often think I could write a criticism on Emerson that would hit the white.

Every man has his Diminisher and his Enlarger in his set.

The most tender, the most radiant, the most sublime landscape is stark as tombstones, except seen by the thoughtful.

What came over me with delight as I sat on the ledge in the warm light of last Sunday was the memory of young days at College, the delicious sensibility of youth, how the air rings to it! how all light is festal to it! how it at any moment extemporizes a holiday! Oh the power of the spring! and, ah, the voice of the bluebird! And the witchcraft of the Mount Auburn dell, in those days!

Bishop Clark, of Rhode Island, told of a dispute in a vestry at Providence between two hot church-members. One said at last, "I should like to know who *you* are."—"Who I am!" cried the other,—"who I am! I am a humble Christian, you damned old heathen, you!"

One capital advantage of old age is the absolute insignificance of a success more or less. I went to town and read a lecture yesterday. Thirty years ago it had really been a matter of importance to me whether it was good and effective. Now it is of none in relation to me. It is long already fixed what I can and what I cannot do.

In youth, the day is not long enough.

Old men are drunk with time.

I delight to see boys, who have the same liberal ticket of admission to all shops, factories, armories, town meetings, caucuses, mobs, target-shootings as flies have; and I desire to be saved from their infinite contempt. If I can pass with them, I can manage well enough with their fathers.

The country is cheerful and jocund in the belief that it has a government at last. The men in search of a party, parties in search of a principle, interests and dispositions that could not fuse for want of some base,—all joyfully unite in this great Nothern party, on the basis of Freedom.

I am at a loss to understand why people hold Miss Austen's novels at so high a rate, which seem to me vulgar in tone, sterile in artistic invention, imprisoned in the wretched conventions of English society, without genius, wit, or knowledge of the world. Never was life so pinched and narrow. The one problem in the mind of the writer in both the stories I have read, *Persuasion,* and *Pride and Prejudice,* is marriageableness. All that interests in any character introduced is still this one, Has he [or she] the money to marry with, and conditions conforming? 'T is "the nympholepsy of a fond despair," say, rather, of an English boarding-house. Suicide is more respectable.

Last night a pictorial dream fit for Dante. I read a discourse somewhere to an assembly, and rallied in the course of it to find that I had nearly or quite fallen asleep. Then presently I went into what seemed a new house, the inside wall of which had many shelves let into the wall, on which great and costly vases of Etruscan and other richly adorned pottery stood. The wall itself was unfinished, and I presently noticed great clefts, intended to be filled with mortar or brickwork, but not yet filled, and the wall which held all these costly vases, threatening to fall. Then I noticed in the center shelf or alcove of the wall a man asleep, whom I understood to be the architect of the house. I called to my brother William, who was near me, and pointed to this sleeper as the architect, when the man turned, and partly arose, and muttered something about a plot to expose him.

When I fairly woke, and considered the picture, and the connection of the two dreams,—what could I think of the purpose of Jove who sends the dream?

Lately I find myself oft recurring to the experience of the partiality of each mind I know. I so readily imputed symmetry to my fine geniuses, on perceiving their excellence in some insight. How could I doubt that Thoreau, that Charles Newcomb, that Alcott, or that Henry James, as I successively met them, was the master-mind, which, in some act, he appeared. No, he was only master-mind in that particular act. He could repeat the like stroke a million times, but, in new conditions, he was inexpert, and in new company, he was dumb.

The vice in manners is disproportion. 'T is right that the hearth be swept, and the lamps right, but never interrupt conversation, or so much as pass between the faces of the inmates, to adjust these things. For you lose the end in the means.

1862

When newly awaked from lively dreams, we are so near them, still in their sphere;—give us one syllable, one feature, one hint, and we should re-possess the whole; hours of this strange entertainment and conversation would come trooping back to us; but we cannot get our hand on the first link or fibre, and the whole is forever lost. There is a strange wilfulness in the speed with which it disperses, and baffles your grasp.

Cannot we let people be themselves, and enjoy life in their own way? You are trying to make that man another *you*. One's enough.

The philosopher speaks over the heads of the contemporary audience to that advancing assembly he sees beyond.

Our only safe rule in politics heretofore was always to believe that the worst would be done. Then we were not deceived.

It is impossible to extricate oneself from the questions in which your age is involved. You can no more keep out of politics than you can keep out of the frost.

Hitch your wagon to a star. Do the like in your choice of tasks. Let us not fag in paltry selfish tasks which aim at private benefit alone. No god will help. We shall find all the teams going the other way. Charles's Wain, the Great Bear, Orion, Leo, Hercules. Every god will leave us. Let us work rather for those interests which the gods honour and promote: justice, love, utility, freedom, knowledge.

The world is full of pot-and-pan policy. Every nation is degraded by the hobgoblins it worships, instead of the eternal gods.

At Washington, January 31, February 1, 2, and 3. Saw Sumner, who, on the 2d, carried me to Mr. Chase, Mr. Bates, Mr. Stanton, Mr. Welles, Mr. Seward, Lord Lyons, and President Lincoln. The President impressed me more favourably than I had hoped. A frank, sincere, well-meaning man, with a lawyer's habit of mind, good clear statement of his fact; correct enough, not vulgar, as described, but with a sort of boyish cheerfulness, or that kind of sincerity and jolly good meaning that our class meetings on Commencement Days show, in telling our old stories over. When he has made his remark, he looks up at you with great satisfaction, and shows all his white teeth, and laughs. He argued to Sumner the whole case of Gordon, the slave-trader,* point by point, and added that he was not quite satisfied yet, and meant to refresh his memory by looking again at the evidence. All this showed a fidelity and conscientiousness very honourable to him.

---

* Gordon was convicted and hanged for this crime.

When I was introduced to him, he said, "Oh, Mr. Emerson, I once heard you say in a lecture, that a Kentuckian seems to say by his air and manners, "Here am I; if you don't like me, the worse for you.'"

Mr. Stanton made a good impression, as of an able, determined man, very impatient of his instruments, and, though he named nobody, I thought he had McClellan in mind. When somewhat was said of England, he said, "England is to be met in Virginia.—Mud! Oh, yes, but there has been mud before. Ah, the difficulty isn't outside, 't is inside."

Mr. Seward received us in his dingy State Department. We spoke as we entered the anteroom, or rather in the corridor, with Governor Andrew and Mr. [John Murray] Forbes, who were waiting. Sumner led me along, and upstairs, and into the Secretary's presence. He began, "Yes, I know Mr. Emerson," and he proceeded to talk a little, when Sumner said, "I met Governor Andrew waiting outside. Shan't I call him in?" "Oh, yes," said Seward. Sumner went out and brought in him and Mr. Forbes. Mr. Seward took from the shelf a large half-smoked cigar, lighted and pulled at it. Sumner went into a corner, with Andrew, and Mr. Forbes seized the moment to say to the Secretary that he saw there was an effort making to get Gordon the slave-trader pardoned. He hoped the Government would show to foreign nations that there was a change and a new spirit in it, which would not deal with this crime as heretofore. Seward looked very cross and ugly at this; twisted his cigar about, and I thought, twisted his nose also, and said coarsely, "Well, perhaps you would be willing to stand in his place," or something like that, and rather surprised and disconcerted Mr. Forbes, but Mr. Forbes, seeing that, though we had risen to go, Sumner still talked with Andrew, went up to him, put his hands about him, and said, "Don't you see you are obstructing the public business?" or somewhat to that effect, and so we made our adieus. Mr. Seward came up to me, and said, "Will you come to church with me to-morrow, at 10¼, and we will go home afterwards, and get some lunch or dinner."

As Judge Chase had invited us to dine with him at five o'clock, we went thither, and saw his pretty daughter Kate, who alone with her father did the honours of the house. He and Sumner appeared to agree entirely in their counsels.

From Mr. Chase we went to General Frémont, but unhappily he had stepped out, and Mrs. Frémont detained us, "because he would surely step in again in a few minutes." She was excellent company, a musical indignation, a piece of good sense and good humour, but incessantly accusing the Government of the vast wrong that had been done to the General.

The next morning at 10¼, I visited Mr. Seward, in his library, who was writing, surrounded by his secretary and some stockbrokers. After they had gone, I said, "You never come to Massachusetts." "No," he said, "I have neither the power nor the inclination." His father died early and left him the care, not only of his own family, but of his cousin's property, three fiduciary trusts, and he had much on his hands. Then he early saw that whatever money he earned was slipping away from him, and he must put it in brick and stone, if he would keep it, and he had, later, obtained a tract of land in Chatauqua (?) County, which, by care and attention, had become valuable, and all this had occupied him until he came into public life, and for the last fifteen (?) years, he had been confined in Washington. Besides, Massachusetts was under a cotton aristocracy, and Mr. Webster worked for them; he did not like them, and had as much as he could do to fight the cotton aristocracy in his own State; so he had never gone thither on general politics. He said, "I am a peacemaker, I never work in another method. Men are so constituted that the possession of force makes the demonstration of force quite unnecessary. If I am six feet high and well proportioned, and my adversary is four feet high and well proportioned, I need not strike him,—he will do as I say. On the day when the political power passed over to the Free States, the fate of Slavery was sealed. I saw it was only a question of time and I have remained in that belief. I was not wise enough to foresee all that has happened since. But it is not important, all was then settled, and is turning out as I expected. All the incidents must follow, both at home and abroad. England and France are only incidents. There is no resisting this. The Supreme Court follows too." But he spoke as if all was done and to be done *by him*, by the executive, and with little or no help from Congress. They do nothing.

We went to church. I told him I hoped he would not demoralize me; I was not much accustomed to churches, but trusted he would carry me to a safe place. On the way we met Governor Fish, who was also to go with him. Miss Seward, to whom I had been presented, accompanied us. I was a little awkward in finding my place in the Common Prayer Book, and Mr. Seward was obliging in guiding me, from time to time. In going out, Mr. Seward praised the sermon. I said that the Doctor did not seem to have read the Gospel according to San Francisco, or the Epistle to the Californians; he had not got quite down into these noisy times.

Mr. Seward said, "Will you go and call on the President? I usually call on him at this hour." Or course, I was glad to go.

We found in the President's chamber his two little sons,—boys of seven and eight years, perhaps,—whom the barber was dressing and "whiskeying their hair" as he said, not much to the apparent contentment of the boys, when the cologne got into their eyes. The eldest boy immediately told Mr. Seward, "he could not guess what they had got." Mr. Seward "bet a quarter of a dollar that he could. Was it a rabbit? was it a bird? was it a pig?" He guessed always wrong, and *paid his quarter* to the youngest, before the eldest declared it was a rabbit. But he sent away the mulatto to find the President, and the boys disappeared. The President came, and Mr. Seward said, "You have not been to Church to-day." "No," he said, "and, if he must make a frank confession, he had been reading for the first time Mr. Sumner's Speech (on the Trent affair)." Something was said of newspapers, and of the story that appeared in the journals, of some one who selected all the articles which Marcy should read, etc., etc. The President incidentally remarked, that for the New York *Herald*, he certainly ought to be much obliged to it for the part it had taken for the Government in the Mason and Slidell business. Then Seward said somewhat to explain the apparent steady malignity of the London *Times*. It was all an affair of the great interests of markets. The great capitalists had got this or that stock. As soon as anything happens that affects their value, this value must be made real, and the *Times* must say just what is required to sell those values, etc., etc. The Government had little or no voice in the matter.

We left the President, and returned to Mr. Seward's house. At dinner his two sons, with Miss Seward, were present. Mr. Seward said that his most intimate friend had been, for very many years, Mr. Thurlow Weed, of Albany. He was in habit of fullest correspondence with him on all subjects, and "every year on the first of January, Mr. Weed's daughter has my last year's letters bound up into a volume. And there they all lie, twelve volumes of my letters on her centre table, open to all to read them who will."

In all this talk, Mr. Seward's manner and face were so intelligent and amiable that I, who had thought him so ugly the day before, now thought him positively handsome.

At six o'clock, I obeyed Mrs. Hooper's invitation and went to dine (for the second time that day). I found Mr. Hooper and his son and daughters, Governor and Mrs. Andrew, and Mrs. Schuyler. Governor Andrew had much to say of Mr. Seward. He thought that he surpassed all men in the bold attempt at gasing other people, and pulling wool over their eyes. He thought it very offensive. He might be a donkey,—a good many men are,—but he didn't like to have a man by this practice show that he thought him one. I told him that I had much better impressions of Mr. Seward, but I did not relate to him any conversations.

Thoreau. Perhaps his fancy for Walt Whitman grew out of his taste for wild nature, for an otter, a woodchuck, or a loon. He loved sufficiency, hated a sum that would not prove; loved Walt and hated Alcott.

The old school of Boston citizens whom I remember in my childhood had great vigour, great noisy bodies; I think a certain sternutatory vigour the like whereof I have not heard again. When Major B. or old Mr. T. H. took out their pocket handkerchiefs at church, it was plain they meant business; they would snort and roar through their noses, like the lowing of an ox, and make all ring again.

War, the searcher of character, the test of men, has tried already so many reputations, has pricked so many bladders. 'T is like the financial crises, which, once in ten or twenty years, come to try the men and institutions of trade; using, like them, no ceremony, but plain laws of gravity and force to try tension and resistance. Scott, McDowell, McClellan, Frémont, Banks, Butler, and I know not how many more, are brought up, each in turn, dragged up irresistibly to the anthropometer, measured and weighed, and the result proclaimed to the Universe.

The war searches character, and acquits those whom I acquit, whom life acquits, those whose reality and spontaneous honesty and singleness appear. Force it requires. 'T is not so much that you are moral as that you are genuine, sincere, frank, and bold. I do not approve those who give money or give their voices for liberty from long habit and the feminine predominance of sentiment, but the rough Democrat who hates Garrison, but detests these Southern traitors. The first class will go in the right way, but they are devoured by sentiments like premature fruit ripened by the worm.

Sam Staples yesterday had been to see Henry Thoreau. "Never spent an hour with more satisfaction. Never saw a man dying with so much pleasure and peace." Thinks that very few men in Concord know Mr. Thoreau; finds him serene and happy.

The first care of a man settling in the country should be to open the face of the earth to himself by a little knowledge of Nature, or a great deal of knowledge, if he can, of birds, plants and astronomy; in short, the art of taking a walk.

In the garden, put pansies that make mouths at you, every one droller and more elfish than the last, as if you had Punch done in flowers.

'T is inexcusable in a man who has messages to men, who has truths to impart, to scribble flourishes. He should write that which cannot be omitted; every sentence a cube, standing on its bottom like a die, essential and immortal.

Henry Thoreau* remains erect, calm, self-subsistent, before me, and I read him not only truly in his Journal, but he is not long out of mind when I walk, and, as to-day, row upon the pond. He chose wisely no doubt for himself to be the bachelor of thought and nature that he was,—how near to the old monks in their ascetic religion! He had no talent for wealth, and knew how to be poor without the least hint of squalor or inelegance. Perhaps he fell—all of us do—into his way of living, without forecasting it much, but approved and confirmed it with later wisdom.

If there is a little strut in the style of Henry, it is only from a vigour in excess of the size of his body.

What a ludicrous figure is a village gentleman defending his few rods of clover from the street boys who lose their ball in it once a day! In a world where a remedy exists for every mischief is there none for the sentimentalist, if it were only a boy's cracker to silence cats under the dormitory windows!

In the caprice and credulity of people, all these rumours and opinions take their rise, to which Whigs and statesmen and cities attach great weight, shaking their heads, and looking grave. "But Kentucky, but Baltimore, but Wall Street, and State Street." "Aye, be sure we had not thought of that." The rumours, the opinions are allowed to have importance, and therefore we must wait, and Congress is

* Died May 6, 1862.

justified and the President is right in caution, and in suspending his purpose. But by listening thus in here, and out there, to each new report, one is left in a chronic puzzle, and incapacity to move. By and by, a strong wind of a battle or of one energetic mind appears, and the whole drift and scud, with all its forms of bears, mountains, and dragons, vanishes out of sight, and the plain way of reason and right reappears once and forever.

A man's connections must be looked after. If he surpasses everybody in mother wit, yet is scholar like the rest, be sure he has got a mother or father or aunt or cousin who has the uncorrupted slang of the street, the pure mud, and which is inestimable to him as spice and alterative, and which delights you in his rhetoric, like the devil's tunes when put to slow time in church-music.

The art of the writer is to speak his fact and have done. Let the reader find that he cannot afford to omit any line of your writing, because you have omitted every word that he can spare.

You are annoyed—are you?—that your fine friends do not read you. They are better friends than you knew, and have done you the rarest service. Now write so that they must.

When you next write on conceit, have the good nature to see it as it is, a balsam, a sugar on the lip of the cup to sweeten the sad potation to all mortals.

How kind this keeping the eyes shut! The little rhymester is just as much pleased with his *vers de société* as the poet with his images; on the whole is happier, for he thinks they are good, and the poet is always wretched at his shortcomings.

As people rise in the social scale, they think more of each other's opinion than of their own. And 't is hard to find one who does not measure his business and daily performance from the supposed estimate. And yet, his own is the only standard. Down in the pits of hunger and want life has a real dignity, from this doing the best, instead of the seemly. The sailor on the topmast in a storm, the hunter amidst the snowdrifts, the woodman in the depth of the forest, cannot stop to think how he looks, or what London or Paris would say, and therefore his garb and behaviour have a certain dignity, like the works of Nature around him; he would as soon ask what the crows and muskrats think of him.

I don't know that the Government can carry on a war; and it has ever been in the minds of our people who know how public action drags, and how efficient is private enterprise, to turn it over to private hands, and let Adams's Express undertake by contract the capture of Richmond, of Charleston, of the pirate *Alabama*, and any other designated parts of the war.

When I bought my farm, I did not know what a bargain I had in the bluebirds, bobolinks, and thrushes; as little did I know what sublime mornings and sunsets I was buying.

George Francis Train said in a public speech in New York, "Slavery is a divine institution." "So is hell," exclaimed an old man in the crowd.

Great harvest this year of apples and pears. I suppose I have sold a hundred barrels of apples, when I add the August and September sales to the winter apples.

What a convivial talent is that of Wendell Holmes! He is still at his Club, when he travels in search of his wounded son;* has the same delight in his perceptions, in his wit, in its effect, which he watches as a belle the effect of her beauty; would still hold each companion fast by his spritely, sparkling, widely-allusive talk, as at the Club table; tastes all his own talent, calculates every stroke, and yet the fountain is unfailing, the wit excellent, the *savoir vivre* and *savoir parler* admirable.

Isaac Hecker, the Catholic Priest, came to see me and desired to read lectures on the Catholic Church in Concord. I told him that nobody would come to hear him, such was the aversation of people, at present, to theological questions; and not only so, but the drifting of the human mind was now quite in another direction than to any churches. But I doubt if any impression can be made on Father Isaac. He converted Mrs. W——, and, like a lion that has eaten a man, he wants to be at it again, and convert somebody.

Poverty, sickness, a lawsuit, even bad dark weather and politics (such as now), spoil a great many days in the scholar's year, hinder him of the frolic freedom friendly to spontaneous flow of thought. And that makes the use of clubs; in the large, discursive, happy talk, truths detach themselves as thoughts, spars flake off from the eternal wall, and not only the company enjoy them, but the scholar most of all; he takes possession of them, and uses them

* Emerson had evidently been reading "My Hunt after the Captain," Dr. Holmes's account in the *Atlantic Monthly* (December, 1862) of his journey to the front to find his son, Captain O. W. Holmes, Jr., of the Twentieth Regiment, Massachusetts Volunteers—later Justice of the United States Supreme Court.

henceforward as powers. Bad politics, the public disasters, instruct us heavily, sober us, cure us of bragging, but they are bad subjects for the muse; they drag us down usually into corners and party views.

1863

How we love to be magnetized! Ah, ye strong iron currents, take me in also! We are so apologetic, such waifs and straws, ducking and imitating,—and then the mighty thought comes sailing on a silent wind, and fills us with its virtue, and we stand like Atlas on our legs and can uphold the world.

Every one stands stupefied at the course of the war. None so wise as to have predicted anything that has occurred.

My interest in my Country is not primary, but professional; I wish that war, as peace, shall bring out the genius of the men. In every company, in every town, I seek intellect and character, and so in every circumstance. War, I know, is a potent alterative, tonic, magnetizer, reinforces manly power a hundred and a thousand times. I see it come as a frosty October, which shall restore intellectual and moral power to these languid and dissipated populations.

War sharpens the eyes, opens the mind of the people, so that truths we were once forbidden to speak, I hear shouted by mobs, saluted by cannon, redacted into laws.

When we quarrel, how we wish we had been blameless!

Machinery is good, but mother-wit is better. Telegraph, steam, and balloon and newspapers are like spectacles on the nose of age, but we will give them all gladly to have back again our young eyes.

Pitch your tone low. A prudent man accepts the lowest name with which his enemies seek to disgrace him, and by native force makes the nickname illustrious. 'T is the way to disarm malignity.

The superlative, so dreary in dull people, in the hands of wit gives a fillip or shock most agreeable to the drowsy attention, and hints at poetic power.

It must be confessed that the new world lies in chaos and expectation until now; that this mad war has made us all mad.

On Friday morning, May 1st, at 3 o'clock, died Mary Moody Emerson, at Williamsburg, New York, aged 88 years, 8 months.

West Point Academy makes a very agreeable impression on me. The innocence of the cadets, the air of probity, of veracity, and of loyalty to each other struck me, and the anecdotes told us confirmed this impression. I think it excellent that such tender youths should be made so manly and masterly in rough exercises of horse and gun and cannon and muster; so accurate in French, in mathematics, geology, and engineering; should learn to draw, to dance, and to swim.

At West Point, I saw a civilization built on powder. It is not quite creditable to our invention that all the instruction in engineering, infantry, cavalry, artillery, rigidly rests on this one accident of our chemistry, gunpowder. A new invention to-morrow would change all the art of war.

Take egotism out, and you would castrate the benefactors. Luther, Mirabeau, Napoleon, John Adams, Andrew Jackson; and our nearer eminent public servants,—Greeley, Theodore Parker, Ward Beecher, Horace Mann, Garrison would lose their vigour.

In reading Henry Thoreau's journal, I am very sensible of the vigour of his constitution. That oaken strength which I noted whenever he walked, or worked, or surveyed woodlots, the same unhesitating hand with which a field-labourer accosts a piece of work, which I should shun as a waste of strength, Henry shows in his literary task. He has muscle, and ventures on and performs feats which I am forced to decline. In reading him, I find the same thought, the same spirit that is in me, but he takes a step beyond, and illustrates by excellent images that which I should have conveyed in a sleepy generality. 'T is as if I went into a gymnasium, and saw youths leap, climb, and swing with a force unapproachable,—though their feats are only continuations of my initial grapplings and jumps.

A picnic is like a "revival"; it changes a man in an instant, and he forgets his home and habits, and thinks he will come and live with Nature. But he returns to his village to put up his horse, stops at the post-office, takes tea with his family, and does not for ten years get a glance at the paradise again.

I went to Dartmouth College, and found the same old Granny system which I met there twenty-five years ago. The President has an aversion to emulation, as injurious to the character of the pupils. He therefore forbids the election of members into the two literary societies by merit, but arranges that the first scholar alphabetically on the list shall be assigned to the Adelphi, and the second to the Mathesians, and the third to the Adelphi, and the fourth to the Mathesians; and so on. Every student belonging to the one or the other. "Well, but there is a first scholar in the class, is there not, and he has the first oration at Commencement?" "Oh, no, the parts are assigned by lot." The amiable student who explained it added that it tended to remove disagreeable excitement from the societies. I answered, "Certainly, and it would remove more if there were no college at all." I recommended morphine in liberal doses at the college commons.

Mediocre people wish to utilize you, to make of Newton a bank clerk, and in all ways act to pull you down from a high career.

Hawthorne unlucky in having for a friend a man who cannot be befriended; whose miserable administration admits but of one excuse, imbecility. Pierce was either the worst, or he was the weakest, of all our Presidents.

School-keeping is a dreary task, only relieved by the pleasure the teacher takes in two or three bright and beautiful pupils. The majority of the children will be brutal, or (to use a milder word) infidels, and the consoler is the appearance of genius and noble nature in one or another.

'T is strange that it is not in vogue to commit hari-kari, as the Japanese do at sixty. Nature is so insulting in her hints and notices; does not pull you by the sleeve, but pulls out your teeth, tears off your hair in patches, steals your eyesight, twists your face into an ugly mask; in short, puts all contumelies upon you, without in the least abating your zeal to make a good appearance; and all this at the same time that she is moulding the new figures around you into wonderful beauty, which, of course, is only making your plight worse.

You can take better care of your secret than another can.

The miller is an idle man and makes the brook or the wind do his work. The poet is an idler man, hates the trouble of consecutive thinking, but observing that these tempestuous passions of his search all his knowledge, all his thought, all his sentiment, in their fury,—he fastens pens on these, and they write songs, prophecies, tragedies, and lampoons that last till the morning of the Resurrection. The daily problem is how to get force.

People do not read much. The beautiful sentence on the 102d page of the printed volume, I know that the hundred pages will protect it, as well as if it were locked in my safe.

He tears into a book for a sentence as a woodpecker grubs into a tree for a worm.

One must thank the genius of Brigham Young for the creation of Salt Lake City,—an inestimable hospitality to the Overland Emigrants, and an efficient example to all men in the vast desert, teaching how to subdue and turn it to a habitable garden. And one must thank Walt Whitman for service to American literature in the Appalachian enlargement of his outline and treatment.

Attitude. Yes, that is all; that is what the orator brings, or he may leave his oration at home. How to make a poor, despised, seedy-looking cause and thin, seedy-looking assembly,—each person in which assembly seems to come in half-ashamed of the company, and only to stay through an odious sense of duty,—how to make these warm, bright, firm, honourable, proud, populous, jubilant, and, in short, the only great cause and assembly in the world,—that is, in each case, the orator's problem.

Concentration indicates control of thoughts, holding them as lanthorns to light each other and the main fact.

Transubstantiation. Every one would be poet if his intellectual digestion were perfect; if the grass and carrots passed through all the four stomachs, and became pure milk. But in Crumplehorn's cream, there is sometimes a tang of turnip; and in the gay pictures of the orator, a reminder now and then of autobiography,—staring eyes of duns, or schoolmasters, or cousins, or critics, who have tormented him, far on this side of heaven. I could guess his griefs better from his poetry than from the polite biography which introduces the book.

People only see what they are prepared to see. Thus, who sees birds, except the hunter, or the ornithologist? How difficult it is to me to see certain particulars in the dress of people with whom I sit for hours, and after I had wished to know what sort of waistcoat, or coat, or shirt-collar, or neckcloth they wore. I have gone to many dinners and parties with instructions from home and with my own wish to see the dress of the *men*, and can never remember to look for it.

This the use of war, to shatter your porcelain dolls; to break up in a nation Chinese conservatism, death in life.

A thought makes solitude in a crowd.

When it comes to divide an estate, the politest men quarrel.

Violent conservatism is more revolutionary than abolition or freedom of speech and of press. 'T is like shutting your window when you have lighted a pan of coals in the un-chimneyed apartment.

A man who makes a speech and does not wish to hurt any-body can be unheard without loss.

Nobody likes a whiffler or a trimmer.

Lincoln. We must accept the results of universal suffrage, and not try to make it appear that we can elect fine gentle-men. We shall have coarse men, with a fair chance of worth and manly ability, but not polite men, not men to please the English or French.

You cannot refine Mr. Lincoln's taste, extend his horizon, or clear his judgment; he will not walk dignifiedly through the traditional part of the President of America, but will pop out his head at each railroad station and make a little speech, and get into an argument with Squire A. and Judge B. He will write letters to Horace Greeley, and any editor or reporter or saucy party committee that writes to him, and cheapen himself.

But this we must be ready for, and let the clown appear, and hug ourselves that we are well off, if we have got good nature, honest meaning, and fidelity to public inter-est, with bad manners,—instead of an elegant *roué* and malignant self-seeker.

In seeing —— the other day, I did not like it that she appeared rather to endure her beauty than to animate or create it.

My humorous friend told me that old age was cheap. Time drew out his teeth gratis, and a suction-plate would last him as long as he lived; he does not go to the hairdresser, for Time cut off his hair; and he had lived so long, and bought so many clothes, that he should not need to buy any more.

In that country, a peculiarity is that after sixty years a certain mist or dimness, a sort of autumnal haze, settled on the figure, veiling especially all decays. Gradually, year by year, the outline became indistinct, and the halo gayer and brighter. At last, there was only left a sense of presence, and the virture of personality, as if Gyges never turned his ring again. It was an immense social convenience.

It is French novels that teach us French, and German that teach us German. The passions rush through the resistance of grammar and strange vocabulary, and facility being once obtained, the feebler appetite of taste and love of knowledge suffice to habituate us in the new land.

We, in the midst of a great Revolution, working through this tremendous ordeal, which elsewhere went by beheadings, of massacre, and reigns of terror,—passing through all this and through states and territories, like a sleep, and drinking our tea the while. 'T is like a brick house moved from its old foundations and place, and passing through our streets, whilst all the family are pursuing their domestic work inside.

Committees don't manage revolutions. A revolution is a volcano, and from under everybody's feet flings its sheet of fire into the sky.

I will tell you why I value Boston: because, when I go to enumerate its excellent names, I do not take down the Boston Directory, but the National History, to find them.

1864

When a man meets his accurate mate, then life is delicious.

Yesterday at the Club, but cramped for time by late dinner and early hour of the return train,—a cramp which spoils a club. For you shall not, if you wish good fortune, even take pains to secure your right and left hand men. The least design instantly makes an obligation to make their time agreeable, which I can never assume.

The single word *Madame* in French poetry, makes it instantly prose.

My physiology would in every point put the real against the showy; as, to live in the country, and not in the town; to wear shoddy and old shoes; to have not a fine horse, but an old Dobbin with only life enough to drag a Jersey wagon to Conantum and there stand contented for half a day at a tree, whilst I forget him in the woods and pastures.

The cannon will not suffer any other sound to be heard for miles and for years around it. Our chronology has lost all old distinctions in one date,—*Before the War, and since.*

Yesterday, May 23, we buried Hawthorne in Sleepy Hollow, in a pomp of sunshine and verdure, and gentle winds. James Freeman Clarke read the service in the church and at the grave. Longfellow, Lowell, Holmes, Agassiz, Hoar, Dwight, Whipple, Norton, Alcott, Hillard, Fields, Judge Thomas, and I attended the hearse as pallbearers. Franklin Pierce was with the family. The church was copiously decorated with white flowers delicately arranged. The corpse was unwillingly shown,—only a few moments to this company of his friends. But it was noble and serene in its aspect,—nothing amiss,—a calm and powerful head. A large company filled the church and the grounds of the cemetery. All was so bright and quiet that pain or mourning was hardly suggested, and Holmes said to me that it looked like a happy meeting.

I thought there was a tragic element in the event, that might be more fully rendered,—in the painful solitude of the man, which, I suppose, could not longer be endured, and he died of it.

I have found in his death a surprise and disappointment. I thought him a greater man than any of his works betray, that there was still a great deal of work in him, and that he might one day show a purer power. Moreover, I have felt sure of him in his neighborhood, and in his necessities of sympathy and intelligence,—that I could well wait his time,—his unwillingness and caprice,—and might one day conquer a friendship. It would have been a happiness, doubtless to both of us, to have come into habits of unreserved intercourse. It was easy to talk to him,—there were no barriers,—only, he said so little, that I talked too much, and stopped only because, as he gave no indications, I feared to exceed. He showed no egotism or self-assertion, rather a humility, and, at one time, a fear that he had written himself out. One day, when I found him on the top of his hill, in the woods, he paced back the path to his house and said, *"This path is the only remembrance of me that will remain."* Now it appears that I waited too long.

Lately he had removed himself the more by the indignation his perverse politics and unfortunate friendship for that paltry Franklin Pierce awakened, though it rather moved pity for Hawthorne, and the assured belief that he would outlive it, and come right at last.

What omniscience has music! So absolutely impersonal, and yet every sufferer feels his secret sorrow soothed.

Within, I do not find wrinkles and used heart, but unspent youth.

The spider finds it a good stand wherever he falls; he takes the first corner, and the flies make haste to come.

I have my advantage in going to a hotel with a task which could not prosper at home. I secured so a more absolute solitude. At home the day is cut up into short strips. In the hotel, I forget rain, wind, cold, and heat. At home, I remember in my library the wants of the farm, and have all too much sympathy. I envy the abstraction of some scholars I have known. All the conditions must be right for my success, slight as that is. What untunes is as bad as what cripples or stuns me. No house is complete without a hiding-place.

The grief of old age is, that now, only in rare moments, and by happiest combinations or consent of the elements, can we attain those enlargements and that intellectual *élan*, which were once a daily gift.

Manners. Their vast convenience I must always admire. The perfect defence and isolation which they effect makes an insuperable protection. Though he wrestle with you, or swim with you, lodge in the same chamber, sleep in the same bed, he is yet a thousand miles off, and can at any moment finish with you. Manners seem to say, "You are you, and I am I."

Old age brings along with its ugliness the comfort that you will soon be out of it,—which ought to be a substantial relief to such discontented pendulums as we are. To be out of the war, out of debt, out of the drouth, out of the blues, out of the dentist's hands, out of the second thoughts, mortifications, and remorses that inflict such twinges and shooting pains,—out of the next winter, and the high prices, and company below your ambitions,—surely these are soothing hints. And, harbinger of this, what an alleviator is sleep, which muzzles all these dogs for me every day? Old age;—'t is proposed to call an indignation meeting.

Each of the masters has some puerility, as Carlyle his proslavery whim; Tennyson, English class feeling. Our faculties are of different ages—the Memory is mature, sometimes the Imagination adult, and yet the Moral Sense still swaddled and sheathed. Yet on the credit of their talent, these masters are allowed to parade this baby faculty, all fits and folly, in the midst of grown company.

We lack repose. As soon as we stop working, or active thinking, we mope: there is no self-respect, no grand sense of sharing the Divine presence. We are restless, run out and back, talk fast, and overdo.

The test of civilization is the power of drawing the most benefit out of cities.

It is mortifying that all events must be seen, by wise men even, through the diminishing lens of a petty interest. Could we have believed that England should have disappointed us thus?—that no man in all that civil, reading, brave, cosmopolitan country, should have looked at our revolution as a student of history, as philanthropist, eager to see what new possibilities for humanity were to begin,— what the inspirations were: what new move on the board the Genius of the World was preparing? No, but every one squinted; lords, ladies, statesmen, scholars, poets, all squinted. Everyone forgot his history, his poetry, his religion, and looked only at his shop-till, whether his salary, whether his small investment in the funds, would not be less; whether the stability of English order might not be in some degree endangered. No Milton, no Bacon, no Berkeley, no Montesquieu, no Adam Smith was there to hail a new dawn of hope and culture for men, to see the opportunity for riddance of this filthy pest which dishonored human nature; to cry over to us, "Up and God with you! and for this Slavery,—off with its head! We see and applaud; the world is with you. Such occasion does not come twice. Strike for the Universe of men!" No; but, on the other hand, every poet, every scholar, every great man, as well as the rich, thought only of his pocket-book, and to our astonishment cried, "Slavery forever! Down with the North!"

The War at last appoints the generals, in spite of parties and Presidents. Every one of us had his pet, at the start, but none of us appointed Grant, Sherman, Sheridan and Farragut,—none but themselves.

We know vastly more than we digest. I never read poetry, or hear a good speech at a caucus, or a cattle-show, but it adds less stock to my knowledge than it apprises me of admirable uses to which what I knew can be turned.

Cows are dull, sluggish creatures, but with a decided talent in one direction—for extracting milk out of meadows: —mine have a genius for it,—leaking cream, "larding the lean earth as they walk along." Wasps, too, for making paper. Then what soothing objects are the hens!

1865

'T was tedious, the squalor and obstructions of travel; the advantage of their offer at Chicago made it necessary to go; in short, this dragging of a decorous old gentleman out of home and out of position to this juvenile career was tantamount to this,—"I'll bet you fifty dollars a day that you will not leave your library, and wade and ride and run and suffer all manner of indignities and stand up for an hour each night reading in a hall"; and I answered, "I'll bet I will." I do it and win the $900.

Why talk of President Lincoln's equality of manners to the elegant or titled men with whom Everett or others saw him? A sincerely upright and intelligent man as he was, placed in the Chair, has no need to think of his manners or appearance. His work day by day educates him rapidly and to the best. He exerts the enormous power of this continent in every hour, in every conversation, in every act; —thinks and decides under this pressure, forced to see the vast and various bearings of the measures he adopts; *he* cannot palter, he cannot but carry a grace beyond his own, a dignity, by means of what he drops, e.g., all his pretension and trick, and arrives, of course, at a simplicity, which is the perfection of manners.

We are such vain peacocks that we read in an English journal, with joy, that no house in London or Paris can compare with the comfort and splendour at Delmonico's in New York. But I was never in Delmonico's.

The Bible wears black cloth. It comes with a certain official claim against which the mind revolts. The book has its own nobilities—might well be charming, if it was left simply on its merits, as the others; but this "you must,"—it is your duty," repels. 'T is like the introduction of martial law into Concord. If you should dot our farms with picket lines, and I could not go or come across lots without a pass, I should resist, or else emigrate. If Concord were as beautiful as Paradise, it would be detestable at once.

A certain slovenliness fits certain persons, but requires perfect *aplomb* and clear, sensible manners and conversation. Cold scholars cannot afford these liberties.

The old sharper said: "his conscience was as good as ever it was; he had never used it any."

1866

The power of manners is a principal agent in human affairs. The rich and elegant and the strong-willed not so much talk down as look down and silence the well-disposed middle class. 'T is fine that the scholar or the red republican defies these people, or writes against them: he cannot get them out of his thoughts. When he meets them in the street, he cannot deny them his bow, and when he meets them in clubs or drawing-rooms, he prizes their attentions, and easily leaves his own set on any advances from theirs.

Quick people touch and go, whilst heavy people insist on pounding. 'T is in vain to try to choke them off and change the conversation to avoid the slaughter-house details. Straightway they begin at the beginning, and thrice they slay the slain; society shall be distressing, and there's an end of it.

It is peremptory for good living in houses in a cultivated age, that the beautiful should never be out of thought. It is not more important that you should provide bread for the table, than that it should be put there and used in a comely manner. You have often a right to be angry with servants, but you must carry your anger and chide without offence to beauty. Else, you have quarreled with yourself as well as with them.

The surprise and dazzle of beauty is such, that I thought to-day, that if beauty were the rule, instead of the exception, men would give up business.

A man of no conversation should smoke.

I find it a great and fatal difference, whether I court the muse, or the muse courts me: That is the ugly disparity between age and youth.

Power is not pettish, but want of power is.

I confess there is sometimes a caprice in fame, like the unnecessary eternity given to these minute shells and antediluvian fishes, leaves, ferns, yea, ripples and raindrops, which have come safe down through a vast antiquity, with all its shocks, upheavals, deluges, and volcanoes, wherein everything noble in art and humanity has perished, yet these snails, periwinkles, and worthless dead leaves come staring and perfect into our daylight.—What is fame, if every snail or ripple or raindrop shares it?

My idea of a home is a house in which each member of the family can on the instant kindle a fire in his or her private room. Otherwise their society is compulsory and wasteful to the individual.

Women feel about men who huddle them aside in the press as geniuses feel about energetic workers, namely, that they see through these noisy masters. In the company of superior women we all know that we are overlooked, judged, and sometimes sentenced.

Man is a rude bear when men are separated in ships, in mines, in colleges, in monasteries. Conversation descends; manners are coarse. Let women sail as passengers, and all is righted. Taste, beauty, order, grace; life is respectable, and has elevated aims.

Wealth is chiefly convenient for emergencies. Day by day, every family gets well enough through its common routine, the poor as the rich. Only now and then comes a pinch, a sudden and violent call for means; as, a marriage or a sickness, or a visitor, or a journey, or a subscription that must be met; then it is fortunate and indispensable to have the new power. But emergencies are in the contract. They will and must occur to every susceptible person. Therefore, you must set your daily expense at the famine-pitch, live

within your income all the year round, to be ready with
your dollars for these occasions.

If I cannot brag of knowing something, then I brag of not
knowing it. At any rate, Brag.

1867

The just pride of a man consists herein, that the recognition
of him by others is no wise necessary to him.

For good quoting, there must be originality in the quoter,—
bent, bias, delight in the truth, and only valuing the author
in the measure of his agreement with the truth, which we
see, and which he had the luck to see first. If another's
words describe your fact, use them as freely as you use the
language and the alphabet, whose use does not impair your
originality.

December 17

Yesterday morning in bitter cold weather I had the pleasure
of crossing the Mississippi in a skiff with Mr. ——, we the
sole passengers, and a man and a boy for oarsmen. I have
no doubt they did their work better than the Harvard six
could have done it, as much of the rowing was on the surface of fixed ice, in fault of running water. But we arrived
without other accident than becoming almost fixed ice
ourselves; but the long run to the Tepfer House, the volunteered rubbing of our hands by the landlord and clerks,
and good fire restored us.

1868

I have no knowledge of trade and there is not the sciolist
who cannot shut my mouth and my understanding by

strings of facts that seem to prove the wisdom of tariffs. But my faith in freedom of trade, as the rule, returns always. If the Creator has made oranges, coffee, and pineapples in Cuba, and refused them to Massachusetts, I cannot see why we should put a fine on the Cubans for bringing these to us,—a fine so heavy as to enable Massachusetts men to build costly palm-houses and glass conservatories, under which to coax these poor plants to ripen under our hard skies, and thus discourage the poor planter from sending them to gladden the very cottages here. We punish the planter there and punish the consumer here for adding these benefits to life.

Henry Clapp said that the Rev. Dr. O—— was always looking about to see if there was not a vacancy in the Trinity. He said that Greeley knew he was a self-made man, and was always glorifying his maker. He said that T. aimed at nothing and always hit it exactly.

We had a story one day of a meeting of the Atlantic Club, when the copies of the new number of the *Atlantic* being brought in, every one rose eagerly to get a copy, and then each sat down and *read his own article*.

The only place where I feel the joy of eminent domain is in my woodlot. My spirits rise whenever I enter it. I can spend the entire day there with hatchet or pruning-shears making paths, without a remorse of wasting time. I fancy the birds know me, and even the trees make little speeches or hint them.

Nature is ever putting conundrums to us, and the *savants,* as in the girls' game of "Twenty Questions," are every month solving them successfully by skillful, exhaustive method. This success makes the student cheerful and confident, and his new illumination makes it impossible for him to acquiesce in the old barbarous routine, whether of politics, or religion, or commerce, or social arrangements. Nature will not longer be kinged, or churched, or colleged, or drawing-roomed as before.

A man never gets acquainted with himself, but is always a surprise.

In poetry, tone. I have been reading some of Lowell's new poems, in which he shows unexpected advance on himself, but perhaps most in technical skill and courage. It is in talent rather than in poetic tone, and rather expresses his wish, his ambition, than the uncontrollable interior impulse which is the authentic mark of a new poem,—and which is felt in the pervading tone, rather than in brilliant parts or lines; as if the sound of a bell, or a certain cadence expressed in a low whistle or booming, or humming, to which the poet first timed his step, as he looked at the sunset, or thought, was the incipient form of the piece, and was regnant through the whole.

1869

The managers of the public conventions, political and other, understand well that they must set the fire going by ready popular speakers, like Wilson, and Russell, and Swift, who will crackle and kindle, and afterwards they may venture to pile on the slow anthracite of argumentative judges and political economists; kindlings first, and then hard coal.

No more irreconcilable persons brought to annoy and confound each other in one room than are sometimes actually lodged by Nature in one man's skin.

Religions are the amusements of the intellect.

Charles Sumner held that every man is to be judged by the horizon of his mind, and Fame he defined as the shadow of excellence, but that which follows him, not which he follows after.

I am interested not only in my advantages but in my disadvantages, that is, in my fortunes proper; that is, in watching my fate, to notice, after each act of mine, what result. Is it prosperous? Is it adverse? And thus I find a pure entertainment of the intellect, alike in what is called good or bad.

The person who commands the servant successfully is the one who does not think of the manner, solely thinking that this thing must be done. Command is constitutional.

All writing should be selection in order to drop every dead word. Why do you not save out of your speech or thinking only the vital things,—the spirited *mot* which amused or warmed you when you spoke it,—because of its luck and newness? If a man would learn to read his own manuscript severely,—becoming really a third person, and search only for what interested him, he would blot to purpose,— and how every page would gain! Then all the words will be sprightly, and every sentence a surprise.

1870

My new book sells faster, it appears, than either of its fore-goers. This is not for its merit, but only shows that old age is a good advertisement. Your name has been seen so often that your book must be worth buying.

The waking from an impressive dream is a curious example of the jealousy of the gods. There is an air as if the sender of the illusion had been heedless for a moment that the Reason had returned to its seat, and was startled into attention. Instantly, there is a rush from some quarter to break up the drama into a chaos of parts, then of particles, then of ether, like smoke dissolving in a wind; it cannot be disintegrated fast enough or fine enough. If you could give the waked watchman the smallest fragment, he could reconstruct the whole; for the moment, he is sure he can and will; but his attention is so divided on the disappearing parts, that he cannot grasp the least atomy, and the last fragment or film disappears before he could say, "I have it."

There is one other reason for dressing well than I have ever considered, namely, that dogs respect it, and will not attack you in good clothes.

Here at Nantasket Beach, with Ellen, I wonder that so few men do penetrate what seems the secret of the innkeeper. He runs along the coast, and perceives that by buying a few acres, well chosen, of the seashore, which cost no more or not so much as good land elsewhere, and building a good house, he shifts upon Nature the whole duty of filling it with guests, the sun, the moon, the stars, the rainbow, the sea, the islands, the whole horizon,—not elsewhere seen, ships of all nations. All of these (and all unpaid) take on themselves the whole charge of entertaining his guests, and filling and delighting their senses with shows; and it were long to tell in detail the attractions which these furnish. The man buys a few acres, but he has all the good and glory of a hundred square miles, by the cunning choice of the place.

The writer is an explorer. Every step is an advance into new land.

The only point in which I regret priority of departure is that I, as every one, keep many stories of which the etiquette of contemporariness forbids the airing, and which burn uncomfortably being untold. I positively resolve not to kill A. nor C. nor N.—but I could a tale unfold, like Hamlet's father.

1871

Nothing in nature is more ideal than the hair. Analyze it by taking a single hair, and it is characterless and worthless: but in the mass it is recipient of such variety of form, and momentary change from form to form, that it vies in expression with the eye and the countenance. The wind and the sun play with it and enhance it, and its coils and its mass are a perpetual mystery and attraction to the young poet. But the doleful imposture of buying it at the shops is suicidal, and disgusts.

The splendors of this age outshine all other recorded ages. In my lifetime have been wrought five miracles,—namely, 1, the Steamboat; 2, the Railroad; 3, the Electric Telegraph; 4, the application of the Spectroscope to astronomy; 5, the

Photograph;—five miracles which have altered the relations of nations to each other. Add cheap postage; and the mowing machine and the horse-rake. A corresponding power has been given to manufactures by the machine for pegging shoes, and the power-loom, and the power-press of the printers. And in dentistry and in surgery, Dr. Jackson's discovery of Anaesthesia. It only needs to add the power which, up to this hour, eludes all human ingenuity, namely, a rudder to the balloon, to give us the domination of the air, as well as of the sea and the land.

Emphasis betrays poverty of thought, as if the man did not know that all things are full of meaning, and not his trumpery thing only.

All conversation and writing is rhetoric, and the great secret is to know thoroughly, and not be affected, and to have a steel spring.

Bret Harte referred to my essay on Civilization, that the piano comes so quickly into the shanty, etc., and said, "Do you know that, on the contrary, it is vice that brings them in? It is the gamblers who bring in the music to California. It is the prostitute who brings in the New York fashions of dress there, and so throughout." I told him that I spoke also from Pilgrim experience, and knew on good grounds the resistless culture that religion effects.

1872

One thing is certain: the religions are obsolete when the reforms do not proceed from them.

The merit of a poem is decided by experience.

Walk in the city for an hour, and you shall see the whole history of female beauty. Here are the school-girls in the first profusion of their hair covering them to the waist, and now and then one maiden of eighteen or nineteen years, in the moment of her perfect beauty. Look quick and sharply,—this is her one meridian day. To find the like again, you must meet, on your next visit, one who is a month younger today. Then troops of pleasing, well-dressed ladies, sufficiently good-looking and graceful, but without claims to the prize of the goddess of Discord.

July 24

House burned.

"*Idlesse* is the business of age. I love above all things to do nothing."

1873

The enjoyment of travel is in the arrival at a new city, as Paris, or Florence, or Rome,—the feeling of free adventure, you have no duties,—nobody knows you, nobody has claims, you are like a boy on his first visit to the Common on Election Day. Old Civilization offers to you alone this huge city, all its wonders, architecture, gardens, ornaments, galleries, which had never cost you so much as a thought. For the first time for many years you wake master of the bright day, in a bright world without a claim on you; only leave to enjoy.

Date Uncertain

Writing should be like the settlement of dew on the leaf, of stalactites on the cavern wall, the deposit of flesh from the blood, of woody fibre from the sap. The poem is made up of lines each of which filled the sky of the poet in its turn; so that mere synthesis produces a work quite super-human. For that reason, a true poem by no means yields all its virtue at the first reading, but is best when we have slowly and by repeated attention felt the truth of all the details.

Fame is a signal convenience. Do we read all the authors, to grope our way to the best? No, but the world selects for us the best, and we select from the best, our best.

Thoughts come to those who have thoughts, as banks lend to capitalists and not to paupers.

The distinction of a man is that he thinks. Let that be so. For a man cannot otherwise compare with a steam-engine or the self-acting spinning-mule which is never tired and makes no fault. But a man thinks and adapts. A man is not a man, then, until he have his own thoughts: that first; then, that he can detach them. But what thoughts of his own are in Abner or Guy? There are clean, well-built men enough to look at, have money, and houses and books, but they are not yet arrived at humanity, but remain idiots and minors.

There is a process in the mind analogous to crystallization in the mineral. I think of some fact. In thinking of it, I am led to more thoughts, which show themselves, first par-tially, and afterwards more fully. But in them I see no order. When I would present them to others, they have no beginning. Leave them now and return later. Do not force them into arrangement, and bye and bye you shall find they will take their own order, and the order they assume is divine.

Religion is the perception of that power which constructs the greatness of the centuries out of the paltriness of the hours.

Even the chickens running up and down, and pecking at each white spot and at each other as ridden by chicken nature, seem ever and anon to have a pause of consideration, then hurry on again to be chickens. Men have more pause.

The best part of truth is certainly that which hovers in gleams and suggestions unpossessed before man. His recorded knowledge is dead and cold. But this chorus of thoughts and hopes, these dawning truths, like great stars just lifting themselves into his horizon, they are his future, and console him for the ridiculous brevity and meanness of his civic life.

INDEX

MODERN LIBRARY GIANTS

A series of full-sized library editions of books that formerly were available only in cumbersome and expensive sets.
THE MODERN LIBRARY GIANTS REPRESENT A SELECTION OF THE WORLD'S GREATEST BOOKS

These volumes contain from 600 to 1,400 pages each